The Grand March

The Grand March

ROBERT TURNER

An EMERALD CITY *Book*

THE GRAND MARCH

Resource Publications
An Imprint of Wipf and Stock Publishers
199 W. 8th Ave., Suite 3
Eugene, OR 97401

www.wipfandstock.com

ISBN 13: 978-1-60899-351-2

Cataloging-in-Publication data:

Turner, Robert.

The grand march / Robert Turner.

ISBN 13: 978-1-60899-351-2

vi + 264 p.; 23 cm.

1. Road fiction. 2. Drugs—Fiction. 3. Love stories—Fiction. 4. Indiana—Fiction. 5. Illinois—Fiction. I. Title.

Manufactured in the U.S.A.

And they shall build the old wastes, they shall raise up the former desolations, and they shall repair the waste cities, the desolations of many generations.

—Isaiah 61:4

"These wipers are about useless," Russell Pinske muttered, partly to himself and partly to see if he could get a response from the woman curled in shadows beside him. She didn't move. He peered through the bug-spattered windshield into the darkness ahead and wondered, not for the first time, what he was doing with her.

Onward to the promise of dawn, he steered the speeding car along an unlit country highway. The two-lane route shot straight across flat Indiana farmland, but he had to compensate continually for the car's tendency to drift left. Dense woods brooded in the moonless night. Fireflies mingled with the Milky Way. The only signal the old AM receiver could pick up was a gospel station broadcasting from a place he'd never heard of. Open windows fanned the stale smell of sun-bleached vinyl car interior. The sleeping woman began to snore again. Gloria Arbogast owned the car.

They had known one another for a couple of years, but hadn't spoken in months when they met by chance on the cross-town bus as both were preparing to leave Cincinnati. Russell had sold almost everything he owned and was off to his hometown of Door Prairie before beginning a trek westward. Gloria was going to Toronto to participate in an intensive summer program studying abnormal frogs. She suggested they leave together, an idea that was funny to him. A month ago he was certain he'd never see her again. Now they were on the road in her cranky old Ford Fairlane in the middle of the night.

He knew the way by heart. The road would curve ahead and enter an uninhabited stretch of dreary marshes that was part of a game preserve.

By his reckoning they'd be in town around sunup. The gospel station grew fuzzy. He adjusted the tuning and then switched it off, wondering why they couldn't pick up any of the stations out of Chicago. The glow of the city should soon be visible, a purple-orange aura on the western horizon. Rank marsh water perfumed the humid air. Gloria sighed and shifted her position, throwing one arm over the edge of the seat. The car roared on.

A large moth hit the glass with an audible splat. He'd long since depleted the car's reservoir of wiper fluid, and was sickened by the dry blades merely smearing the gummy remains into the mélange that had been accumulating for hours. Not that there was much to see in this swampland, nothing but a scum-ridden slurry of shallow streams. He eased off the accelerator, mindful that some bored state trooper might be out hunting for a fool like himself. Something about the thought of being stopped by a cop made him need to urinate, so he pulled off the road near a bridge that crossed the Kankakee River. After finding relief on its banks he returned to the car for a cup, intending to fetch some water and wash the windshield. Gloria awoke as he rummaged through his pack in the back seat.

"What are you doing?" she asked with a drooping mouth, her head propped on the window. Her voice startled him.

"Sorry," he mumbled, struggling with a strap on a compartment of his pack. "I'm going to clean the windshield. I can't stand looking at bug guts anymore."

He grabbed a cup and a rag.

"I used up all your fluid, there wasn't much left," he said, backing out of the car. He leaned into the front seat to tell her, "Man, you need new wipers."

She looked at him placidly and shut her eyes. He left the door open and went back to the river. She reached over and closed it, then stretched out on the bench seat.

"Hey, can you turn the light on?" he called out upon his return. She lifted a weary hand and flipped the switch. He cleaned the glass and the wipers, then stashed his gear and started the motor. They rolled back onto the road and got up to speed.

"Car's pulling to the left pretty bad. Could be your front end."

She grunted. He looked at her and continued.

"Hope it makes it to Detroit."

"I'm going to Toronto," she said with a sigh, her head resting on her hands and her eyes tightly closed.

"Yeah, well, I'm saying I hope it makes it to Detroit."

She yawned and buried her face in her arms.

———————◆———————

A hint of light touched the eastern sky. They approached a town that greeted its visitors with large stone markers mounted with rusted ship anchors. Whenever he came through here, he wondered what significance these anchors held for this landlocked farming community. He'd never bothered to find out, but now thought that his open-road adventure ought to include learning about places like this. He stopped at the next junction. The route they were on went through the lake counties and into Chicago. He turned north. Straight ahead lay Door Prairie, and Michigan beyond. Stars faded in the blushing dawn. The moist air was strangely sweet.

He looked at her in the light from the dashboard. Her face wore an unguarded expression, one he saw as stern, even dour. Together they had formed a relationship of convenience. He valued their conversations, and the witty acuity she brought to them. She found in him a quality of canine fidelity. He was attentive and loyal and she thrived on that companionship, not having many close friends in her life. At one time she tried to buy into his laid-back lifestyle, but couldn't work up much enthusiasm for it. He was a line cook, without any apparent desire to advance beyond that. Whatever ambition he had came in fits and starts, and seemed to her to be misplaced anyway. She was a serious person, now beginning graduate work in the field of environmental science, specializing in wetlands ecology.

Problems arose when they tried to move beyond using each other, when they sought to forge a stable platform for their disjointed lives. That platform collapsed last winter, after many creaks and groans, when it became apparent that he had some idealized notions of their romance that she did not share. She wouldn't even call what they had a romance, and scoffed at his sentimental earnestness, hoping to snap him out of it. But when he continued to lay bare his innermost soul, she hardened against what she considered to be his gratuitous sincerity. The depth of his feeling unnerved her. She simply had never felt swept off her feet, certainly not in the way he claimed to have been. He accused her of indifference, which she refused to dispute. When he began insisting that she start caring about him, it was clear they were done. Done for good, he had thought, yet here they were.

After their breakup Russell began to spend more time with people he hadn't seen much during his year of preoccupation with Gloria. He sought out one friend in particular, Johann, a woodworker by trade. Johann ran his shop out of the basement of his house, which became Russell's primary hangout. He appreciated his friend's craftsmanship, and found it satisfying to watch him create a piece from beginning to end. The idea of a completed work appealed to him. Although he took pride in his cooking, his meals didn't last. He began to long to accomplish something lasting.

Johann suggested he start writing a journal, advice Russell took and practiced daily for a few months. When he read back over everything he'd written, he was depressed by the banality of it all. It was then he decided to hit the road. Things needed shaking up, and he couldn't think of a better way to do that than by packing up and leaving town. He had always wanted to see the Pacific Ocean, so that was something he could accomplish. If nothing else, his journal entries would certainly become more interesting.

Russell quit his job, gave notice to his landlord, and sold everything he couldn't carry with him. While he waited for his final paycheck he took long walks around the city, trying to work up a properly adventuresome spirit. The best he could muster was a combination of exhilaration and trepidation. It was on one of these expeditions that he ran into Gloria. He was happy to go along with her idea to leave town together, not only because it saved him money on a bus ticket, but because he thought it would do him some good to leave on friendly terms with her. The plan was for him to drive through the night while she slept; then she could take over and continue on fresh in the morning.

Yesterday he stuffed his belongings into his backpack and went to see Johann one last time. There he was presented with an ornate walking stick that Johann had made for his journey. The top was carved into an over-large acorn, supported by the tails of four grinning squirrels. Oak-leaf scrollwork twined down to a thick bronze tip. It was an accomplished work, and Russell gratefully accepted the gift. He took his first walk with it when he hiked over to Gloria's with his backpack. They had dinner together, then got on the road. She fell asleep around midnight, shortly after they crossed into Indiana. He'd driven almost the entire length of the state and was nearing the southern curve of Lake Michigan, the place where he had grown up that now seemed so foreign.

He was laying rubber across land once covered by glaciers, and marked by prehistoric tribes with their mysterious mounds. Trappers had tramped with the Potawatami until both were displaced by garrisons of soldiers who built forts and trading posts to supply westward wagon trains. Towns slowly accreted on what they called the portal to the prairie, and with the railroad came more schemes and scams, successes and failures, loves and losses. His own people, drifting in from all over, decided to make a go of it here, at least for a while. He wished he knew their stories, but all his relations were scattered and distant. He could imagine them, though: plainspoken folks in their kitchens, their perfect flaws intimately warping the space around them.

Gloria snorted and snapped her eyes open. "Where are we?" she asked with a yawn. She sat up and ran her hand through her tangled hair.

"Just about twenty miles away or so."

She cleared her throat and fished a fresh pack of cigarettes from her purse. Last he knew, she had quit smoking. He smiled to see her light up with the Zippo that he'd given to her. She lazily exhaled out the window. The silence wearied him.

"Over there used to be a barn," he started, indicating a field to the right. "The Party Barn. All through high school we'd go out there and get drunk and stuff. Nobody owned the place; it was just abandoned property. But a couple years ago some kids were partying a little too heartily and burned it down."

She recoiled at the thought of a party barn, at the notion of cheap booze and sweaty teenagers. He rambled on, oblivious to her displeasure.

"A neighbor of mine, kid I grew up with, got killed on these tracks coming up. Train dragged him, like, a quarter mile or so before it stopped. Sixteen years old and wham—"

He snapped his fingers, then read the look in her eyes and shut up. She snuffed her cigarette, then took out a compact and primped a bit. They entered Door Prairie.

About thirty thousand souls dwelled in this county seat that had thrived during the heady days of the Rust Belt and had declined along with it. Some manufacturing remained, most famously production of the meat slicer found in delicatessens across the country, but lately the town council had begun to focus on revitalizing the languishing tourist economy. Back in the Jazz Age it had been one of Chicagoland's bucolic retreats, and the plan was to resell it as such.

He drove along the old Lincoln Highway that served as the main street. A downtown beautification project was underway around the monumental courthouse towering over modest buildings of brick and stone. Groups of migrant workers stood around in parking lots, either waiting for a ride or seeking a job in the fields. Every spring waves of wandering farmhands came through, most from Mexico. Two of the friends he was here to see, Carmela Contreras and Manny Fuegas, were part of the resident Hispanic population, as was the current mayor.

While they waited at a red light, he offered to buy her breakfast. She accepted with thanks. Somehow he liked her better when he could do something for her. He felt an echo of the satisfaction that had filled him in their early days, when it was clear he was providing her with something she needed. They drove to a restaurant where the hospital he'd been born in had once stood.

He ordered up a mess of protein; she asked for fruit and oatmeal. After testing her coffee with a sip, she excused herself and left the table. Forms of cars glided across the shaded windows. A man in a business suit read a newspaper at the counter. An elderly couple ate wordlessly in the next booth. The decor relied on neutral colors, brass rails, and hanging baskets of silk plants. He peered through the rough weave of the shade. For the first time he felt wobbly facing his future, acknowledging the range of things he could do and places he could go. The air conditioning felt good. It was going to be a hot day.

She slid back into the booth and smoothed her hair. He watched her bony wrist as she stirred an ice cube into her coffee. Her dull nails were chewed and ragged. The whirlpool in her cup absorbed her black eyes. With her face turned down in the warm morning light, she looked like a stranger to him. And she was. For all her foibles and follies he could enumerate, all her preferences and moods he knew so well, he realized as they sat together in this restaurant that she was more mysterious to him now than when they first met. He knew that he might never see her again.

She was trying to calculate how far her US dollars would stretch in Canada.

"When are you going back to Cincinnati?" he asked, because he felt he had to say something. She stopped stirring and sipped her coffee.

"Over Labor Day. Why?"

He shrugged. "Curious."

"Where do you think you'll be?" she asked while glancing out the window.

"I don't know." He raised his brow and shook his head. "California, I'm guessing. I'm going to stay here awhile, look up some friends."

Their food arrived. She asked for skim milk to add to her coffee. He caught sight of a familiar face behind the counter. The cook was someone he knew, but the name escaped him. He turned his attention to his omelet. The old folks finished their meal and shuffled off. Gloria and Russell ate in silence. He wolfed down his eggs and was attacking his toast when she asked him for directions.

"You can get out of town on this road here. It'll take you to 94 north into Michigan. Got me from there. Do you have an atlas? I've got a pocket one you can have."

She bit a piece of cantaloupe before answering. "No, there's one in the car. So this goes straight to the highway?"

"Yeah, it's about ten miles. Maybe more. Less than twenty." He paused and set his toast aside. "Listen, I want to thank you for getting me up here, even though it was out of your way."

With a dismissive wave she said, "That's OK. I'm happy to help you out. Besides, it's shorter for me to drive from here than it would have been to drive the whole way."

"Well, anyway, there's a gas station up the road—I'll fill up your car."

"OK," she said, after a spoonful of oatmeal. "Thanks."

He swigged the last of his coffee. She ate her cereal. When the waiter came around, Russell got a refill and asked for the check.

"So, you were born here?" she asked, dropping her spoon in her bowl and wiping the suggestion of a smile away with her napkin. He thought to tell her that this was, in fact, the very parcel of land that marked his entrance into the world, but refrained from informing her of the specifics.

"Yeah," he began. "I haven't been back in a few years. Still have good friends here. Family's all moved away. It's a weird place. I'm thinking I'll get caught up with my friends, see what's up, try to find a ride out west. Just see what happens. Who knows?"

The waiter brought the bill. Russell finished his third cup of coffee; Gloria left half of her first cup. A steamy parking lot greeted them as they stepped out the door.

"So, the gas station's just up here," he said, nodding in the direction.

She leaned close and whispered, "You have the keys."

He barked out a little laugh and fumbled for the keys in his pocket. She walked behind him as he approached the passenger-side door. Before he unlocked it he stopped, turned, and kissed her.

In a flash she struck out in a roundhouse slap that connected with his temple, sending his glasses flying. He dropped her keys and went scrambling for his glasses.

"What the hell," he spluttered.

She snatched the keys off the pavement and glared at him. "What do you mean? You tell me what the hell."

He squashed his glasses back on his face. She opened the car door, grabbed his backpack and hurled it to the pavement.

"I'm sorry," he said, going for his pack. "It was just an impulse."

He picked up his pack and quickly scanned around to see if anyone was watching this scene. The lot was empty. They faced each other. To him, it looked like she expected something.

"Can I still buy you gas?" he tried with a weak smile.

"Goddamn," she blurted, then slammed the door and cranked the ignition.

"No, really," he said, reaching out a hand. The transmission coughed and the car lunged into reverse. He stepped aside and watched her leave. As he slouched over his backpack and pondered his next move, it occurred to him that she'd driven off with his new walking stick.

2

The hot pavement shimmered under a climbing sun. Russell sighed and looked down the road where Gloria had left, then strapped on his pack and walked slowly, trying to find the posture that most comfortably carried the weight on his back. That walking stick would be useful about now, and he regretted its loss. He'd already grown fond of it, as he did with certain objects. By nature he was something of an animist. He once had a bicycle that he would pat and stroke like a pet, and he had even been moved to hug a mailbox after dropping in a letter. Down the road he came to the small grocery store that used to deliver orders to his grandparents' house. A sturdy old woman struggled out the door, a wagon filled with goods squeaking behind her. She stopped, kicked the rear axle and walked on, the wheels now rolling silently.

He meandered past the house where he'd grown up. Things had sure changed since his great-grandfather settled here after emigrating from Russia at the outbreak of the First World War, but the house he'd built and the neighborhood he'd built it in remained largely the same. It was a place of simple wood-frame homes and small garden plots. Russell was the third generation to be raised in the house, after his grandfather Charles and mother Liz, and he was the last. That was about all he knew of the history of his family, one that had disintegrated by the time he was aware enough to be curious.

What little he did know, he'd pieced together from fragments of stories that had stuck in his memory. He knew he was an accident, one that his parents did their best to put behind them. His birth did briefly unite

Dick Pinske and Liz Czanderra in matrimony. The marriage, tenuous at best, didn't last long. By the time Russell was five, his father had remarried and relocated out of state, dropping out of Russell's life for good. His mother, about that time, entered graduate school at Northwestern, then began an academic career there. She told her parents that she didn't want to uproot Russell, and she arranged to keep him with his grandparents indefinitely.

So his childhood unfolded in the kind indulgence of Charles and Alma. They kept him fed and in school and provided for him as best they could, with Liz sending money but showing up rarely. Russell was an easygoing kid content to hide away for hours with his books and the worlds they took him to. He cultivated his fertile imagination and developed a knack for making friends, talents that would serve him well.

Charles died when Russell was fifteen. Alma couldn't cope on her own, so Liz had to step in. She moved back and began commuting the sixty miles to Chicago each day while Russell finished high school. She hated it in Door Prairie, and spent as little time as possible there. Once Russell was on his own, Liz beat it back to the city for good. Alma sold the house and went to live with her diabetic sister in northern Michigan. It was during this time that the deep friendships he'd formed nourished him in ways his fractured family could not.

The idea of going to college was appealing, but even with scholarships he balked at the expense. A friend told him about a culinary school in Cincinnati and he went to check it out, reasoning that kitchen skills would prove practical. He liked it there and decided to stay. The city seemed romantic to him, a well-worn place of sagging brick that stood like a natural outcrop on the eroded hills. There was something dreamy in the air of that river valley, and indeed the years passed as in a dream. It was nice while it lasted, but it had come to a dead end.

He wound his way in the shade of trees by the renovated marina and praised the town's investment while making use of the newly built public toilets. The breeze came cool off the lake as he sat in the park under a leaning oak. From there he could see the extent of the development: rows of new condominiums and docks. He got up and walked along a trail. The woods were still moist with dew, the foliage and spider's webs jeweled with sun-glazed droplets. He came to a swimming beach, where he took off his pack and sat on a bench by a playground. The beach was empty, except for a man playing with his dog. Russell searched through his gear for a canteen he'd packed away. He pulled out half of his stuff before he found it, and spent a good deal of time re-packing, trying to make it all fit again. He filled the canteen from a water fountain then headed toward the fairgrounds and the last known address of Helen Kolopnok.

Russell and Helen had met six years ago, when he had just turned eighteen and she was going on twenty-five. They were introduced at a high-school graduation party thrown by the parents of Carl Paulette, one of Russell's closest friends. Helen had been invited to the party by Carl's older sister, who was a nurse at the hospital where Helen volunteered. They hit it off right away, and spent most of the evening making wry observations about the increasingly inebriated partygoers. Before she left she gave him her phone number. He called the next day and they became fast friends that summer, sharing their stories and enjoying each other's company.

They had last seen each other four years ago, when she'd gone with him to Carmela and Manny's wedding. That night she told him all about a difficult relationship she'd been in that had recently ended, and thanked him for lifting her spirits. He was glad to oblige. They'd stayed in touch, but gradually the frequency of their communication declined. Now while he walked down her street, he felt bad that he wasn't even sure she still lived here.

He consulted his old pocket watch. It was pretty early, but she always made a big deal about being a morning person, so he thought she'd most likely be up. She might even be at her summer job, if she had one. Her main livelihood came from managing the rental properties of her parents, but most every summer she took a part-time job for both supplemental income and experience. A carpet of wildflowers surrounded the house, colorful evidence that this was still her place. He climbed the steps and read the names on the two mailboxes, one for H. Kolopnok and another for M. Petersen. That would be Myrtle, he figured, the upstairs tenant Helen had described as "splenetic." He stood on the porch. Her door was slightly ajar. Wind chimes tinkled. The butt of a cigar rested in an old tuna can next to a wicker chair. Her collection of blown-glass paperweights had grown. They used to line the window ledges, but now also adorned most of the porch railing.

"Helen?" he called out as he knocked on the screen door. "Hello, Helen?"

The interior door jerked open. He was confronted with a gaunt, blotchy old woman whose blue hair twisted wildly out from her scalp like extruded strands of gunmetal. She took a step back, her floral-print muu-muu billowing about her shrunken form.

"What do you want?" she demanded, scrutinizing him through squinty eyes.

"I was looking for Helen. Is she home?"

She put her hand on the edge of the door and replied sternly, "I don't know you."

"I'm Russell," he gave a halfhearted wave. "Russell Pinske. A friend of hers. Are you Myrtle?"

"I said I don't know you."

"Well, I'm a friend of Helen's. She mentioned you once to me."

She thought about this, then said, "She never said anything about it."

"Yeah, I haven't actually talked to her in a long time."

In a niche on the far wall stood a statuette of St. Christopher that Helen had always displayed. It was something he'd entirely forgotten about, and the sight of it set him adrift in a flood of memories until the old woman responded.

"Doesn't sound too friendly to me."

He shifted the weight of his backpack and returned his attention to the conversation. "Is she home? I just got in town and I'd like to see her."

"I'm not saying a thing," she said, closing the door a little and placing more of herself behind it.

He craned around to more fully face her. "Could you tell her Russell came around? I'm sure she'd like to know."

"Don't be so sure," she told him, then slammed the door and loudly threw the bolt.

Either he'd forgotten that downtown was pretty noisy, or there was more traffic running through here than there used to be. A few blocks along Lincoln Way, the town's thoroughfare, he came upon a local furniture dealer and was greeted by a novel sight. In the parking lot was a king-sized canopy bed with a high mattress and fluffy comforter. A sign hanging from the canopy identified it as "The Celestial Bed." Beside the bed stood a fat man in a tasseled nightcap and flowing nightgown, waving to passersby with a glittery wand topped by a silver star.

Russell walked on and was glad to see the usual contingent of bums loitering around the Red Rooster Inn, open for business already. Carl used to tend bar there, but now he worked an office job in Chicago, commuting from the town of Stillwater, about twenty miles southeast, where he and his girlfriend, Ellie Sellers, lived. He talked to Carl a week ago and told him about what he was up to. They'd get together somehow, but it was uncertain when, as was just about everything else in his life.

In the window of a shop he saw one of the posters that was part of the new tourist initiative, reprints of advertisements first produced in the Twenties. They were stylish renderings of bobbed beauties and dapper gents enjoying the charms of the Indiana duneland. A couple of years ago Carmela had sent him a print depicting well-heeled couples on Door Prairie's lawn-bowling greens. During the years he'd been away she'd kept him abreast of local developments, like the old tractor factory being turned into a shopping mall and the expansion of the marina on Long Lake, largest of the town's nine lakes. He called her the day he sold the poster, and they discussed his planned trip. She insisted that he come see them before heading off to points unknown, so here he was.

He left the main drag and made his way down a cobblestone alley behind old warehouses, then crossed the tracks and cut through the parking lot of the roller rink on his way to where he thought his friends lived. Twenty-one Melon was the address he had for the house they'd bought shortly after their marriage. He didn't know exactly where Melon was, but knew it was by Lily Lake, on the east side of town.

The street took him past a foundry and a scrap-metal yard, then into a residential area built on a low rise above the blue ellipse of Fox Lake. Bulging roots of sycamores buckled and broke the sidewalks. He took the road that wound out to Lily Lake, a fair-sized body of dark, still water ringed by lily pads. He stopped in the weeds on the side of the road to get his canteen from his pack. As he drank he looked across the street at the overgrown acreage that was once owned by Door Prairie's most notorious citizen, known locally as Nellie Widow. Her gruesome exploits were popularized in all manner of lurid publications and duly chronicled by the county historical society.

Early in the twentieth century a woman calling herself Nellie Harper advertised in lonely-hearts newspapers for eligible bachelors to come visit her at her farm, luring them with livestock and land. She used a hatchet to dispose of seven unfortunate suitors, along with three children and two farmhands before the brother of her last catch took his fears to the police. Her house burned to the ground as an investigation got underway. The remains of her victims were found in a pit in the cellar, chopped up and covered with quicklime. A female corpse was recovered from one bedroom, but it had been decapitated, and a positive identification was impossible. Witnesses said the body belonged to a woman much smaller than beefy Nellie. She was reportedly seen in California the following year, and sightings persisted along the West Coast for a decade or so. The case was never resolved.

Melon was to his right, directly opposite the heavy steel gate that barred vehicles from entering the desolate, old farm. Hot and tired, weighed down and unsteady, Russell trudged in dirty gravel beside broken asphalt. So far the exhilaration of the open road had proven elusive, while a profound weariness was inescapable. He questioned the wisdom of his enterprise, this so-called adventure that now seemed like a played-out folly. On his first day he was already despairing. The house to his left was a ramshackle, cinderblock eyesore whose mailbox bore no address. House numbers here were apparently assigned at random. Next to number 9 was number 14, across the street from number 11. Seventeen was next to 14, across from 12 and 15. An empty lot on his left flanked what turned out to be number 21, on the corner.

The place was real nice, right across from the lake, a two-story, old, craftsman-type house with a wrap-around porch and a climbing rose on a trellis. It looked like it had been painted recently, a clean, creamy white with lavender trim. Behind the house was a barn-like garage. Three large maples and a tulip tree stood in the open yard, the property demarcated by a pile of rocks at the curve in the road, and by a weed-entangled fence next to the empty lot. Up by the steps they'd stationed the pink flamingoes he'd given them on their wedding. He took off his pack and set it on a stool painted in fine Carmela style. On the seat she'd drawn a menacing crab, and between the outstretched pincers were the words: "Sit At Own Risk." He knocked. A fish-shaped windsock hung limply from the eaves. The blanket of lilies heaved in rhythmic ripples. He knocked again. There was no car in the driveway. He sighed, more pessimistic than before about his prospects here. A corner of the curtain was drawn back, then the door opened and Carmela stepped out.

With a little squeal, she wrapped her arms around him and exclaimed, "You're here! We were just talking last night about what you were up to. I even called down there, but your phone's disconnected. Manny said you'd blown us off and you were probably in Timbuktu already, but I knew you'd come."

She stepped back, bobbed her head, and shimmied her shoulders. Sunlight poured across her smooth cinnamon skin; her dark eyes danced above high, smiling cheeks. She wore her black hair in a thick braid that hung down half the length of her spine. The bridge of her proud nose crinkled as her smile spread, dissipating any gloom still shadowing his thoughts.

"I'm glad you're home," he said. "Hope I'm not showing up too early."

"Oh no, not at all. Manny's at work already. I didn't know if I heard you knocking or not. I'm in my sewing room in the back. We usually use the side door." She turned and waved him into the house. "Come in. I'm right in the middle of something."

He placed his pack inside and closed the door after him. The room was appointed with furnishings that were threadbare in a genteel fashion, a funky array of rummage-sale finds. A faded oriental rug covered the central portion of an oak floor. Carmela had decorated the top foot or so of the walls with the intricate designs she was always doodling, a variegated band of geometric patterns that twisted and flowed with a suggestion of movement. The whole effect was subtle but striking. It must have taken a long time to complete.

"You've been busy," he commented, stopping in the middle of the room. She turned and followed his gaze up to her handiwork.

"Yeah, I did that last year. I've started the kitchen cabinets. See?" She walked into the kitchen and pointed to the outlines sketched on the corners of the cabinet doors. "But I'm kind of stalled out on it."

He nodded to indicate that he knew what it was like to be stalled out.

"Hey," she continued, "I'll show you around later, OK? I'm doing some alterations for my mom now—I've got to get them down there by nine, when they open."

He raised an eyebrow and pulled out his watch. "It's almost nine now, isn't it?"

"No, quarter till eight." She indicated a clock on the far wall.

"Oh, man." He smacked his forehead. "You guys are in a different time zone, aren't you?"

She laughed. "Time zone. I don't know why, but that makes me laugh. Time zone." She repeated it once more in a slow monotone, then shook her head and said, "Come on."

She led him through a set of French doors into a small room down the hall from the kitchen. "This was just a closet, but Manny and my brother Felix expanded it for me to work in. I was set up in one of the bedrooms, but if we ever have babies, we'll need all our bedrooms."

She sat behind her sewing machine and took up her work with a whispered sigh. Folded clothes sat on her table, among scraps of material, boxes of thread and other items of her craft. An iron stood steaming on its board. The shelves held linens embroidered with her motifs. A needle-point sampler she'd made when she was a child was framed on the wall.

"It's nice in here," he observed.

"They did a good job," she said, tinkering with her bobbin. "Manny got the cool old doors from a salvage yard. He got these natural spectrum lights for cheap, too. They're great—I can see true color in here when I do my needlework, like working in sunlight."

He sat in a plush armchair, feeling comfortable in the moment. She zipped along in her sewing.

"I'm sorry I didn't call and tell you what was going on," he said. "I had to wait for my check, then I hung around to cop a ride off Gloria."

"What's the deal there, you and Gloria?" she asked, head bowed to her task.

He rolled his eyes and slumped. "Oh, I'll tell you about it later. I can't even think about it now. It's just too stupid is all."

"OK," she replied.

Her machine ratted and tatted, her eyes were fixed in concentration. Russell noted the proximity of their place to the old widow's farm.

"Actually, that's one of the reasons we bought this place," she told him. "It's really a beautiful piece of land, and the city owns it. The real-estate agent said they were going to annex it to the rest of the park, but I guess the deal hasn't been worked out yet, 'cause nothing's happened so far. Remember going out there and being scary and stuff?"

She grabbed a pair of pants from the stack in front of her and held them up. They had an enormous waist. About three Carmelas could have fit inside them.

"Now that's scary."

She folded the pants and said, "Hey, go get the phone book. It's in the kitchen on top of the fridge. I'll show you something funny I noticed the other day."

"All right," he said as he stood. "But explain your street numbers to me."

"Talk to Manny about that. You know him. It drives him crazy."

He returned with the book and stood leafing through it.

"So you see what they've done," she said, directing his attention to the format of the listings. "They strung together the name and the street, and it's just odd the way it reads. Look up Manny."

He read: "Fuegas Manuel Mr. Melon." It made him smile.

"Now check out W, the last Weaver," she suggested.

"Weaver Wanda Mrs. Walnut."

She snorted. "Don't you think they were made for each other?"

He put the book down. "Oh, Carmela, you even make the phone book fun."

"It's all in how you look at things," she let him know.

His mood now fully brightened, he poked through her work on the shelves and pulled out some linens to admire.

"These are lovely."

She stopped working and addressed him with a serene expression. "Thank you."

"Hey, you know things that make you laugh, like time zone and Mr. Melon?" he asked, folding her things and putting them back on the shelves. She looked at him gamely, and he continued. "I walked by the roller rink coming down here. Is that old guy still there on the Wurlitzer?"

She confirmed the continuation of the organist at the establishment, and he resumed his discourse.

"Just about anything that guy says will make me laugh. It's that drone he has, I guess, when he calls out the skating routines, or whatever they're called—you know? When you have to skate a certain way?"

"Couples skate. Promenade two by two." She imitated his hypnotic drawl perfectly.

"Yeah, that's it. There was one, I forget what you were supposed to do, but I cracked up when he said it: 'Let The Grand March begin!' It all just seemed so absurd somehow—that cheesy organ playing, people skating around, everybody doing their thing. I don't know why it was so funny, but it was. I totally lost it."

"Guess you had to be there," she said distractedly, putting the final stitch in her last article. She got up and unplugged the iron. The phone rang.

"It's my mom," she predicted as she walked into the kitchen to answer it. He followed and helped himself to a glass of water.

"Yes, Mom," she was saying while making goofy faces at him. "Yes, I just finished. As soon as I get off the phone with you, Mom."

She hung up and returned to her sewing room. He stayed in the kitchen, drinking his water and checking out her sketches on the cabinets. She packed her work in a milk crate, then took it through a door off the kitchen and strapped it to a rack on her bike. She returned, quickly went down the hall and came back with a helmet on her head.

"Help yourself to anything," she offered. "Manny might be home for lunch. I'll be home this afternoon. I've got errands to run for my mom, then I'm going over there to start cooking for this big family thing tonight, all the kids and cousins and everybody. You can come, too, if you want."

He nodded and placed his empty glass in the sink, then followed her out the door. They stood on the porch.

"If you leave, just pull the door closed behind you and it'll lock, but you have to slam it pretty hard. There's a foldout kind of couch-bed thing in the room right next to my sewing room. Get some rest. You must be tired."

She smiled at him as she coasted off. Near the end of the driveway she turned and waved.

"I'm glad you're here, Russ."

3

Russell was tired but couldn't sleep, his mind abuzz with speculative scenarios of what the summer would bring and where this trip was heading. It occurred to him that it might be a good idea to record his thoughts. But he'd captured enough drivel in his notebook already. He would wait for inspiration before he picked up his pen again, knowing that it might remain capped for a long time. He resigned himself to staying awake and folded up Carmela's couch-bed thing. Then he went roaming around their house.

The two rooms upstairs were being used for storage. It was hot up there, and he went down again quickly. To the right of the staircase was a door that opened to their bedroom. It was sparsely furnished, very airy, with a gleaming oak floor. He turned and walked through the living room again, past a wall of photographs: Carmela and Manny in Mexico on their honeymoon, them standing with a number of her extended family, a candid wedding shot, Carmela's parents in their youth, snapshots of her nieces and nephews. Among all the pictures displayed there was none of Manny's family.

Manny and his mother, Olivia, had moved here from Chicago when he was eight, a year after his father was killed in an industrial accident. Russell had been to their house a few times, but only briefly. Olivia did not welcome visitors, especially Manny's friends, none of whom she liked. Manny himself more often than not fell short of her expectations. But she was not without a sense of humor, expressed in an acerbic sarcasm that was hard to laugh off. Manny inherited her sharp tongue.

Workbenches in the basement were piled high with all manner of electronic component: stacks of circuitry, spools of wire, miscellaneous hardware. Pegboards held specialized tools whose functions mystified Russell. He walked back upstairs. Above the clothes washer in the utility room hung a Door Prairie poster like the one Carmela had sent him. This one showed a beauty on the beach, in full-body suit and cap, someone he'd surely enjoy spending a day at the beach with. He walked past the guest room, then by Carmela's sewing room. Noting that the lights were still on, he switched them off and went into the kitchen. A cool breeze blew through the open windows, calling him out to the porch.

Milky clouds smeared the sky. Water lilies shimmered on the lake. An image of the house swirled around the surface of a blue reflecting ball on a concrete pedestal in the front yard. Russell stretched out on the porch swing, closed his eyes, and let the birds sing him away.

He was roused by the sound of car tires on gravel. The engine shut off, a door opened then closed. Russell willed himself upright, groggy and stiff. Manny was startled at first when he saw someone sitting and stretching on his porch. It took him a moment to recognize his old friend, then he ran to the stairs.

He came to a dead stop and assumed a wild fighting posture. His lips moved rapidly and soundlessly, mimicking a poorly dubbed film, then he blurted out, "I told you if you ever returned you would die!" He stood locked in his stance while his lips continued moving a few seconds more.

Years before, when Russell and Manny were getting to know each other, they were amused to learn that they had independently developed the same parlor trick of speaking while moving their lips in a way that produced the effect of being overdubbed. They had both spent too many hours of their youth watching low-budget martial-arts movies and learning to do things like throw their lips out of synch with what they were saying. So this was the game they played now, a display of their peculiar bond.

With a whoop, Russell nimbly leaped onto the porch railing, adopted a similarly exaggerated position and dubbed over himself, saying, "Listen to me! We need to form an alliance!"

Manny chopped at the air, crazily kicking and flailing his arms about. Then he stopped, spit on the ground and said, "Do you think your Kung Fu is better than mine?"

"Why do you want to forfeit your life?" Russell responded, feverishly moving his mouth. "If we band together we will never be defeated."

Manny drew himself up, squared his legs and placed his fists on his hips, like a warrior at ease, then announced, "Today we are friends. Tomorrow, we fight to the death."

Russell laughed and hopped off the railing. Manny climbed the stairs and greeted him with a casual, "Hey, man," as if they saw each other every day. He patted Russell's shoulder as he walked past him and sent the door to his kitchen flying open.

"I'm hungry," he bellowed. "You hungry?" He turned to Russell briefly, then stepped into the kitchen and called out, "Get me some food, woman." He stood in the middle of the kitchen, thumbs in his belt loops, a self-satisfied smirk on his face. Then he slumped and drawled, "Oh, that's right. Got to get it myself."

Russell sat at the table while Manny rummaged through the refrigerator, his pants creeping down as he bent over. He yelled, "Meat!" and tossed a packet of ham over his shoulder. It slid across the table and Russell prevented it from slipping off. "Lettuce!" came the next cry, and half a head landed on the table. With a shout of "Tomato!" Manny turned around and fast-pitched one right at Russell, who ducked. It splattered on the counter.

"Dude," Manny berated him, "What did you have to go and do that for?"

"What? You threw it."

"You were supposed to catch it."

"You hurl the thing at me and I'm supposed to let it explode on me? No thanks."

Manny picked a chunk of tomato off the floor and examined it. "Nah," he muttered, "I don't even like tomatoes." He ran a dishrag over the mess, then turned and began to assemble his sandwich.

"Help yourself," he offered the food to Russell. "There's soda in the fridge, and some filtered water, too. The shit out of the tap's nasty—don't drink it."

"Tasted all right to me," Russell said, spreading mustard on a slice of bread.

"Loaded with a hundred years of factory waste," Manny responded. "Drink enough of it and it'll kill you dead, and that's no joke." He crunched a pickle, then ran his tongue along the trimmed mustache he'd taken to wearing. His hairline was definitely receding, a fact he accentuated by wearing his hair longer in the back.

"Got everything there OK?" Manny nodded toward Russell's plate. "Want some chips?" He pushed a bag toward him. Russell took a handful.

"Let's go eat on the porch," Manny suggested. "It's stuffy in here. One of these days I'm going to install central air, when I get the time and the money."

They sat together on the porch and ate from the plates on their laps.

"So, where are you working now?" Russell asked. "You past being a journeyman or whatever it was last I knew?"

Manny finished chewing before replying. "Oh, you bet. IBEW, certified commercial and residential electrician. Working for Charlie Jenner. You know, the big contractor?"

Russell didn't know.

"Well, he pulls in all the big contracts around here. We built these condos on Long Lake, part of the big marina renovation down there. I'll take you by it."

After a bite of sandwich, Russell told him, "I've already seen it."

"Oh yeah?" Manny replied. "What were you doing down there?"

"Hanging out. I got in early, didn't want to wake you."

"Don't have to worry about that now. I've got to be on site at dawn."

"What site is that?" Russell wanted to know, finishing the last of his sandwich.

"Big, big site. Warehouse store outside of town. City wouldn't let them put it in town, so it's just over the line. Pretty funny. We've got an election coming up this fall. I hope we vote in some realists who aren't afraid of progress."

Russell crunched a chip and raised an eyebrow. "Warehouse store?"

"Yeah, 'Mega Cart' it's called. There's one in South Bend. It's wild. They, like, rent forklifts to people so they can buy full pallets of deodorant and toilet paper and stuff."

"Oh, that's horrible," Russell said.

"What do you mean?" Manny asked, wiping his mouth with the back of his hand.

"Those places kill local businesses," Russell opined.

Manny belched. "How can you say that? It's local business building it. A lot of good work for me. Pays the bills and then some."

"Well, sure, it's good for you building it," Russell conceded. "But places like that put small downtown shops out of business."

Manny dismissed this with a snort and shook his head. "You been downtown lately? Most everything moved into the new mall. What's left is antique shops, craft stores, places like that. Stuff they don't sell at the Mega Cart."

Russell considered this point while polishing off the last of his lunch.

"Is Ajax Novelties still there? I bet the Mega Cart doesn't sell whoopee cushions."

"They might be able to get you a gross of them," Manny answered, putting his empty plate aside. "But Ajax, yeah, I was by there not too long ago. Thought about buying a joy buzzer, but didn't. Should have."

"We all have our regrets," Russell rejoined.

They sat for a moment, quietly enjoying a faint breeze.

"So, what are you doing?" Manny asked.

"Sitting here."

"And, what are you going to do next?"

Russell shrugged.

"You got everything in your kit?"

"Yep," Russell affirmed, his eyes cast across the lake.

"Got everything you need? Camping gear? Tent, stove, all like that?"

"I got everything, man. I'm handy, you know."

Manny scratched his chin, then fished a box of cigarettes from a pocket. He took one and held the box out to Russell, who declined. Manny lit his, got up and sat on the porch railing, leaning back against a post by the stairs.

"How long you sticking around?" he asked.

"I don't know. Until I feel like leaving. Or until you kick me out."

Manny smiled through the cloud of his exhalation. "I just couldn't do that, man, pick up and take off like that. I mean, it's cool that you can—but I'm just not wired that way, you know?" He looked around. "I'm digging my roots deeper here."

Russell nodded in agreement. "It's a great house, and you guys are looking good. It suits you." He stretched out on the swing. "So what's next? Kids?"

Like a spouting whale, Manny tilted his head back and directed a stream of smoke into the sky. He cleared his throat and spat over the side of the porch.

"Ah, yeah, maybe. I don't know how much Carmela's talked to you about it."

"She's mentioned wanting kids, that's about all."

"OK. Well, about a year ago we decided we were ready, right? I mean, she was ready a long time ago, but I wasn't until we had it more together. Then I decided I was as ready as I'd ever be, so she went off the pill. But, hey—nothing yet. I don't know. I'm beginning to think there's something wrong. Know what I mean?"

Russell frowned. "I don't know much about that."

"What? You don't know how babies are made?" Manny replied, taking another drag.

Russell shot him a tired look. "Fertility problems. I've only ever cared about making sure I don't get anyone pregnant. I've never had to worry about trying to make it happen."

"Uh-huh," Manny contemplatively intoned. "Well, she wants to see a doctor, and I'm not so sure I like that idea. I mean, if something's wrong with her, she's going to feel like shit. It's become so important to her in the past couple years. She wants lots of them, too, like four or five. She's got names all picked out, and she's been making baby clothes and stuff." He got up and snuffed his cigarette in an ashtray on a windowsill. "And then, if it's me, how's that going to change how she thinks about me? Maybe she'd start thinking she married a dud, you know—firing blanks. It would definitely change things between us."

Russell came within a breath of offering to try to get Carmela pregnant. He held his tongue, with the thought flashing in his mind that a few years ago he would have gone ahead and made the joke. Of course, a few years ago there would have been no context in which to make it. He changed the topic and inquired about Victor Van Donkersloop, their old friend who surprised everyone in their little coterie a few years ago when he joined the Navy.

"I see his mom around sometimes, but haven't heard from him since forever," Manny said, shaking his head. "I think Carmela wrote to him once but never heard back. You know how he is, though—we probably won't hear from him until he just shows up one day."

Their conversation was interrupted by a low, distressed moan. They walked across the porch and saw a large cat on the grass. Two swallows flew around, twittering loudly and harassing it by buzzing overhead. It hunkered down, ears folded back, and kept groaning.

Manny cheered on the birds. "That's it. Get her. Get her good."

"Poor cat. Why doesn't it run away?"

"Too fat and stupid. Get her. Pluck her whiskers out."

Russell shot him a look.

"Oh, I hate that cat and it knows I do. I want a dog, but Carmela hates dogs. Never mind that I hate that cat, but Carmela gets her cat and I don't get a dog." He grinned out one side of his mouth and scowled out the other. "That's married life, I guess."

He turned his back on the little drama of nature in his yard and walked to the door, saying, "Hey, Russ, can you put those dishes in the sink? I gotta take a leak and get out of here."

Russell was washing the dishes when Manny returned, carrying a pair of socks.

"Hey, that's cool—I didn't mean for you to wash them, but thanks."

Manny sat at the table and began to unlace his boots.

"So, how much money you got for your little trip?" he asked, peeling off his socks and dropping them on the floor. Russell leaned against the sink and paused before answering.

"About seven hundred bucks."

Manny snorted. "Really? How long do you think that's going to last?"

"I don't know. As long as it lasts."

"Have you even thought this thing through?" Manny asked, spreading his toes and airing his feet. "You don't know how long you're staying in town, or where you're going, how long your money's going to hold out, or how you're going to keep going when it's gone."

He looked at Russell, who shrugged and said, "I'm playing it by ear, making it up as I go along. I've been doing the same thing for, what, five years now? And I don't feel like I've done anything, really. Nothing important anyway. Got to the point where I was in a real rut. I needed to shake things up. So here I am, shaking it." He did a sort of jig while Manny put on his fresh pair of socks.

"Yeah, I can see that." Manny laced up his boots. "But seven hundred bucks ain't squat, and you're going to get sick of camping out. You're going to run out of cash and end up somewhere else besides Cincinnati doing the same thing and falling in the same rut, and all you've done is change the scenery."

"Well," Russell began, getting a little annoyed at his friend's critical analysis, "that's one way it can turn out."

"I just call it like I see it, you know? I want to things work out for you. All I'm saying is, you should think about what's going to happen and be ready for it. Of course, I suppose you can always find work at a restaurant, right?"

Russell slouched. "Yeah, if I have to, but I'm in no hurry to get stuck back in a kitchen again."

Manny walked to the utility room and tossed his sodden socks in a basket on top of the washer. He offered further commentary upon his return.

"Could get seasonal work, keep from getting tied down that way. A lot of the pickers around here end up in Texas and Florida in the winter."

Russell nodded to signal that he was listening, but he was in no mood to seriously consider any advice. He was content to deal with things as they came up, to tend to his survival on a daily basis and devote himself more to the present than the future. It was novelty he needed, not stability. But he didn't feel like explaining himself, so he suffered Manny to continue.

"You know Felix, Carmela's brother?"

Russell shrugged. "By name, yeah. I don't think I ever met him. I only know Carmela, Isabel, and Nestor. There's two older brothers, right? I think they were already out of the house by the time I started coming around."

"Felix and Luis. Luis is set to take over the dry cleaners whenever the old man retires. But Felix is a manager out at the gravel quarry now—he's always bitching about how hard it is to get good workers. Want to swing by there? No harm in seeing if he's got anything open. It's hard work, but it'll keep you in shape, give you something for your resume. Come on, and then I'll take you out to the Mega Cart. It's really pretty cool."

Russell couldn't object. He had nothing else to do and didn't think he could insist on staying behind. Besides, he didn't want to discourage Manny's concern for his welfare.

"Pull that door hard so it'll lock," Manny said, loping down the steps. Russell slammed it hard enough to rattle the windows, then checked to make sure it was locked. The door opened, so he slammed it harder. This time the lock caught and he walked down to the driveway. He smiled to see the car. It was the same one Manny had driven in high school: a cherry red '63 Impala that Carmela had named "The Imp." It had been well cared for. The chrome was polished, and the waxed body glinted in the sun.

"Water lilies are ancient plants," Russell observed as they drove along the shore of the lake. "Been around a couple hundred million years at least."

Manny looked at him over the top of his sunglasses, his wrist resting on the steering wheel. "You notice the new paint job on The Imp? Original color, new paint. Took it to Earl Scheib—any car, any color, ninety-nine dollars. Dropped a new engine in her a few years ago." He rubbed the upholstery on the seat. "Had this cleaned, the whole thing detailed. It's like new. I want to keep this car forever."

They turned and headed downtown on their way to the gravel quarry.

"I saw the weirdest thing this morning," Russell remembered as they approached downtown. "In the parking lot of Fisker's Furniture. This fat guy in a nightgown and one of those long nightcaps standing next to this big old bed. He was waving a wand and there was this sign that said, 'The Celestial Bed.' It was freaky. I just kind of looked at it and walked on."

"Let's check it out," Manny said. With a jerk of the wheel he changed lanes and made a hard right, racing through a yellow light. They pulled into the parking lot. It was empty. As they idled there, Manny looked carefully around him.

"What are you talking about? Celestial Bed, my ass. I ain't seeing no Celestial Bed, pal."

"I'm telling you I saw it earlier. Go in and ask if you want."

Manny shifted the transmission into park and shook his head. "Right. I'm going to go walk into Fisker's Furniture and ask to see 'The Celestial Bed.' Yeah, right. What do you think I am, some kind of fool?"

"I'm just telling you what I saw."

"Well, you see it now?"

"No."

Manny clicked his tongue. "Say it," he ordered.

"What?"

"Say, 'There ain't no Celestial Bed.'"

Russell barked a bemused laugh and repeated, "There ain't no Celestial Bed."

"Say it again," Manny insisted.

"Oh, come on."

"Say it again, and mean it this time."

"There ain't no Celestial Bed."

"All right," said Manny, now thoroughly humored. "Let's get out of here."

Abruptly reversing, he spun the car around and squealed out across four lanes of traffic, gunned it through a red light and sped out of town.

———•———

A guard walked toward them as they approached the gate to the quarry.

"Flip him off," Russell sneered, poking Manny in the ribs. "Flip him off and ram the gate."

Manny swatted him and leaned out the window. "We're here to see Felix Contreras."

The guard nodded, opened the gate and waved them through. Men covered with dust worked among roaring machinery. Mountains of sand and gravel rimmed the pit. They drove slowly to a corrugated tin building where they were directed to Felix's office. He was on the phone when they walked in and greeted them with a hesitant wave, holding his hand in the air while he continued his conversation with a strained expression. Noise from the machines outside vibrated the fake wood paneling of the windowless room. Fluorescent tubes glared from a cracked fixture. A fan tried to ventilate the room, but succeeded only in rustling the pages of a company calendar tacked on the wall behind the desk. They remained standing, although they could have seated themselves on a sagging couch. Felix hung up and loosened his tie. Sweat beaded on his brow as he addressed Manny.

"Hi. What are you doing here?"

He turned to Russell and nodded, letting his gaze linger on him a moment.

"Hey, Felix. You know Russ Pinske?"

"Afraid not." He extended his hand. "Good to meet you."

"Yeah, Russ is an old friend of ours. He just got back in town. I told him about you always looking for help."

Felix sighed. "Guys, I wish you'd been here about a month ago. I got a full crew now. Nothing open except for haulers." He looked hopefully at Russell. "You got a commercial license?"

Russell considered whether he should reveal that his ordinary license had expired a while ago, but said only, "No."

"That's all I need now. But who knows—a week from now could be different. Here," he reached under a stack of papers on his desk and handed over a card. "Give me a call if you don't find anything else. Jobs open up all the time."

Relieved, Russell turned to leave. Manny stayed behind.

"You coming by tonight?" he asked.

"No," Felix said. "I'm coaching Ernesto's Little League tonight. We'll probably stop by, but it depends on Liz. She's feeling tired all the time these days."

Manny nodded. "All right. Later on." He walked to the door where Russell stood.

"Take it easy," Felix called out from behind his desk. "Thanks for coming by."

Manny cranked the volume on a disco station as they jostled along back roads. A hawk circled in the hazy, humid sky. Fields of corn and beans blanketed the rolling land, interspersed with clumps of trees. Russell didn't know exactly where they were, but Manny seemed to know where he was going, and he seemed to want to get there in a hurry. He muscled the wheel and swerved onto another road, sending gravel and dust flying behind them. They crossed a bridge over a creek and Russell recognized the road they were on.

"OK, I know where we are. I went to grade school out here."

Manny turned the radio down. "Yeah, I want to show you something."

Kingsford Elementary School used to be out in the country. New houses now sprawled across land that had once been dairy farms and alfalfa fields.

"Charlie Jenner built this whole subdivision," Manny boasted. "I wired a lot of them back when I was an apprentice."

"Wow," said Russell, at a loss to say anything else in the face of the countryside's transformation. Manny smiled and shot down the road to the highway. They drove to the job site and pulled into a dirt lot next to a couple of trailers.

"There it is," Manny said, cutting the engine. "Used to be a soybean field. Look at it now."

Russell looked. Rebar twisted out of concrete pilings sunk deep into the fertile loam. Men worked on scaffolding along a partially completed wall, while earthmovers cleared and leveled the perimeter. Manny opened the door, leaving the keys in the ignition.

"I can trust you with The Imp?"

"You know it," Russell assured him, glad to be offered wheels.

"Pick me up at four-thirty. Don't be late." He reached in the back seat, grabbed his hard hat and tool belt, got out of the car, and walked to one of the trailers. Russell slid into the driver's seat.

The car glided into a space right in front of the Red Rooster Inn. Back when Carl tended bar here, he lived in one of the apartments upstairs. It was there that Russell first met Guy Bogel and Gary Pierce, who shared a place with an ever-changing rotation of shiftless creeps. They were always on the make, working the angles of one scam or another, and in his few interactions with them he had been fascinated by their reckless energy. He climbed the worn, creaking stairs to the third floor. All the apartments were empty. The door of their old unit had been torn off its hinges. Trash covered the floor. A rat skittered through the litter. He returned to the street.

He had a notion to walk around downtown, see what it was like these days, maybe pick up a joy buzzer for Manny. A couple blocks along he spied Helen's scooter. It was hard to miss, with a big wicker basket strapped to the handlebars and an orange pennant fixed to the rear fender. At some point it had been painted yellow, but that paint was scratched and chipped in places, allowing the original blue to show through and giving it a sort of mottled look. He walked slowly down the street.

"You're not going to just walk right by me like that, mister."

The voice stopped him. Slowly he turned. She stood akimbo and stared at him sternly, tapping a sandaled foot under her long silk skirt. He took a step backward; she took a step forward. Her green eyes flashed like the first ray of sun on the sea.

"So are you even going to try to make excuses, or are you just going to stand there?"

"I was looking for you," he began, leaning toward her. "I saw your scooter. I just got in town. I stopped by your place, but you weren't there." She continued to stare him down as he approached. He threw his arms up and admitted, "I'm the world's worst friend. I totally suck."

A single blonde curl fell out from under her bandanna and dangled in front of her ear. "The truth's a pity," she quipped with a crooked grin, "but there it is." Her grin broke into a smile, her endearing malocclusion widening as she beamed. She wrapped her arms around him and picked him up off the ground.

"Whoa," came his surprised response. She put him down.

"I've been working out." She flexed her arms. "Pumping iron. What do you think?"

"Impressive," he said, truly impressed. "Hey, what are you up to? Summer job?"

"Oh yeah." She said with a tone of exasperation. "Retail job. Hadn't really planned on it, but this old friend of my folks, Wayne Edwards, opened up an antique shop last spring. I ran into him a while ago and he needed help, so here I am for the next couple months." She tapped his upper arm. "What are you up to, stranger?"

"Well, I left Cincinnati for good. Just got into town this morning. I'm on the road, looking for somewhere to go, something to do." What he heard himself saying sounded absurd, so he added a modifying, "Or something like that."

"And what are you doing for fun?" she asked with a smile.

He gave her a good long look, then hugged her.

"Oh, Helen, I'm glad you don't hate me."

She patted his back and broke the embrace, saying, "I'm glad I don't, either."

"You know, I stopped by your place this morning. Actually, you were the first person I looked up. But you weren't there, and Myrtle wouldn't tell me where you were."

"Myrtle?" She looked startled. "You talked to Myrtle?"

"Yeah, she was in your apartment when I knocked."

Her eyes narrowed. "Myrtle was in my apartment?"

"Yeah, the front door was open, she was in there. At least, I guess it was her—she wouldn't confirm or deny that she was Myrtle."

"Scrawny old bird with a blue fright wig?"

"Yep," he said, his affection for her rekindling as they talked.

"That stinker. I'm going to have to have a talk with her."

"So, you didn't know she was in there?"

"No, I didn't. And I didn't give her permission either."

She stared into middle distance and recalled, "I gave her a copy of my key a few months ago so she could water plants and stuff when I was up in Michigan." She wagged a finger as she declared, "And I got that key back, I know I did. She must have made a copy. That stinker!"

He snickered. She huffed and pointed at him.

"You're good for something after all—letting me know that's been going on all this time. I'm going to chew her out good, boy."

She fumed a little, then calmed down and said, "Hey, I've got to get back. I'm the only one here today. Let me give you my number. Call me tonight. I don't have any plans, except maybe slapping Myrtle around. But we'll get together and do some catching up."

He found a scrap of paper in his pocket and wrote the number she recited.

"That's unlisted," she added.

He told her he'd call her later, then she got back to work. He walked to the novelty store and bought a joy buzzer.

After an aimless drive around town, he ended up on a county road out by Bass Lake, where Guy's father, Frank, lived. He knew better than to stop if Frank's car was there. Once on a carouse with Guy and Gary he'd been in the house while Guy raided the refrigerator and liquor cabinet, something he did on occasion. Although he'd never met Frank, he'd heard enough of Guy's stories to steer clear of him. Frank had seen action in Vietnam, and the house was filled with military paraphernalia. Things had gotten really bad when Guy's mother abandoned them all. Guy was eight at the time; his autistic brother Bob was six. That was the same year Frank lost most of his right foot when a bucket of hot tar spilled on him. The boys were pretty much left to their own devices while he drank and popped pills. Guy left the house at fifteen. Frank lived off illicit arms sales, supplemented with Bob's welfare checks.

The driveway was clear, so Russell stopped to see if Bob was home, and if he knew where to find Guy. When his persistent knocking went unanswered, he turned to leave. The door opened behind him, and Bob stuck his head out.

"Hey, Bob," he said, turning. "I'm Russ Pinske, used to hang out with Guy a little."

"Uh-huh." Bob eyed him with suspicion.

"Know where I can find him?" He smiled, consciously using his most friendly tone.

"Nope."

"Have you seen him? Is he still around?"

"I don't know. My dad's coming back, and he gets mad at Guy's friends." With that he closed the door.

Exhausted, Russell drove back to Carmela and Manny's. He tried several of the dozens of keys on Manny's ring before he found the one that let him into the house. Tossing the keys on the kitchen table, he went back to the guest room, unfolded the bed from the couch, and rummaged through his backpack for an old alarm clock. He wound it, and set it to get him up in time to retrieve Manny.

His deep, dreamless sleep came to an abrupt end. Carmela was jumping on the bed in her stocking feet, her long ponytail flailing about her bobbing head. She giggled and squealed while bouncing around. He regarded her with mouth agape and groggy eyelids drooping.

"Come on," she said brightly. "Get up and take a shower. We're going to my folks' for dinner. Put on some good clothes—you know my mom can't stand sloppy."

"What the hell's going on here?" Manny's voice boomed down the hall. Russell sat up. Carmela stopped bouncing. He stepped into the room, arms crossed over his chest, looking pissed.

"I let you use my car, tell you to pick me up, and this is how you thank me? Leaving me stuck out at work while you lie around here stinking up my house, snoring like a pig?"

Russell gasped. "Manny, dude, I set my alarm." He grabbed his clock and shook it. Manny burst out laughing, and Carmela rolled her eyes.

"You can never pull anything off," she said with a disappointed shake of her head.

He laughed and nodded in agreement. "You're right. I always crack up."

Carmela began bouncing again, acting goofier than before. Russell held his clock.

"Don't hurt your clock," she told him. "I came home and saw you and turned it off, and went to pick him up." She dived off the bed toward Manny, shouting, "Catch me!"

He did, and carried her out of the room in his arms.

Russell rifled through his backpack, found the best clothes he had and threw them on the bed. They were pretty wrinkled, but they'd have to do. He stepped into the shower. A breeze came through the open window, carrying a hint of rain that blended sweetly with the water splashing on cool tiles. He wrapped himself in a fluffy towel and returned to the guest room. The bed had been made, his clothes had been ironed and laid out. He dressed, ran a comb through his mop of hair, and stepped out to join his friends.

4

"So, how are your folks?" Russell asked Carmela as they rode together to the Contreras' family home.

"Oh, my mom's beautiful as ever. She's still at the alterations shop every morning, to make sure everything gets out, but she leaves around noon, instead of staying around all day like she used to. That's good for her, I think. My dad's still my dad. He's got two new shops in Michigan City, so he's there a lot. Mom keeps telling him to take it easy, let Luis take over, but he just works all the time still."

"He's a walking heart attack," Manny commented.

She turned to him and said sharply, "Don't say things like that."

"It's true," he persisted. "The way he eats, always working—what did your mom say his cholesterol was? Something crazy, way up there. Blood as thick as pudding."

She stiffened, stared straight ahead and stated, "We're done talking about my father's health now."

Manny cast a glance over at Russell, who avoided his eyes. They came to a stop at a red light. A decidedly unstable-looking fellow loped into the crosswalk. He stretched his scrawny neck, thrust his head over the hood of the car and stared at the three occupants with a yellow-toothed snarl. He narrowed his eyes on Manny, who imitated his expression and leaned over the wheel, staring back. The guy crossed slowly to the curb, eyes fixed on Manny's. He stood there and continued staring at them. Manny kept his eye on him.

"What's that guy's problem?" he muttered.

"I don't know," answered Carmela, "but let's not make it ours."

The light changed and they drove on.

"How's Isabel?" Russell continued inquiring about her kin.

Manny snorted.

"What's so funny?" Russell wanted to know.

"Just thinking about when you had a thing for Isabel," Manny explained. "It's funny."

Carmela looked at her husband with something just shy of scorn, then turned to Russell and said brightly, "Isabel is fine, thank you. She's teaching English at a school in Mexico, living with my Aunt Rosa. We write to each other every month or so. I'll tell her you asked about her."

Manny snorted again, and Russell leaned across Carmela to tell him, "I don't know about having 'a thing' for Isabel, but I like her all right. All the Contreras women are charming."

Carmela planted a kiss on Russell's cheek as Manny laughed approvingly.

"And how's Nestor?"

"Oh, Nestor, now let me tell that one," Manny started. Carmela cast him a sideways glance as he launched into a story that he obviously relished.

"You know he married Lisa Strube, right? Just out of high school—bam—and her dad buys them a house, a real nice house. She was going to school, but Nestor just plopped his ass down. She started riding him, so he got this band together, right? Only they sucked and could never get any gigs, and it was just an excuse for him to party anyway. So she kicked him out, and he went bonkers. I mean, seriously bonkers. He spray painted crap on the house, smashed her car with a sledgehammer, ran around screaming, got picked up downtown butt naked one night. The works. Mom and Dad sent him away someplace downstate. He got back last year and he's living with them, not doing much of anything that anyone can tell. He's a lot mellower now, on his meds, but man, get him talking and he's a pure, unadulterated freak."

Carmela piped up. "What's your problem with my family tonight?"

"I'm just saying the guy's a freak. I like him, but you got to admit he's out there."

"He's my brother. And your brother-in-law."

"Oh, I know. I love your family. Really I do. They're just funny to me is all."

"Well, I'm glad we can amuse you," she said coolly.

Manny shot another look at Russell, who returned it this time.

They parked next to a bunch of cars angled together on one side of the house.

"Is that new siding?" Russell asked.

"Nope," Manny answered, setting the brake. "Painted a couple years ago, though."

Her parents had a nice spread with their three-story house on a sizable piece of land, complete with a duck pond in the backyard. They were both first-generation Americans, born to Mexican families that had moved here in the 1940s. Alejandro, her father, had graduated from business school and started the dry cleaners that provided their family income. Her mother, Letitia, was an equal partner in the business, in charge of alterations and repairs. They had been married for thirty-five years, and had lived in this house for thirty.

Dad was at the barbecue on the patio. Four picnic tables were joined together and laden with dishes of food. A few guys tossed a Frisbee. A croquet match was underway in the backyard. Children gamboled about, playing games and chasing ducks.

"Who's this?" Dad nodded as Russell approached. He was a short, stocky man with eyes that squinted above his broad cheeks. His short, thick hair was still mostly black, but flecked with gray.

"Russ Pinske," Carmela said, giving her dad a quick peck on the cheek.

"Good to know you," he said, holding his hand out to Russell.

"Russ has been here before, dad," she said as she headed to the door with a sack of corn she'd brought.

"Oh, sure, I remember," he said, although it was clear he didn't.

Dad got back to the grill, and Russell followed Carmela into the house. Manny had meanwhile joined the Frisbee game.

Letitia was a great collector of things, and adept at their artful display. Russell stopped at the kitchen door to admire a collection of eyecups.

"Russ Pinske," Letitia said from across the kitchen. He came in. Fortunately the daughters had inherited the fine features of their mother. With Carmela standing there beside her, it occurred to him for the first time that the kids all stood a good head or two taller than their parents.

"Russ Pinske," she repeated, looking him square in the eye. Without the slightest trace of a smile she asked, "What are you doing here?"

He looked at Carmela, then back to her mother and answered, "I'm back in town for a while."

She considered this with a tight-lipped hum as she continued chopping ingredients for a huge salad bowl. Without looking up, she said, "Russ, get out of my kitchen. Nothing personal, but men get in the way in my kitchen. You want to be useful, go clean this corn. Outside."

He took the bag of corn and two empty bags and went to the kitchen door. Carmela winked at him as he left, then busied herself in her appointed tasks. He sat on the stairs, the bag of corn at his side, the two empty bags open at his feet. A screened-in gazebo stood halfway between the stairs and the pond. He could see part of the croquet game, and the Frisbee players occasionally drifted into view. The grill was out of his line of sight, but the smoke reached him where he sat, quite contented with his shucking.

Nestor stepped out of the gazebo, letting the screen door slam behind him. He lazily crossed the lawn, lifting a lanky arm in a sort of half-wave, half-salute to Russell.

"Hey, Russ," he said, sitting down on the stairs. "When did you get in town?" He blinked his eyes rapidly, as though something irritated them. He looked tired. His clothes were wrinkled, and he needed a shave.

"Just this morning."

Nestor ran a hand through his long black hair and said, "Yeah, Carmela said something, like, a month ago about you maybe coming to town."

"Took me a while to get my act together, but here I am." He tossed a clean ear of corn into a bag and got to work shucking another.

"She said something about you going on a road trip, something like that."

"Yeah, that's what I'm telling people. I just want to get out and see the country, you know? See what's happening out there."

"Any real reason, or just to say you've done it?"

"Well, I'm hoping I'll find something to get involved in, maybe someplace cool I want to live, some community to be part of. But I'll be damned if I know what I'm looking for."

Nestor grunted. "You might be more damned if you find it."

Their eyes met.

"Well, what the hell you hanging round this shit-hole for?" Nestor blurted. "Get out—get out while you can. Go!" He grabbed Russell's arm and mock-dragged him down the stairs. "Try to get to the county line before it's too late!"

They shared a laugh, then Nestor continued. "Seriously, though, man, you stay around too long, and this place will get its hooks in you. Suck you right in. Suck you in so good you'll forget you ever wanted to leave. That's when it starts to quietly digest you from the inside out." He paused, contemplating whether to continue in this vein, then pointed to the bag of corn. "Give me one of those. Shame on my mom, putting her guest to work."

"Oh, it's cool," Russell shook his head and finished another ear. "I don't really know anyone here. And I can hardly charm them with my Spanish."

"I suppose," Nestor agreed, husking the corn with muscular efficiency. "Well, you got your whole assortment here this evening. A few friends of the family, few aunts and uncles, cousins, nieces, nephews. All like that."

Having vigorously stripped the husks, he now meticulously began removing the silk strand by strand. Russell watched his delicate movements.

"So, Manny told me on the way over here that you went nuts."

With his intense concentration focused on one particular strand, he softy stated, "Man, you don't know nothing till you've been through the wringer like I have. Goddamn." He peeled off the thread and moved to another, isolating it from a tangle. "And now I'm always going to be 'Crazy Nestor.' Someday, 'Crazy Old Nestor.' As long as I'm around all these people, who keep thinking of me as 'Crazy Nestor,' see me as 'Crazy Nestor,' how can I not be 'Crazy Nestor?'"

He removed his current strand of concern, and with a triumphal flourish cast it to the wind. He immediately singled out another strand and continued talking, almost in a whisper. "All I know is I got to get out of here any way I can, get away from all these eyes pinning me down as 'Crazy Nestor.' Got to make a clean break and head off where no one knows me. I think East Coast."

Russell finished the remainder of the bag while Nestor continued his futile attempt to remove each tassel individually. He handed the uncompleted ear to Russell and said, "You finish it. I just can't." He got up, walked down the steps, stopped and said, "I don't know if I'm going to make the big feed, so if I don't, stop by the gazebo before you leave. I'll be out there."

Russell took the cleaned corn to the kitchen. Carmela met him at the door, set the bag on a counter and ushered him back out onto the landing.

"I saw Nestor out here helping you. He's really been looking forward to seeing you, I know, ever since I told him you were coming. He seems all right to you?"

"Well, he's Nestor," Russell began. "You know, but he seems kind of nervous and distracted. But he's always been kind of nervous and distracted, I guess, so who's to say? He's definitely still Nestor."

"Yeah," she said with a sigh. She wrapped her arm around him. "Hey, I want to thank you for your compliments on my embroidery work this morning. You really like it?"

"Sure, Carmela, it's great." He felt her enthusiasm swell, and he liked pumping it up. She unhooked her arm and leaned out over the railing.

"You know, like on consignment or something. It'd be great if some of them sold. I like to think about people wearing them, putting them on their tables, giving them as Christmas gifts or whatever. I just want to get my stuff out there in the world."

One of the croquet players gave a shout that sent some ducks flying. She turned and smiled at him.

"I'm going to go boil that corn. Why don't you play Frisbee? I see Manny down there with Luis."

She went back inside, and he took himself over to the game. Dad waved when he walked by. Manny saw him and yelled, "Russ—go long!"

He sent the Frisbee flying. Russell ran to intercept it, fell short and dived for it, touching it with his fingers but not grabbing hold. He got up, brushed himself off and picked up the disc, to the evident delight of Dad, who shouted, "Hey, he plays fetch! Hey, Fido! How you like it?"

Russell ignored the comment and walked toward Manny, who indicated that he should turn around, just as Dad's voice rang out again.

"Hey, how you like it?"

Russell turned to see the man holding a steak above the grill.

"Rare," he answered. Dad started laughing.

"Rare. Rare. That's him all right," he called out to Manny and Luis. "He's a rare one all right!"

It took a while for the crowd to be seated when dinner was called. Russell had gotten separated from Manny and Carmela, and was surrounded by strangers. They all held hands as a white-haired man said a prayer. Although Russell's Spanish was limited, he followed the gist of the blessing, heavy on the gratitude for family, making him even more self-conscious of being a stranger among them. After the meal began, he felt a slap on his back, and Nestor appeared at his side.

"I decided I'm hungry after all," he said with a broad smile.

A plentiful meal was set before them. Platters were heaped with grilled meat and shrimp. Bowls overflowed with salads of every stripe— bean salad, lettuce salad, potato salad, egg salad, macaroni salad, fruit salad. There were plates of corn, beets, biscuits and bread. Carmela made sure Russell tried a dish she'd concocted with melon and walnuts. Dishes clattered. Children shouted, giggled, and carried on. Everyone talked at once, a babble largely unintelligible to Russell, who concentrated on his plate. The food looked especially good to him, and he dug in. Nestor nudged him.

"See the redhead?" He tilted his chin and drew Russell's attention down the table to a woman whose flaming mane was hard not to notice. "Luis's girlfriend, Cheryl," Nestor continued. "Check her out."

Her complexion was pale and freckled. There was almost no food on her plate, and she wasn't eating any of it. Her watery eyes bulged from their sockets and stared beyond the table. Russell followed her far-off gaze and saw that she was watching a duck waddling on the lawn. Suddenly she grabbed a soda can and raised it to her lips, then closed her eyes and jerked her head back as she took a quick swallow.

"She's one weird girl," said Nestor in a confidential tone. "And you know, if I'm calling someone weird, well, keep your eye on her. She's nuts. Takes one to know one, you know."

Russell looked at her again. This time she noticed him. They looked at each other for a moment. Then she rolled her eyes back in her head, picked up her soda and took another bird-like gulp. Russell returned to his meal and devoured a pile of shrimp.

A cooler of ice cream was presented for dessert. Russell ignored the sweets and began to help clean up. He was dismissed by a woman who told him not to bother, so he started to walk off to the gazebo to which Nestor had already retired. On his way he remembered with a start that he hadn't called Helen. He sought out Carmela for permission to use the phone. She led him into the kitchen and left him there. He picked up the receiver and searched his pockets for her number, then realized he'd left it behind. He really didn't want to blow her off again, but he slouched and hung up.

Out in the gazebo, Nestor was writing. He glanced up as Russell came in.

"Hey, grab a seat. I'm just taking a few notes here. Something on my mind."

Nestor sat at a desk, surrounded by a futon and a chest of drawers. Crates full of books were piled everywhere. Russell sat in a folding chair.

"What, do you live out here now?" he asked.

Nestor answered while he continued to write. "Yeah. My dad kept telling me I should move out of the house, so I did." He looked up with a smirk on his face. "Moved out here. For the summer at least." He capped his pen and moved over to the futon, where he stretched out.

"Dad mostly just ignores me now. Whenever he does notice me he calls me a kook. But Mom's cool. She knows I'll probably just disappear one of these days. 'Crazy Nestor' getting lost in the crowd in New York City."

The horizon turned yellow and the air thickened. A charge built in the atmosphere, like a storm might be coming. The air was still, without the slightest breeze. Slanting light cast the scene in a greenish tinge.

"I've been concentrating on my music," Nestor said. "Let me play you something I've been working on." He reached behind the futon and pulled out an electronic keyboard, then looked through a crate for a long orange extension cord. Russell followed him to the house.

"My dad hates it when I do this. Let's go round the back and avoid a freak out." He led him to the rear door and located an outlet. Russell turned to head back out, but Nestor stopped him and waved him up a set of stairs.

"Come up here for a second and check out my mom's latest craze."

They stood in a little alcove of shelves filled with shuttlecocks.

"See this one?" Nestor handed him a bundle of cork and feathers. "Passenger pigeon feathers," he said. "They used to blacken the sky. Now this is all that's left."

Russell handed it back. "Pretty wild."

"Yeah." Nestor started down the steps. "You want to know something wild—you know about Isabel?"

"Carmela said she was living in Mexico."

"Right, with Aunt Rosa." They left the house and headed across the lawn. "Did she tell you about the unsuitable suitor?"

Russell shook his head.

They entered the gazebo and sat together on the futon. "Maybe she doesn't know," he began. "But my mom got a weird-ass call last week about this guy Isabel was dating. I guess he creeped Rosa out, she said she got this bad vibe off him. So Isabel's going out with this guy, and then Rosa finds out he's married. She tells Isabel and she puts the guy out. Then he comes back the next day with a big bouquet of flowers, only Isabel wasn't home. Rosa grabbed the flowers and threw them on the ground and—this is what my aunt told my mom—then the flowers turned into hissing green worms."

"What?" Russell exclaimed.

Nestor laughed and continued. "I know. That's what she said, big hissing green worms. The guy ran off and she stepped on them and squished them and she said they were full of black blood that smelled like sulfur."

"OK," Russell slowly intoned, trying to determine by Nestor's expression if this was some sort of joke.

Nestor laughed again, then stood and shrugged his shoulders. He set up his keyboard and began cranking out swirling chord progressions. He closed his eyes and swayed rhythmically, leaned across the keyboard and chanted in a slow drawl, "All skate! Everybody skate!"

"No way!" Russell shouted.

Nestor continued playing, then trailed off and said, "What, no way?"

"I was just talking about that this morning," Russell excitedly explained. "I walked by the roller rink and thought about that guy and his 'all skate, everybody skate' thing."

"Well," Nestor chuckled, "I've been working for a while on a concept, sort of a take-off on *The Phantom of the Opera*, maybe something like, *Phantom of the Roller Rink*."

Russell stared at him. "That's just weird."

"Yeah, it's a weird world," Nestor sanguinely affirmed, then launched back into his homage to the maestro of the rink.

Carmela gave a perfunctory knock and walked in. "Hey, guys."

Russell stood as she entered. Her brother kept playing, his eyes closed and his whole body swaying.

"Manny's ready to go," she said.

They stood together a moment and Nestor's keyboard faded out. He walked over to his desk, picked up an envelope and handed it to Russell.

"Good to see you again, man." He slapped him on the back. "Come on out here and see me again before you leave town. We should talk more."

As they stepped out of the gazebo, Nestor pointed at the envelope and said, "That's a little souvenir from dinner for you."

Carmela and Russell caught up with Manny near the front porch, where he stood talking to a middle-aged man wearing a wide-brimmed hat. Three other hatted men stood in an adjacent cluster, talking amongst themselves. Manny noticed their approach and hailed them.

"Russ, here, meet Arturo."

Russell took a couple of steps forward to shake hands with the man, who looked him up and down and asked, "You work?"

Manny put his arm around Russell's shoulder. "I told Art you were looking for work. He's the lead man on a field crew. Turns out he needs a few new hands."

Arturo again addressed Russell. "You work hard? It's hard work. Out in the sun. Sunrise to sunset. Forty dollars a day, paid cash at the end of the week."

"Work for a month and you'll more than double your roll," Manny nudged him. "Keep you moving a lot longer."

Arturo continued explaining the terms of employment. "You start Monday. Be at the Five Star parking lot at five-thirty. Truck takes you out, brings you back. We got water. Bring a bottle to carry with you. Bring food. You'll burn out there, so bring a hat."

Russell nodded, not knowing how to get out of this without looking like a shirker.

"OK. You be there Monday at five-thirty."

"All right," said Manny as they walked to the car. "I feel better about that now."

They drove slowly past the handsome estates on one of the town's wide boulevards. Most dated from the nineteenth century: spacious old mansions set among towering maples and sycamores. Russell thought about the families and all the generations that had inhabited them, about stories told and lives lived.

"Hey, take him by the free house," Carmela said.

Manny took an abrupt right.

"Free house?" Russell asked.

"Yeah, free if you can move it. You tell it, Manny."

"I heard from some guys at work about this guy, Jim Ryan I think his name is, a businessman—"

Carmela interrupted with a little snort.

"What?" Manny asked.

She tried to explain. "Businessman. That word is funny to me."

"What's so funny about it?" Manny wanted to know.

Russell gave her a knowing look and said, "Time zone." They both giggled.

"What?" Manny said again, thoroughly perplexed. "You two talking in some kind of weird code now?"

"Some words are just funny," Carmela said.

"Businessman," Russell repeated, and she snickered.

Manny glanced at them and continued where he left off. "Anyway, this businessman—go ahead and laugh—he, well, owns a business, and he wants to expand to the next lot. So he buys it, but there's this old house on it. Needs some work, nobody's lived in it for a while, but it's a nice old house and he really doesn't want to tear it down. So he put out the word that anyone who'll move it off the property can have it for free. He's not going to expand till September, so someone's got to take him up on it before then."

They pulled up and idled in front of a peeling but proud Victorian house sitting in the middle of a yard gone to seed.

"How much to move it?" Russell asked.

"I heard someone say forty grand just to jack it up, then you have to move the utility lines, and haul it at, like, five miles an hour to wherever it's going to go. It'd be pretty cool to see. Hell, I'd take it if I had a place to put it."

Carmela liked that idea. "Oh, that's good. You know how some people have cars up on blocks in their front yards? We could have houses up on blocks in our front yard! Lots of 'em!"

They drove away and headed toward the center of town.

"Can you believe they wanted to tear down the train depot?" Carmela said as they passed by the stately old building.

"No," Russell gasped. "Why did they want to do that?"

"Parking," she responded with a disgusted tone. "This town is obsessed with parking. Tear it all down and pave it over!"

"Well," Manny interjected, "the traffic is getting pretty bad. Sometimes you can't find a decent spot anywhere."

Carmela raised a finger. "But we can't keep losing nice old houses and tearing down things like the train depot. Too much is getting bulldozed lately without too much getting said about it, if you ask me."

"Run for office," Manny said, as though they'd had this conversation before. "Run for mayor. I'd vote for you. I'd even work on your campaign a little."

They cruised along Lincoln Way for a few blocks, then turned and went past the Masonic Temple and the old Rumacher Hotel.

"Now there's something they've done right," Manny said with civic pride. "Remember it used to be all worn down? Complete restoration, inside and out. It's beautiful in that lobby, man. Go in there sometime and just sit. They've got these murals on the walls that tell the whole history of the region. It's cool."

"That was a good move," Carmela agreed.

They continued meandering through the town. Russell took out his pocket watch, but it had stopped. He reset it and wound it.

"Got someplace to be?" Manny asked.

"Oh, no. I thought if it was earlier I'd ask to get back to your guys' place so I could call Helen, but it's too late to call now." He sighed, disappointed in himself for blowing her off, even if it was inadvertent.

"Helen?" Carmela asked. "Didn't you call her from Mom and Dad's?"

Russell frowned. "I tried, only I didn't have her number with me, and it's unlisted. I just saw her today and I told her I'd call her tonight." He trailed off into a shrug.

"You brought her to our wedding, didn't you?" Carmela asked. "I remember her dancing barefoot."

Russell smiled at the recollection.

"So you guys are still friends?"

Russell rolled his eyes. "I hope so. I haven't talked to her in a while, but looked her up this morning and ran into her later, downtown. It was good to see her, and I hate dogging her tonight."

Manny and Carmela exchanged a look.

"Should we get home?" she suggested.

"Oh, not on my account," Russell insisted. "I'm liking this little drive. I'll call her tomorrow."

They resumed their slow cruise.

"So, you never did tell me about you and Gloria," Carmela prompted Russell, who immediately began to squirm.

"Oh, God—do I have to talk about that?"

Manny chuckled. "Women, Russ—they love to get the dirt on one another."

Carmela swatted him. "You're in fine form tonight." She turned her attention to Russell and said, "I'm afraid you bring out the worst in him."

Manny winked. "You're a bad influence."

They stopped at a red light.

"Aah!" Carmela cried. Both men jumped.

"What?"

"Oh, whew," she whispered, holding her hand to her breast. "It was nothing. Just that guy, see him?" They followed her pointing finger to a man wearing camouflage fatigues. She began to giggle as she continued. "I couldn't see his body—it was completely camouflaged—I just saw this head go floating by."

Manny wiped his brow. "Damn it, woman, don't do shit like that. You make me all nervous."

"If it gets any greener it'll puke on ya!" Carmela taunted Manny as he lagged behind the changing light. She was giggling hard now.

"All right, all right," he said, slowly pulling into the intersection. "Not like I'm holding anyone up."

"Look out!" Russell shouted in alarm as a big old boat of a car hurtled through the intersection on an obvious collision course.

With a cry of "Shit!" Manny assessed the situation and gunned the accelerator, hoping to clear the intersection and avoid getting broadsided. The front end of the other car hit the Imp in the right rear fender and spun it around.

"Goddamnit," was all Manny could say when he climbed out of the car.

"Calm down, it's OK. No one's hurt," Carmela reassured him.

He stormed over to the other vehicle, where he was met with the squinting sneer of an elderly woman.

"Well, I don't know how you drive where you're from," she scolded him, "but around here we stop at red lights."

Manny stood dumbfounded a moment, then informed her, "I come from here. And my light was green."

"Look, look here," she said, "You just got your paint scraped. You should consider yourself lucky that I don't report you."

"Holy moley!" Manny roared. "Lady, you're paying for a new fender."

A nearby homeowner called the police, who came and talked to Manny and the other driver, a Mrs. Enid Kartch. They were given an incident report and the advice to be careful.

———— • ————

"Damn," Manny mumbled as he paced around the porch. "Damn, damn, damn."

"We'll get it fixed, it's OK."

"But it was perfect—perfect when I got it, and perfect until now. Until tonight, when old lady Kartch rammed into it with her lame-ass old Caddy. Damn."

Carmela tried to calm him down. "Lighten up, man."

Manny was having none of it. "See that car?" he pointed into the darkness. "That's not the same car anymore. That car used to be perfect, and now it's not anymore."

Carmela arched an eyebrow. "It's just a car, Manny."

"I know, I know," Manny said. "It's just a car. But goddamn, I've kept it like I wanted it for this long and now— just like that—it's totally altered. From this point on, it's a different car. Thanks to old lady Kartch. What the hell kind of name is that, anyway?"

By way of distraction, Russell offered the comment, "Looks like that storm's passed by us."

Lightning sparked in the distance, too far away to resonate on this calm porch. Carmela and Russell watched Manny walk out to his car and disappear into the shadows. They heard him walking in the gravel, then silence, then the striking of a lighter. As a pinprick ember glowed in the driveway beneath them, Russell turned to Carmela.

"You want to know about Gloria," he began, scratching his chin. "I just remembered something. Once we were in bed and we were fighting about something—who knows what, we were always fighting about something—and at one point she just gave me this lame crap like, 'You're right. You're always right. I should know better than to ever voice my opinion.' God, that just irritated me. I shouted, 'No, I am not always right. In fact, I am frequently wrong!' And then I punched the wall. Only the wall was weaker than I thought, or I was stronger, and my fist went right through it. Then I punched it again and made the hole bigger and I yelled, 'See? See? I am not always right!'"

Carmela stared at him with a wide grin, then broke into a deep laugh. "You're funny, Russ." She hugged him. "I'm so glad you're here."

Manny shuffled back up the walk and onto the porch. He stopped by the door and offered a beer to Russell, who accepted. Carmela got up and followed him into the kitchen. They were inside awhile as he sat lazily swinging, watching the flashing sky. The night droned with cicadas, crickets and frogs. A mosquito bit him. Manny came out with the beers.

"Here," he said, handing one over, and seating himself on the railing.

They sipped their beers in silence. Then Manny came over and sat beside Russell on the swing. He took his shoes off and urged Russell to do the same. Then he put his left foot against Russell's right foot and said, "Look at that."

"What am I looking at?" Russell wanted to know.

"At our feet. See mine, and how regular the toe progression is? From the big toe—"

"That's the one who went to market," Russell interrupted.

"Right. From the big toe to the little toe—"

"Wee, wee, wee!" squealed Russell.

"Yeah, well, you see how regular all the toes are? Perfect, you might say. Each one proportionately smaller than the next. Now, you take yours. Boy, look at your toes. Those are some ugly toes you got on your feet. Are you a human, or a marmoset?"

Just as Russell was withdrawing his unworthy feet from the scrutiny of his perfect-toed friend, Carmela came out on the porch. Seeing Manny sitting with his toes splayed, she made an assumption and asked, "Is he getting off on his toes again?"

She sat between the two men, patted her husband on the knee and said in an overly patronizing tone, "We all know your toes are perfect, dear."

They swung together silently, until Russell spoke up.

"Hey, what's with the house numbers on this street?"

"Oh," Manny began with a low growl. "I don't know, but if I ever get my hands on the person responsible I'm gonna slap some sense into him. I talked to the postman, or postwoman, I guess, and she said she didn't know how it got to be so screwed up, but it's been screwed up so long that no one's going to do anything about it at this point. So I'm thinking I'll just change our address randomly. Right now it's 21. Tomorrow I'll change it to 32. Next Thursday it'll be 1508. Why not? It obviously doesn't matter."

Carmela got up and went inside again. They sat and drank their beer.

"Say, Russ," Manny turned to him. "Did you turn off the lights in the sewing room?"

Russell nodded that he had.

"OK. Just leave them alone next time. They're special fixtures with a ballast that should be turned on and off only once a day. Carmela knows that, and she takes care of it herself."

With this point understood, Manny moved to another topic of interest. "Hey, did she show you The Wiggler?"

"The what?" came Russell's reply.

"The Wiggler. It's in our basement, left over from whoever owned the place before. It's this antique exercise device. It's got this kind of platform you stand on, and there's this big rubber belt you put around your waist, and when you fire it up the belt starts moving and jerks your body around like a spaz. It's supposed to, like, vibrate your fat off or something. It's major machinery—I can see why they left it behind for someone else to deal with. Want to try it out?"

Russell shrugged and consented. As they were getting up, Carmela came back out and said, "What now?"

"I was going to introduce Russ to The Wiggler."

"No," she insisted. "God, no. Don't go down in that basement and get that thing going. It shakes the whole house. Sheesh—just give it a rest."

They all settled back. The sky was purple, the air was heavy.

"Hey," Russell began, "Nestor totally freaked me out tonight with something out in the gazebo. You know what we were talking about this morning, the roller-rink organist? Well, it turns out Nestor's been writing a piece of music about him, calling it *The Phantom of the Roller Rink.*"

She looked at him with a slightly skewed smile. "He's putting you on, Russ. I talked to him this afternoon, told him you were in town. He asked what you were up to, and I got to talking about what we talked about, and told him you'd mentioned the skating rink. He's goofing on you, pulling one of his jokes."

Russell rocked tranquilly, then said, "So, what should I make of the story he told me about the flowers turning into worms?"

With his friends staring at him, he related the story as he'd heard it.

"That's a new one on me," she said. "But I don't doubt it. I know for a fact that my Aunt Rosa has heard the voices of dead people on her radio."

The night quietly absorbed this statement.

Russell looked around for a minute, assessing his surroundings. "Your house is just great, guys, just great. And right over there is old Nellie Widow's."

"You know, I told you all her property went to the city, and now it's getting annexed to Fox Lake Park," Carmela said, gesturing into the darkness. "So there'll be one big park from the lake all the way up the ridge and out past here. Permanent green belt. Perfect for kids."

Manny stretched and yawned. "I'm getting tired."

"Oh, hey," Russell hastened to ask, "have you seen Carl or Ellie recently?"

Carmela, now also yawning, said, "I haven't talked to Ellie for a couple of weeks. But they're still living out at Stillwater. Carl's working some job in the city, sales rep or something."

"Yeah, remember last time they were out here?" Manny asked his wife. "Remember Carl freaking out about that rock pile out there by the road? He was about to go out there and tear it apart. I don't know what his problem was."

Carmela's cat came puttering across the porch and laid itself down at her feet. From where Russell sat he could clearly see the animal was pregnant.

"She's pregnant," he stated.

"Yep," she said softly while stroking her pet.

"Oh," he said, looking at Manny, who averted his eyes. "I just didn't know, that's all."

A breeze came off the lake, rustling the windsock a bit. Carmela patted her cat's head, then got up and gave Russell a quick kiss on the cheek.

"Good night, Russ."

The two men sat awhile, staring out at the black water.

"Seen Guy Bogel or Gary Pierce around?" Russell ventured to ask.

Manny face expressed disdain. "No, and I don't want to. Last time I saw those guys was when they came around here with a couple of AK-47s they were trying to get me to buy. What the hell do I want with one assault rifle, let alone two? Who knows where they got them, but I don't like that business. Those guys are bad news."

Russell accepted this and finished his beer. Manny got up and cracked his knuckles.

"I'm hitting the hay, Russ. You got the back room there, and anything you want. Just slam the door hard when you come in, so it locks. Don't worry about slamming it—I'll worry if I don't hear it slam. OK?"

They hugged. Manny smiled, squeezed his shoulder, and said, "See you tomorrow."

In the back room, as he was preparing to turn in, he remembered the envelope Nestor had given him. He opened it and read:

> The graceful curve of subatomic particles, unresolved musical sentences, subtle intonations eliciting resonant memories of the warning: Do not eat shellfish when the glow of the dinoflagellates can be seen from shore. She sat at the picnic table and looked out across the pond. Scum bobbed on the waves, and she tried to remember her name. At a loss, she drank her soda and turned to the conversation at table. Forty people were talking at once. She could grasp words, but they had no context. She thought two cousins may have been discussing whether an individual's name was Paco or Pablo. More voices joined in. Above the noise she heard the voice of Aunt Flora, who said, "Once I roped a wild horse and named him Paco." Aunt Flora's voice faded again into the confusion. An Eskimo Pie melted on a paper plate. Her amorphous mind continued to assimilate as she sipped soda and tried to conceal her swelling delight.

He folded the page, replaced it in the envelope, and tossed it on the nightstand. When undressing, he discovered two stickers on the back of his shirt. In thinking over the day, wondering who might have stuck them there and when, it seemed that everyone he'd been with had handled him in some way. It was Nestor's work, he decided, looking closely at the stickers. One was a severely crosshatched and demented rendering of the Big Boy mascot of the diner chain. The other depicted a stick figure pedestrian, like the one on signs at crosswalks, only this figure was hunched over, its feet in waves, and on its back was a lumpy bag labeled, CATS. He got out his journal, peeled off the Big Boy sticker and put it on the front cover. The other sticker ended up on the back. He set everything aside, turned off the light and shut out the world.

5

Carl Paulette awoke slowly, only gradually becoming aware that he was not where he'd been dreaming he was. That place was peaceful, full of light. Now he regained his senses in Mira's apartment. Mira was about the worst housekeeper he'd ever known. Her apartment had an innate dinginess, here in an old building on Chicago's North Side, and she sure hadn't done anything to brighten it up. Dreary light oozed through yellowed shades, falling on walls of an indiscriminate color. Piles of stuff squatted in every room—piles of clothes, newspapers, books, magazines, mail. Every inch of the place was marked with the detritus of daily life. It was a rat-hole, compared to the house he shared with Ellie. But this rat-hole was his retreat. He kind of hated it mostly, but sometimes it was just what he needed.

He rolled over and looked at the alarm clock. The digital display read 7:28 a.m. That was one thing he was consistently good at—every time he set an alarm he'd get up exactly two minutes before it went off. Always. He'd set Mira's alarm for seven-thirty, knowing that if he slept as long as he really needed, he'd wake up this afternoon. He couldn't afford to sleep in today. He had to get back to Ellie as soon as he could. She had expected him home last night, and he hadn't called. It wasn't the first time this had happened. Certainly not. In the past year it had happened too often. Big problem this time was that it had happened last only a couple of weeks ago. This was not a good trend.

The shrill beeping of the alarm sent his blood pressure soaring. He silenced it by giving it a good slap. The ruckus caused Mira to stir. The last thing he needed was to have to deal with her first thing in the morning. He had enough to deal with trying to concoct some sort of story for Ellie. God, he hated this. So why did it keep happening? This time it was Mira's fault for sure. Usually they'd get together in the afternoon, whenever Carl could sneak out of work. They'd do their thing and hang out until Mira went to work at the bar. Last night she decided she'd call in sick, and although he tried to weasel out of it, he was stuck with her all night.

She stretched and yawned, then blinked her eyes. He practically ran to the bathroom. He faced himself in the mirror and shook his head in disapproval. What he needed was a good shower to wipe off any trace of Mira that Ellie might pick up. Once he had come home and Ellie had surreptitiously sniffed him all night. She didn't say anything, but it was then that he decided he'd better not test the ability of her nose to detect another woman. His shower filled the small bathroom with steam. He opened the medicine cabinet and took out his razor. He wiped the mirror with a towel and looked at himself again. How could this have gotten to the point where he kept toiletries here? He slathered aftershave all over his body, then returned to the bedroom to dress. Mira sat up in bed.

"Where are you going?" she asked.

He zipped his trousers and muttered, "I told you. My sister. I have to make sure she takes her medication."

With a heavy sigh, she flopped back on her pillow. "Why doesn't she live with your parents? Or at least have a nurse, or be in a home or something?"

Of course, this 'sister' didn't exist. All this convoluted subterfuge was pure crap designed to explain why he always needed to be seventy miles away in Stillwater. The 'crazy sister' story served the purpose of dissuading Mira from calling him at home, or, if she did call, to conceal Ellie's true identity should she answer. He had it sewn up pretty neatly, but the effort he had to make to keep his stories tight was exacting a toll on his nerves.

He shook his head as he buttoned his shirt. "What I haven't told you," he said, making it up as he went along, "is that she was married once, when she was twenty. Eloped. Didn't last long, though." He stalled by clearing his throat as he tucked in his shirt, not certain where this new lie was taking him. "She broke down right after that, and the folks sort of disowned her. That's when she came to me. And I don't have money for a nurse."

That was good. Pam, his real sister, was a registered nurse. His career achievements ranged from janitor to bartender to salesman at a ball-bearing factory.

Mira sighed and sat up a little. "Well, I just don't understand why you always have to be there, taking care of her." She crossed her arms and glared at him.

He didn't have time for this nonsense. But he had to keep cool.

"Because she's my sister," he said, playing the sensitivity card, "and if she didn't have me to keep her on her medication she'd slip away. I can't let that happen."

Where did this bullshit come from? He glanced around the stuffy little room, at the big, oppressive mess of it all. That sagging old bed had wrenched his back, and his hangover was in full swing. He had to get out of here. This all just had to stop. But he couldn't put an end to it now. Now he just had to get out the door. He'd deal with everything else later.

Mira softened, smiled, and beckoned him over for a kiss. "OK," she said.

For a moment he felt peaceful, light, almost like in his dream. But he had to go. He grabbed a small pipe from her coffee table and filled it with some of her pot, saying, "I'm taking this with me."

"Just bring it back tonight. We're supposed to be there at seven."

He had no idea what she was talking about, or where she expected him to be tonight at seven. She wasn't going to see him again for a while. Maybe not ever.

"Right," he replied, tucking the pipe in a pocket. He hated the clothes he wore to work.

He turned to her to take his leave. God, she looked like hell this morning. Her hair was frizzed out, her eyes had that raccoon thing going on, her face was puffy from too much liquor. But he shifted a soulful look into his brown eyes, leaned forward and kissed her. She sighed. His head felt like it was about to explode.

"Got anything for a headache?" he asked, knowing Mira was always good for pills.

She nodded to her lumpy bag on a chair. "Some codeine in my purse."

He took two tablets and put them in his shirt pocket.

"I have to cruise," he said, heading for the door.

"OK. Come back as soon as you can. We have to catch the train by six-thirty to get there at seven."

He left, still wondering what she was talking about. The street was empty. A sullen haze hung over the city. At eight o'clock in the morning it was already stifling hot. It was going to be one hell of a day. His head pounded. Those pills might knock him out on the way home, but damn it—he needed relief. He stopped and choked them down dry. In an hour or so he'd be home and feeling all right. He'd sweet talk Ellie and smooth things over. It was becoming routine.

Where the hell was the car? He couldn't remember where he'd parked it, or much else of last night. He had sneaked out of work in the afternoon and gone over to Mira's. They fucked, then got drunk; then she decided to call in sick. They went out, ate, drank way too much, came back and fucked some more. All in all a pretty good night, he guessed, but the details were sketchy. And the little detail of where he parked the goddamn car was pretty aggravating. This all just had to stop.

They had turned the corner last night at that building with the flower boxes. There was the park they walked past, and they'd gone under the train line, then up a couple blocks. He approached his old hatchback with trepidation. There was glass all over the sidewalk, and around his car. The rear window was smashed. His fancy tape deck and speakers were gone. Sure, they were hot when he bought them, but that didn't mean it was OK for them to be stolen from him. He climbed in his car and sat there, picking up fragments of his window and tossing them in the gutter. Why couldn't anything just go right and work out for him?

He meandered along gray streets. All the loose litter in his car was sucked out of the windowless hatchback as he brought the car up to speed on the freeway. The wind and noise were downright intolerable. Couldn't use the air conditioning—not that it worked all that well anyway. It was going to be a long ride home. He felt sick, and the exhaust fumes circulating in the car weren't helping. Maybe the carbon monoxide would kill him before he made it home. Or maybe he'd conk out from that codeine. He gripped the wheel and headed down the road.

What was he going to tell Ellie? What was he going to do about Mira? This had to stop. Mira was smart enough to know what was going on. Surely she was. So she was waiting for him to break it off with his 'sister.' But he couldn't. He and Ellie had been together since high school, and he had moved in with her last year. Just last week they'd talked marriage. Of course, he'd talked marriage with Mira, too, but he didn't mean it with her. At least, he didn't mean it as much as he meant it with Ellie. Oh, he was a mess.

Ellie must know too. She must. So why did she stay with him? Maybe it was one of those things where she didn't even know why, but one day she'd get fed up and split. Except she wouldn't split—she'd kick his ass out is what she'd do. Maybe today. He couldn't entertain that thought now. He needed her. She was good to him, and he wanted to do right by her. And he usually had, until Mira got him drunk that first night he'd stayed with "Tom," a fictional co-worker, who either didn't have a phone, or whose phone was never operational for one reason or another. How lame.

What was wrong with him? Ellie was stable, a real practical partner. Mira was a flake with no assets other than a quick wit, a hot body, and access to free booze. Ah, but he liked her for that. And how could he begrudge himself that fondness? He knew it wasn't right at all, but it certainly wasn't all wrong. All he knew was that it had to stop.

He fished in his pocket for his lighter, and pulled out that pipe. Lighting it was going to be tricky in this wind. Fortunately it was early Saturday morning, and the traffic was light. He crouched down around the pipe with his lighter, sort of generally guiding the wheel with his shoulders. He sparked the bowl, inhaled deeply, and quickly resumed a proper driving position. He then coughed his lungs out and spat onto the passenger seat. His madness had never been more apparent.

The stench of heavy industry blew through his violated vehicle. A few miles down the road his low-grade nausea became a gnawing hunger. Maybe he needed something on his stomach. He was coming on Lake Station, where there was a diner he'd eaten at a few times before. A big sign on the roof said, "Eat." Just the ticket.

A patchwork of mismatched linoleum squares covered the floor. The walls were coated with vaporized oil and tobacco residue. He plopped himself on a tired old stool at the battered counter. A bunch of sad sacks accompanied him there, yawning, staring hypnotically at their coffee, devouring their food.

Sweet Jesus, who was this hot little brunette pouring him coffee? Those eyes, those lips—oh, he did have an appetite.

"Know what you want?" she asked, snapping her gum.

What a loaded question.

"What's good?" he asked, openly checking her out.

"Everything's good," she said, impatiently looking around while straining to keep hold of the coffee pot. "Should I come back in a minute?"

"No, no," he told her, waving a hand. "I'll take some pancakes. And maybe some bacon."

"You can get the special of pancakes, bacon, and eggs for less than pancakes with a side of bacon," she advised him.

"OK, then. Scramble my eggs, all right?"

She nodded, turned, and slid the coffee pot onto a burner while simultaneously slapping his order onto a wheel at the window to the kitchen.

He sipped coffee and pondered his predicament. There was no way he could just dump Mira, just dispose of her. But he couldn't keep pushing things with Ellie. Everyone knew that Ellie was the best thing that ever happened to him. She kept him in check, or mostly did. She balanced him. He really did like Mira, though. Hell, he even loved her, and he sure didn't want to hurt her. But it was clear things couldn't go on as they were. He and Mira could never make it together—they were too much alike. They stood on the same side of the scale, and they each needed someone else to even them out. He'd be doing both of them a favor by calling it off. No question about that. The question was how to do it. He was searching hard for an easy answer.

The car was another matter altogether. He'd have to file a police report and call his insurance company. Since he already left the city, he guessed he'd have to pretend it happened in Stillwater and file a report there. Unlikely thing to happen in Stillwater, though. Nothing much ever happened there. But he couldn't very well file a report in Chicago—he would have spent the whole morning there if he had. Besides, he couldn't remember where he told Ellie that this "Tom" lived. He had to make sure all his stories meshed, but his mind was in no state to sort through his tangled webs right now. Why couldn't things just be easy? Just once he'd like something to work the way it should. Just once.

Well, at least his head was numb now. He'd been drinking way too much lately. If he wasn't careful he'd turn into his old man, drunk all the time. Or not even drunk, really, just always loaded. Right now he had to load up on the coffee if he didn't want to pass out. That sweet waitress came by empty-handed, but she could come any way she wanted as far as he was concerned.

"Can I get some coffee when you get a chance?" he asked her.

She hoisted a rack of coffee cups to her midsection, turned, looked at him without answering and marched to the kitchen. A minute later she returned and filled his cup.

"You from around here?" he asked in the cheeriest voice he could manage. She replaced the coffee on the burner and hesitated before she replied.

"Yeah."

"Well, I come through here every now and then. Maybe you could show me around sometime."

Brilliant move. Good thing to hit on her while trying to figure out how to drop his mistress because of a newfound fidelity to the woman he lived with. And he was high as a kite to boot, in order to mask one hell of a hangover. Yeah, he was doing all right.

"Look," she said, leaning close to him. "I'm sure you're real nice and everything, but my boyfriend's the cook and I can tell you one thing— you don't want him pissed at you."

She walked away. Couldn't blame a guy for trying. Except, of course, in his case you really could blame him. Could blame him quite a bit, as a matter of fact.

He ate eagerly, and just as eagerly sought to relieve himself after-wards. For a moment there, sitting on the can, he actually felt good. All that dope now freely coursing through his blood helped him gain a little altitude over his troubles. His chemically induced solace needed a little reinforcing, so he pulled out the pipe, intending to take a hit and stand on the toilet to exhale through a vent. He sucked the smoke in deeply, then froze as someone walked into the room. The guy moseyed over to the urinal and stood there for a seeming eternity. A cough burst out of Carl's chest. His attempt to hold it back resulted in snorting and sputtering that fanned the cloud of smoke filling the stall. He sat still while the other occupant of the room finished, and took his time washing up. Before he left he coughed loudly, sending Carl into quite a state.

He was certain that as soon as he opened the door he'd be arrested. Should he just bolt, try to run out of the joint? No, it was always better to play it cool. He walked back to his seat, trying to keep it together. Was everyone looking at him, or was he just imagining it? It sure seemed like all eyes were on him. Someone coughed. His mouth dried up and his knees got wobbly. He slapped ten bucks next to his plate, then left in a hurry.

After dropping his keys and scraping his knuckles to retrieve them, he peeled out and hightailed it to the freeway.

OK, that was about as uncool as anything he'd ever done, but it was over. And that's how things would have to be with Mira: over. It was an uncool thing, but it was over now. He had to try extra hard to repair the damage with Ellie. Things could work out for everyone. He and Ellie could be stronger. Mira could find someone better for her. And he could grow up.

That codeine was kicking in now, slowing him down and taking the edge off his brief panic. He cruised on in his temporary elation until a sudden realization slapped him down. It was Ellie's birthday today. No. No, it couldn't be. When was her birthday anyway, the twenty-third or twenty-fourth of June? And today was Saturday the what? Goddamn. Oh, why couldn't anything be easy? He didn't need this. No, he most definitely did not.

He vaguely remembered buying something for her a while back, a silk scarf he found in a shop somewhere. But maybe he had already given that to her. It seemed like he'd seen her wearing it. But come to think of it, he had actually given that scarf to Mira. Oh, he was screwed all right. Why did he have to deal with this on top of everything else? He got off the freeway and stopped in Door Prairie, where he knew of an antique shop.

The first thing he saw was a fanciful fish made of orange glass. At twenty bucks, it was just about what he wanted to spend. He gave a perfunctory look around the place before coming back to it. What the hell. It was OK. He'd get it for her as a quirky objet d'art. She'd like it. Probably. Besides, he didn't have the time or the inclination to hunt around. It would have to do.

Now if he could just get someone to take his money he could get out of here and be home in twenty minutes. His head felt thick, and his dry eyes burned. He hoped he could muster up some energy when he tried to make peace with Ellie. Right now he felt like he was going to faint. He rang a bell on the counter and a wiry, white-haired man walked over.

"Interesting piece," he said, turning the fish end over end to find a price.

Carl didn't register a word.

"So, is this a gift?" the man asked, writing a receipt.

"Huh?" Carl grunted, snapping to. "Yeah. For my girlfriend."

The shopkeeper nodded. "I'll wrap it for you then, if you want."

Carl accepted the offer and stood unsteadily as the guy set about finding supplies.

"Interesting color," he commented, putting the fish in a box. "You don't see much orange glass." He began wrapping the box and continued to try to engage a stupefied Carl in conversation. "So, your girlfriend likes glass fish?" Lagging close to a full measure behind, Carl concentrated and answered slowly, "Uh-huh. She's crazy about them."

"Collects them?" the man asked, cutting some ribbon.

Carl's eyes glazed over as he spoke. "Yeah. Got a whole room full of 'em."

Why was he lying to this guy? For the sake of convenience. After all, the alternative was to lay out the truth of the matter. He could explain that he was picking up the first piece of junk he found because he thought it might be his girlfriend's birthday. But he couldn't quite remember whether it was her birthday or not, because he was too stoned. And he'd gotten stoned in order to dull his hangover from the night before, which he'd spent getting drunk and bedding down with his other girlfriend. No, his fictions were more expeditious than the convoluted truth.

"A whole room, you say?" the shopkeeper replied, tying the ribbon.

All right, just stop with the room full of glass fish already and wrap the damned thing up. He had better things to do than shoot the breeze here. Like crashing his car on the way home, for instance. His eyelids were getting heavy.

"Yeah, she's got 'em all over the place," he heard himself say.

"Well, she'll be glad to get this one," the shopkeeper opined, tying a bow. "Might be the last one round these parts. You see, I've never seen one before. Thought it was one-of-a-kind."

Carl reeled a bit as he picked up the package. "Keep your eyes open," he said, making to leave. "Every once in a while you see a glass fish."

With gift in hand he walked past his car and went to a bookstore with a coffee bar. What he really wanted was to chain smoke about a dozen cigarettes. But he'd quit only a month ago and was determined to quit for good this time, so a double espresso would have to do the trick. As he waited for his coffee he saw someone he knew sitting in the back of the room, and turned his head so he wouldn't be noticed and drawn into a conversation he didn't want to have. He downed his shot and left. Propped up by caffeine, he drove out of town and headed home, his buzzing mind marinating in melancholy.

He made it home. Ellie was gone. Good. He was all for putting off the inevitable as long as possible. He opened the garage door and drove his car in. He usually parked in the driveway, but he wanted to shelter the car from the storm clouds rolling in. The air in the house was stale. He walked around, opening windows and turning on fans before shedding those horrible work clothes, and was asleep before his head hit the pillow.

When Ellie pulled into the driveway, she surged with the anger and anxiety that she had suppressed since last night, feelings that she had stopped engaging until now. They flushed through her again as she both cursed Carl and hoped he was all right. Upon finding his damaged car in the garage, she stood perplexed for a moment, looking at the smashed window and wondering what had happened. The thing was a piece of junk when he bought it, and he'd beat it up pretty hard. She stood there a moment longer, twisting a strand of her long brown hair and growing utterly despondent over his inability to take care of anything.

She brought in bags of groceries from her car and set them just inside the door. Worn out and lightheaded, she went to sit in the living room. After a minute on the couch she felt better. So Carl was around here somewhere, probably snoring away in the bedroom. Just as well. Now that she knew he was all right, she was in no real hurry to see him. She got up and unpacked the groceries. The refrigerator needed to be cleaned out in a big way, and she started clearing off the shelves. It felt good to get this done, something she'd meant to do for a while. Busy with her task, she inwardly jumped when Carl shuffled into the room, but managed to maintain her outward composure.

"There you are," she exclaimed in a brighter and livelier tone than she intended.

While he walked toward her he started in on his apologies, like she knew he would. There was nothing he could say now that she particularly wanted to listen to, so she blurted out an efficacious, "Don't," which stopped both his advance and his tongue.

With the refrigerator door separating them, she looked at him and said, "I was worried about you last night, when you didn't call. I was mad, too, but I'm not now. I'm just glad you're OK." She did her best to mean it. And she did, mostly.

He stood silent as she returned her attention to the refrigerator. Now that there was no talking to be done, he looked around for something else to do. A pile of dirty dishes caught his eye, and he tended to them. The sky darkened with storm clouds. Mindful of the uneasy silence, he switched on the radio and tuned it to a station that played old R&B and Soul, seeking to mellow the mood. She wasn't listening to the music, though. Her own heartbeat commanded her concentration as she tried to cope. What she couldn't do was lose her cool. She figured out last night how to deal with this, and she just had to follow through.

She carried some limp lettuce to the garbage disposal. They stood side by side at the sink. He was nervous, and she could tell it. She knew he wanted to absolve himself by talking his way out of it, and she knew it was eating away at him. Well, he could just fret awhile as far as she was concerned. She really didn't feel like talking right now. Maybe because she knew it would relieve him, or maybe because she didn't want to hear him lying anymore. Just as she was wondering how long it would take him to start spilling his guts, he turned to her and started in on what passed for a confession in his book.

"Look, I'm sorry about last night. I sure didn't mean for it to work out that way. I went out with Tom after work and—"

She interrupted him. "Carl, we can talk about all that later, if there's anything to talk about. Right now I just want us to be together in our kitchen on a Saturday night."

She shut off the disposal and went about tidying the counter. The radio took a commercial break. He found it hard to believe that she wasn't angry, but she was expressing it in an oddly quiet way. It was fine by him, though—much better than the loud way she'd done on previous occasions. Done with the cleaning, she washed and dried her hands, then touched him on the small of his back. She spoke softly and noticed how tense he was.

"Are you hungry?"

"Sure," came his quick reply, and he shook his head vigorously, involving almost every muscle in his upper body. He wasn't hungry at all, really, but it seemed like she wanted to be busy, and cooking dinner was about the safest thing she could busy herself with at the moment.

She smiled at him sincerely as she turned to the stove. It had been a long time since she'd confused him, and she proceeded slowly.

He washed the last of the dishes and watched her as she started preparing their meal. OK, she was being good to him. That was fine, too. If she didn't want to bitch him out, he certainly wasn't going to insist that she do so. He was all for just forgetting about it. Maybe things were finally going his way at last, and he could skate away scot-free. But he felt bent out of shape and anxious. He wanted to talk to her, but what else was there to talk about besides this big elephant in the room that she refused to recognize?

The phone rang. Ellie was closest to it and answered.

"Hello?" She paused, then repeated, "Hello?" and stood there with the receiver to her ear, waiting for a reply. She could hear someone on the other end of the line, and tried again with another hello. The caller hung up without responding.

Carl sighed.

With the last of the dishes done, he wiped his hands on his pants and thought of something to discuss. He considered telling her about the damage to his car, but it was too closely linked to the subject that was off-limits now. Work was something he always talked to her about, but he hadn't spent much time there yesterday, and there wasn't much he could remember anyway. The radio began playing music again. She turned her full attention to peeling potatoes.

Lightning flashed through the windows, followed by thunder that rumbled through the floor. They were in for it tonight. He stepped outside through sliding glass doors and stood on their little patio. Something was definitely blowing in. Purple clouds roiled and flashed. The wind picked up, and he went back inside. Ellie was focused on preparing food, with an intensity she rarely displayed. He searched for something to say or do, then remembered his gift and went out to the garage to get it.

His buzz had long since worn off, and he felt like getting another one going. He grabbed the pipe from under the seat and sucked up the last smoke he could burn out of the bowl. He stashed it away, then picked up the fish and headed to the refrigerator they kept in the garage. It was stocked with beer and he opened a bottle, put the package beside him and leaned against a workbench to drink.

He wondered why he felt he had to get high to deal with his girlfriend. At least that was one thing about Mira: he didn't have to hide his habits from her. Not that Ellie was a prude. She could get loose with the best of them, but only when occasion called for it. For Carl, just making it through a day was occasion enough. It was Ellie who first pointed out to him that his parents were both problem drinkers, and he'd better watch out. Fact of the matter was that most of his relatives—a bunch of rowdy Canucks who'd been settled in these parts for umpteen generations—were bona-fide drunks. But she'd never come out and say that. And tonight he didn't really want to think about any of it. Tonight he wanted to numb his extremities along with his anxieties.

The lights flickered after a clap of thunder. He chugged the remainder of the bottle and started back to the house. When he turned the knob to open the door he remembered why he had ostensibly come out here in the first place, and went back to pick up his gift. He was on edge as he approached the kitchen. If he could make it through this night he'd be all right. The morning would bring a fresh start.

"Here you go," he said, tapping her on the shoulder. "For you."

She spun around rather sharply, startled out of her concentration. With his proffered gift before her, she smiled weakly and said, "But, it's my birthday tomorrow."

"Oh, I know," he said, although he didn't, "but I thought this was just the coolest thing and wanted to give it to you now."

She looked at him, knife in hand. "Should I open it?"

"Whenever you want," he shrugged.

She put down the knife and took the package. "It's heavy."

He nodded. She placed it on the cutting board and unwrapped it. A long moment passed as she scrutinized it at arm's length.

"It's a glass fish," she said finally. He nodded again.

"What do you do with a glass fish?" she asked, still holding it far from her body.

He shook inside as he shrugged again. "It's for decoration. You know, maybe a centerpiece."

"It's heavy," she repeated, placing it on the countertop. "We'll have to find a place for it. It can live here for now."

He stood frozen as she returned to her cooking without further comment. He was mortified by this latest stupid move of his. There could be no doubt that he was an ass. And he ought to have a tattoo that said, 'Kick Me.'

Dinner was begun in silence, save for the radio and the growl of the approaching storm. He went out to get another beer. She poured herself a glass of milk. Neither of them thought they were hungry, but both ate heartily.

"Guess you saw my car," he ventured to start a conversation. Ellie nodded.

"They got my stereo and speakers," he added.

"That's too bad," she said, trying to feign interest. "I know you liked them."

Silence resumed.

Just what was going on here? He could handle it a lot better if she was screaming or crying or totally giving him the cold shoulder. But what was this business of her cooking for him, saying she wanted them to spend a quiet night at home together like everything was OK when it obviously wasn't? Well, she was being awfully quiet, all right, and it was really annoying. He was just miserable all around. Something had to give.

Rain began falling, beating against the windows of their kitchen. Another flash of lightning, with immediate thunder, and the lights went off for a few seconds, then came back on. The rain fell heavier, the lightning and thunder grew more intense. The power went out again and stayed out this time. They looked at each other in the darkness. He got up and searched for a flashlight, then brought some candles back to the table. Ellie was fully savoring her peas and carrots while he lit the candles and sat down to finish his beer. He thought about commenting on how romantic it was to be dining by candlelight with her, but he figured that would go over as well as his other attempts at conversation tonight.

The meal ended with nothing more said. He gathered the dishes off the table and took them over to the sink. The storm was in full force now, seemingly hovering right above the roof. He directed the flashlight to the sink and began washing the dinner dishes. She picked up a candle and came over to his side.

"Leave that for now, Carl. We've got to talk."

With a hand cupped around the flame, she walked to the living room and cleared a spot on the coffee table for the candlestick. He followed and sat beside her on the couch, instantly launching into excuses. He paused for breath and she interrupted.

"Whatever happened last night happened. Whatever's been happening for however long doesn't matter now. It's not important anymore." Her voice cracked as she choked back a sob and continued. "What's important now is that I'm going to have your baby. That's what's important now."

She didn't hold back, and began crying in earnest. He sat there dumb-founded. When she leaned toward him, he stiffly put his arms around her. His mind was numb. After a while she stopped crying and pulled away from him. As she sniffed and wiped her eyes, he asked, "Are you sure?"

She nodded her head. "Positive."

His next question was, "What are we going to do?"

"We're going to have a baby."

They sat a long time in silence, neither of them knowing quite what to think or say. The rain was gradually dying. At length he said, "I guess we should get married?"

Her chin quivered as she gave her answer. "Yeah."

Flooded with too many emotions to sort out, they sat by the light of a single candle. The storm had mostly passed, but the power was still off. Out here, it would be hours before it was restored.

"Your parents know," she said, watching the wax pool on the table.

He came to as if slapped. "What?"

"I found out for sure yesterday afternoon. I couldn't stay here alone. I went over there and spent the night."

He sat up abruptly, and the candle flared. "You told them before you told me?"

Her wet eyes turned to live coals. "Well, Carl, you weren't here."

They were both drained when they wordlessly parted. She took the remnant of the candle and got ready for bed. She was glad the lights were off, because she didn't want to look at herself in the mirror. For just over twenty-four hours now she'd known that she was going to be a mother. At first she was exhilarated. That exhilaration deflated when the father of her child failed to show up, failed to call her and tell her what was going on, failed once again to earn her trust. Why did she let him walk all over her? Why hadn't she sent him packing long ago? Why couldn't she reform him? Why couldn't he live up to his capabilities? Why didn't they use birth control? Exhausted, she climbed into bed, wondering how different things would be in a year.

He found his way outside. The air smelled of wet concrete and grass. Crickets resumed their chirping. The storm had moved on, blowing over the distant woods. It was so quiet out here in the country. His heart beat in his ears as he walked off the patio and sank to the warm, wet earth. What a pathetic figure he cut there, alone in the dark night. For too long he'd been a selfish, careless, mean, and sloppy jerk. He had to shape up.

He had to. He'd been thinking about quitting the job he hated, but now he couldn't. Not only did it pay better than anything he'd be likely to find, but once they got married, Ellie and the baby would be covered by company insurance. So he was stuck there. And he'd better shape up there, too, if he didn't want to get fired. A train whistle blew somewhere far off. It was a sound that he had always been fond of, a sound that he had always associated with a feeling of hope. Tonight it sounded mournful. He was sick at heart, and he had no idea how to get well. For the first time in years he thought to pray, but the only prayer he could croak out was a muted sob.

6

Like a kid with a good report card, Manny couldn't wait to get home and show off. He never could keep a secret, and he'd had a terrible time these past few months refraining from telling Carmela about a really good thing, not wanting to let her in on it until he was certain it was going to happen. He'd gotten the news this morning, and all day he'd been bursting to tell her. She wasn't home at lunch, and he didn't want to tell her over the phone, so when quitting time came he tore out of the parking lot and raced back through town.

Today he learned that he had a guaranteed job in the spring, and he knew Carmela would be pleased. Their income depended on his being hired on major contracts. The remainder of the year was mostly secure, with the new warehouse store and the hospital expansion, but after that it was going to be on-call work. Until now, he'd heard only rumors about a big contract. This afternoon it was confirmed that he'd be working on a new housing project that would begin next March. This job security had produced in him a great euphoria, and now Carmela's appreciation would top off his brimming cup of self-worth.

Carmela sat in her sewing room, transfixed by her work. She was finishing the embroidery on a shirt that she'd started days ago. When this one was done she'd have two dozen ready to sell at the county fair. It was still several weeks away, and by then she would have another dozen or so, along with her previously completed stock of linens. At the fair she would be sharing space in the grange with a woman who'd been selling her knitting there for nearly forty years.

The shirts were a consummate Carmela creation. She designed them herself, making generous use of the bolts of fine cotton cloth she bought wholesale through her parents' business. With a palette of vibrant threads, she richly embroidered them with her characteristic motifs, stitching bands along the button line, collar, pockets and cuffs. She had mastered her craft, and these shirts were proof of it.

So absorbed was she in her stitching that Manny was able to enter the room and walk halfway across the floor before she noticed him. Startled, she jumped in her seat and pricked her finger. She drew that finger to her mouth, preventing blood from staining her nearly completed work. He walked around behind her and planted a noisy kiss on her cheek.

"How's tricks?" he asked with a little chortle.

By the unusually playful nature of his greeting, she knew something was up. She removed her fingertip from her mouth and held it flat, watching a little drop of blood pool as she responded.

"You scared me. You're home early." She put the finger back to her lips. He hummed to himself as he meandered over to a chair in the far corner. He sat down, a grin plastered on his face.

"Could you get me a Band-Aid?" She got impatient when he refused to get to the point. He jumped up, always eager to accommodate her, and returned with the package unwrapped. She thanked him and waited for him to speak, which he did at length.

"I've got work lined up for the beginning of the year. Big new housing project, guaranteed income."

He stood there beaming at her. She looked up at him with a smile. He was so earnest. She had to love him.

"Way to go," she said, wrapping the bandage around her finger. "That is good news."

"Best thing is," he added, "I can walk to the site—won't even need the car. You can use it during the day."

"Really? Where?"

He nodded in the direction of the old farm and said, "Nellie Widow's."

She stopped tending to her finger. He just kept smiling.

"What?" she asked, not willing to believe what he'd just said.

"Yeah, they're putting houses up there."

Again she said, "What?"

"What do you mean, 'What?' What's the matter?"

"They're going to build houses on Nellie Widow's farm?"

"Yeah. Thirty-some to start with, with an option to build more once the first round sells." He added rather boastfully, "We could be making money off this for a couple years at least."

She shook her head, trying to dispel the reality he was stating. "But they can't."

"What's the matter?" he repeated, feeling flustered all of a sudden. "Why not?"

The look of disbelief on her face made him shrink. He knew why not.

"It's supposed to be a park. Remember? Remember we bought this place so we'd be right next to a nice, big park? Now we're going to be down the street from a nasty new subdivision? That's terrible."

His fuse was lit. "Sheesh! And here I thought I had good news, coming home with two years' work wrapped up. Guess I should've known that would piss you off."

She disregarded his sarcasm and asked for an explanation. "How can they do that—build houses on a park?"

"It never was a park," he stated, glad to have the facts of the matter well in hand. "It was going to be part of Fox Lake, but there's a strip of land in between that's owned by the county, and the county won't sell it. But the city put their part up for sale, and the developer who built the Long Lake condos bought it. He's using us again to do the work. And I got hired on." He paused to emphasize the point he really wanted to get across: "And that work is keeping us in this house."

Her vision of children scampering on a hilltop park dissolved into a cluster of bland tract houses. "Why didn't I ever hear anything about this? How can something like this just happen?"

She wasn't talking to him, necessarily, but he had the answer. It was a backroom deal. Charlie Jenner, the contractor he worked for, was the chief crony skulking around the old-boys' club at city hall. Upset as he was, Manny still had enough presence of mind to realize that revealing the shadowy nature of the land acquisition wouldn't help his case, so he only replied, "Well, all I know is I've been busting my ass to get in on this job, and I thought you might appreciate that."

"I know, Manny. I know, I know—it's just, I wanted it to be a park. I thought it was a park. Someplace we could take walks, where our kids could play. It just seems so wrong."

"Why wrong? I don't get it. We've got Fox Lake just right up the street. We can walk and play there all we want."

"Yeah, but it's not the same as having it right there, nice green open space at the end of our street. Besides, building houses up there where people got killed? That's just not right."

"But building a playground up there is OK? Come on!"

She shot him a stern look. "Don't yell at me, Manny."

"I'm not yelling. I just don't get it. I'm supposed to turn down work? I can't do that. Why should I?"

She said nothing, just shook her head. He stood there a moment, then left the room in a huff. He went to his basement workshop and got a pair of gloves, safety goggles and his chainsaw. These he loaded these into his car and came back to the sewing room, where he announced, "I'm going over to my mom's. I told her I'd cut back that tree by her driveway."

Her only response was a sigh. She just sat there, eyes cast down. He hated it when she got all mopey like this. He wanted to storm out. Instead, he held back and simply turned around and left. He couldn't resist peeling out of the driveway, though.

She looked down at her unfinished shirt but couldn't pick up her needle again. As lighthearted as she had felt before, happily stitching away, so now she felt weighted down, her creativity stymied. She got up to leave and paused at the doorway, then switched off her lights, knowing she wouldn't feel like doing anything in here again until tomorrow.

She rode her bike part of the way up the hill, then walked it to the top. The deep grass hummed with insects as she made her way along a mossy stone wall to the remains of the foundation sticking out of the ground. This was a place she had come to often since she was a child, to wander in the shade of mature oaks and maples, to be alone and stare out across the lakes. It should remain like it was. Manny was right about the work and all, but no way should this hill be paved over into a sterile subdivision. Somehow it could be stopped. The mayor was a family friend. Maybe her parents could help. She rode off to seek their advice about what could be done.

The pickup hit a crater-like pothole, almost sending Russell flying out of his perch in the bed. His fellow fieldworkers were all sitting on the floor of the bed itself, but he'd taken to sitting on top of the wheel well, finding the position more comfortable. Now that he'd practically gotten thrown from the truck, he slid down onto the floor with the rest of them, much to their evident delight. Jokes in Spanish circulated around him. He was the only gringo on board, and mostly he loved the anonymity of not being able to communicate with the rest of the people he worked with. Moments like these, though, rather soured the whole experience. He'd lately started wondering just what he was doing, hanging out here for so long instead of getting on with his big adventure.

They came into town. At the first light he hopped off, even though the truck was taking them to where the week's pay was being distributed. He'd get his money later. He waved to his co-workers as they pulled away, his precipitous departure generating another round of jests at his expense. He'd gotten off a few blocks away from where Helen was working this summer. Her scooter was nowhere to be seen, but he walked to the store anyway. It had been a couple of weeks since he'd come to town, and apart from their initial conversation he hadn't talked to her. He figured if he wanted to be her friend it was about time he started acting like it.

She was seated on a stool behind the counter, reading a magazine. She finished a paragraph before she looked up in response to the tangle of cowbells tied to the door. Without changing her expression or position, she sized him up with a piercing gaze.

"You're something, you know it? You totally blow me off for how long? Now you come back and blow me off again?"

"I lost your number," he began, feeling rather lame. "I thought I put it in my wallet, but I didn't. I put it in a shirt pocket and it went through the laundry. And you're unlisted, and, well, I started working and stuff."

She arched her brow to express her skepticism.

"And I'm a total jerk-off."

"For starters," she readily concurred, setting down her magazine and sliding off the stool. She stepped out from behind the counter. "So, are you out shopping for antiques, or what?"

She was casually attired in a tank top, shorts and sandals. There was something strange yet familiar in her voice and demeanor, something that both set him on edge and put him at ease.

"I just came in to see if you were here," he said, and continued his apologies. "Look, I've been a real lazy friend. Not just to you, but to a lot of people. But I was hoping while I'm here we could do something together sometime, like, soon."

"Let's do something together sometime, like, now." She lifted her voice and called out over her shoulder, "Hey, Wayne?"

"Yeah?" came the reply from another room.

"I'm taking off early. It's been dead here all day. You got it covered?"

"Sure thing," he called back, then added a chirpy, "Thank you, Helen dear."

"You bet," she shouted, then nudged Russell out the door. As they started down the street, she nodded back in the direction of the unseen Wayne and said, "That guy knows his business. If you ever do go shopping for antiques, talk to him."

He nodded, feeling pleased to be in her company and glad that he'd jumped off that truck.

She led him up the street, saying, "We're going to pick up Bob."

"Bob?"

"My scooter," she answered. "One day I figured I'd had it long enough it should have a name. I looked at it and said, 'Bob.' So now it's Bob."

He accepted this with a nod.

"Yeah, I got a flat on the way in this morning—didn't realize it until I tried to go home at noon. I walked it up to the service station to get repaired." They waited to cross the street and she added, "So, I didn't know if you had already breezed through town, or what. You said you were working?"

"Uh-huh," he started as they walked on. "I kind of got roped into it by Manny, my friend I'm staying with. He got this bee in his bonnet on the first day I was here about my not having enough money to live off. So he found me this job, and I couldn't really turn it down after he went to the trouble."

She interrupted the conversation momentarily as they entered the service station and she inquired about her tire. As someone went to fetch her scooter, she turned back to Russell and asked, "Well, what are you doing?"

"Today I was helping to mend a fence, but usually I'm out detasseling corn, from one field to another. Crazy kind of job. Gives you lots of time to think. First week, though, I fried in the sun, and that corn made me itch all over. Now I've got a tan, and I've stopped itching, so it's OK I guess. I'm out there all day, not talking to anyone, moving up and down these rows of plants, pulling off their reproductive apparatuses."

"And you're OK with that?"

"I don't know. I'm doing it."

Her scooter was brought round. She inspected the work, then went to pay.

"Ever think about selling it?" the guy asked as he wrote out a receipt for her.

"Nah, I like it too much," she answered.

He nodded, and continued writing the bill. "Thing is, they're hard to come by, and getting harder. I know a guy who'll take it for parts. What is it, anyway? Seventy-four?"

"Seventy-three. And I'm not ready to scrap it. I've kept it going too long."

He handed over her copy of the paperwork and said, "Well, you change your mind you know where to bring it. And hey—here's what we pulled out of it." He produced a triangular piece of metal from a pocket of his overalls.

"Nasty," she proclaimed.

"Yeah," he grinned. "Your tread's still pretty good, but it's not going to stop that."

Russell stood back, watching this exchange, noting how easily she interacted with people. It was so different from his hesitant, halting manner. The transaction completed, they walked to the scooter. He started talking more about his work.

"Besides, maybe Manny's right. As long as I'm here I might as well be making some money. Thing is, I don't want to get stuck here. So it's good it's seasonal work—at some point I'll be out of a job and forced to move on."

She took her helmet out of her basket and put it on. "Let's talk about it later," she said, straddling the scooter. "You hungry? Let's go to my place. Only one helmet, though, and I'm wearing it."

He hopped on. She stomped on the starter a couple of times before it fired up. Her hand released the clutch and with a barely perceptible lurch they were off, the two-stroke motor whining at first then easing into a puttering pace. The wind felt good on this hot, muggy day. He held her waist. She smelled faintly of hyacinth.

Helen was born to her parents late in their lives, thirteen years after her brother, Jim. Jim had already run afoul of the law by then, having blown up a phone booth with a pipe bomb late one night. When Helen was ten, Jim was sent away to prison for his part in the bungled holdup of a pharmacy. She grew up at the County Home, where her father was the administrative director. The County Home was an assemblage of brick dormitories, originally built as an orphanage in the nineteenth century, later expanded to serve as a tuberculosis sanitarium, then an insane asylum before being run by the county to house elderly citizens who couldn't afford to go anywhere else. Around town it was known as the Poor House. Helen was given free rein of the place and was doted on by staff and denizens as well as her parents, she being a source of consolation in the midst of Jim's travails.

In college she earned a degree in social work. There was an incident where she ran off to New Mexico to live with an artist there, but she kept the details of that affair pretty sketchy. She'd been working at a school for the blind in Indianapolis when her father suffered a heart attack. During his recuperation she lived at home, helping her rather addled mother cope. Her father retired from the County Home and they lived on the income from rental houses they owned around the area. Helen moved into the bottom floor of one of these houses, and began managing all their properties.

Helen's roundabout route became more of a ramble as she went past the turnoff to her street and headed out on a country road. Russell was along for the ride, confident that she knew where she was going. They disembarked at a fruit stand, where they bought strawberries, blueberries, and cantaloupe, which they carried along many more miles of country roads. After circling three lakes and passing through four townships, she brought them back to her place on Marquette Avenue. Bob spluttered to a halt in a driveway lined with wildflowers.

She took off her helmet and shook her head, saying, "Whoa. That was a good ride, eh?"

They carried themselves and their goods to the side door and entered through the kitchen. As they settled in, she waved a finger at him and said, "I'll have you know that Myrtle hasn't spoken to me since you came to town. So, thanks for that!"

He set the cantaloupe on a counter and asked, "And the deal there was what?"

"Was that Myrtle's a total fruitcake. I cornered her on that day, you know, and told her that I'd seen you, and told her what you said happened. And she gets all antsy and starts trying to spin a yarn about how you were trying to break into my place and she fought you off or something."

She got out a colander to rinse the blueberries and continued. "So I called bullshit on that right away. Like, Myrtle, who's always pulling this 'poor, frail me' thing—yeah, I'm supposed to believe she's leaping to my defense when she spies this strange man breaking in through my front door in broad daylight." She turned off the water and looked at him with a scowling smile. "And then I told her to give me her keys, and—surprise, surprise—I found the copy of my key that she made."

He laughed, and so did she, then she set her jaw and snarled, "And then she tried to pull the 'poor, frail me' thing again. She actually said to me, 'Oh, you have to understand. I'm dying all alone upstairs, with nothing and no one.'"

Helen smacked her lips, angrily remembering the encounter. She drew a paring knife from a drawer and began cleaning the strawberries as she went on.

"So I called bullshit on that, too. I mean, she's been talking for years about how she's dying, but she's healthy as a horse as far as I can tell. She's always moving around up there, doing God knows what, and she never sees a doctor that I know of. I still volunteer at the hospital, and I know she's not receiving treatment for anything in this county. So I told her that I was really disappointed, that I had trusted her to take care of my things while I was away, and that she had really betrayed me. You know?"

She looked at him. He knew.

"And she was just looking at me, all pathetic, and I kept getting more and more pissed off." She shook her head, her voice softening as she continued. "And then I couldn't be a hard-ass anymore, and told her she could come talk to me sometime, but that she had to understand how upsetting this was to me."

She sighed as she ran water over the berries. "Haven't heard from her since. Scared her off by the confrontation. If I were any meaner, I could find a reason to evict her. But part of what she says is true—she doesn't have any friends I know of. She's a lonely old woman with nothing going on. That doesn't make it all right for her to break into my place, but I do sort of feel sorry for her."

With a weary shrug she dropped the subject and asked him to slice up the cantaloupe as she rummaged through her refrigerator for the makings of a salad. She set out the salad and fruit, and searched her pantry for something else.

"Rye toast?" she proffered, holding up a box of crackers. He took a cracker.

"Smoked salmon?" She handed a package to him. "And some of these," she said, holding out a jar of olives. He put the stuff on the table. She followed with the remains of a bottle of champagne. As she poured their glasses, he went to wash up.

He stood over her bathroom sink and looked in the mirror. To his surprise, he didn't look as grubby as he thought he might. His hand hovered over a wire basket filled with soaps of various shapes, colors and scents. It was good to be at Helen's place again, after being away for so long. He frowned at his reflection as he washed his face, contemplating the fact that he'd spent the past few weeks like he'd spent the past few years—just wasting time. Sure, he'd been having some fun and all, but it was becoming increasingly important to have something to show for it. He splashed some water over his head, then ran his hands through his hair. A breeze blew through the door as he opened it. He closed his eyes and stood there, feeling comfortable, cool and refreshed.

She was chowing down and waved at him when he returned. "I didn't stand on ceremony. Sit down; help yourself."

He fell to. As he ate, he thought about the last time he was here, and what had changed since. The dining room wore a light wash of ochre. The living room was painted a faint peach with a glossy black picture rail. A bookcase covered one wall, a couch sat in front of a picture window that looked out onto the porch and the street beyond. The oak floor gleamed in the afternoon sun. It was warm, but the open windows and ceiling fans kept the air moving.

"Your place hasn't changed much," he commented.

"Except the wall colors. I painted them a couple of years ago, with a friend one summer." She shifted her eyes and gazed past him, raising her glass to her lips and smiling.

When she was done, she picked up the bowl of blueberries and walked over to the couch. She kicked off her shoes and stretched out, placing the bowl on her lap. He took his glass of flat champagne and joined her in the living room, easing into a chair near the couch. She tossed a berry in her mouth and savored it fully, then turned to him.

"So what are you doing, Russ? I thought you said you were off on a joyride across America or some such thing, no?"

He drank before answering. "Yep. And I've made it from Cincinnati all the way back here." He rolled his eyes and shook his head. "You know, I wanted to come here to see some friends and hang out awhile. So far I've only been hanging out with Carmela and Manny. I've tried to connect with a few guys who don't seem to be around anymore. I've talked to my friend Carl on the phone. You know, Pam's brother. He's out in Stillwater with his girlfriend now. We were supposed to get together last week, but he crapped out on me. You know how that goes."

He looked at her. She knew.

"Hey," he continued. "I've finally gotten together with you, and that's good. But I didn't think I'd be here this long, and, well, I just don't know. Maybe I shouldn't have spent all this time here. Maybe I should be hundreds of miles down the road. Maybe I'm just totally deluded. I really don't know. I just basically really don't know what I'm doing right now."

He sipped wine while she ate berries.

"But one thing I know," he said, "I know I don't want to get stuck. And I think I'm prone to getting stuck. So that's why I think I should keep moving. I mean, this town is full of people who were on their way somewhere else but stayed here because it's pretty good, or at least not too bad. They settled here because it was OK. That's something I can totally see myself doing. Pretty good is pretty good—I can settle for it easy. You know, I was in Cincinnati for years, and doing all right. Comfortable, settled. Then all of a sudden it became important to get out and not be stuck anywhere anymore. But here I am, maybe getting comfortably stuck again."

After popping a few more berries, she offered her thoughts. "I think you're talking about different things here, two things you're confusing. You're talking about being stuck and being settled. They're different states. Being settled is not the same as being stuck. Seems like you've been stuck, and you're worried about getting stuck again. But you've never been settled. When you're really settled, it'll be a good thing—you'll know you're someplace you belong."

She lifted the bowl from her lap and placed it on the coffee table, then leaned toward him and continued. "I understand what you're saying about needing to keep moving, but just because you're not as far down the road as you think you should be doesn't mean you're missing out. It could very well be that you're exactly where you're supposed to be right now. You're an aware individual, and if you remain aware, you'll find your way."

With an audible exhalation, she sank back on the couch. "You're young. There's a time to be lost. That doesn't mean you should sit around and wait for your ship to come in, wait for the world to figure things out for you, but don't worry—the show's just starting."

The room hummed gently as a train went by on the tracks that ran between her place and the town's largest park, on the south end of Long Lake. He waved a fruit fly away from his glass. Specks danced in sunbeams. In one fluid motion, she rose from the couch and crossed the room to a bookshelf, where she removed a photo album. She returned to the couch and patted the cushion beside her.

"Come check these out."

He sat on the couch and looked at photos of her engaged in various occupations.

"My summer job scrapbook," she told him, flipping through the pages and offering commentary. He saw photos of her wrapping cellophane around boxes in a candy factory, cutting sheet metal, painting traffic signs, planting shrubbery, and silk-screening T-shirts. The latest entry showed her in what appeared to be a sort of space suit.

"What's that?" he asked, almost expecting her to say she'd been working in a nuclear power plant. She smiled.

"Last year I was an exterminator. Learned how to handle a tank of nerve poison. Killed a lot of things that once crept and crawled upon this good earth."

She snapped the book shut and put it back on the shelf.

"You know what I've always wanted to do?" she asked, returning to sit next to him. "I've always wanted to try my hand at diamond cutting. I'm hoping before long I can at least go watch one work. It's such an interesting thing to me. You have this rough gemstone. You study it, figure out how it will fall apart, figure out where to put your chisel—or whatever it's called in the trade—figure out how much force to use and a whole bunch of things, I'm sure. You do it right and there are these beautifully shaped jewels ready to be polished and perfected. Do it wrong and you smash the thing to slivers and dust. The tension must be something else."

He could tell this was exciting to her. Her eyes sparkled. She leaned back on a pillow and told him a story.

"I once read about the guy who cut the largest diamond ever found—mined in Australia, I think, round the turn of the century. Something like six inches long, and weighed close to a couple of pounds. It's given over to this diamond cutter in the Netherlands—they seem to breed them over there—and he's got to cut it into jewels. From what I read, he prepared it as best he could, then the day came when he had to cleave it. He hit it once, and the tool broke. So he had to hit it again. He did, and fainted on the spot. He came to and found he'd done it right. What a moment that must have been!"

Her laughter washed over him like a wave, and when he laughed along he bobbed with a new-found buoyancy. She was relaxed, in her element. The vicissitudes of thirty years had done little to diminish her delight in living, a delight she openly expressed and freely shared.

"So, what do you want to do, Russ?" She looked out the window. "Want to take a walk in the park? There's going to be a good sunset."

The sky was mellowing above the treetops.

"You know what, though? I should really get back. I want to get the dishes done for those guys—I meant to do them last night. I've been crashing at their place, and they haven't asked me for anything. I try to do what I can, you know, to earn my keep and all."

She sprang off the couch. "OK. Let's go out the front. I'll lock up in back."

"I remember that statue of Saint Christopher from that first day I ever came over here," he said as they stepped out on the porch. "It's in the same place. I remember it because when I was little I was given a Saint Christopher medallion from some friend of my grandmother's. I kept it as a sort of good-luck charm for a long time, then I lost it somewhere along the line. I always felt bad about losing it. Nice to see him still there."

She smiled, but had to say, "He's not really a saint, though. He was desanctified, if that's the term, but he's no longer a saint."

He shot her a look of disbelief.

She nodded with conviction and closed the door behind her. "Really. You didn't know that?" They walked to the scooter and she explained. "It happened back in the '60s. The church took him off the rolls, him and a lot of others. Or at least they dropped his feast day from the calendar. I guess since there's no historical evidence that he actually existed, he got bumped."

"You're a freak," is all he could think to say in response.

"Thank you," she said, strapping on her helmet. "But what do you mean by that?"

"Just that you have all this information on all sorts of subjects that you can rattle it off just like that." He snapped his fingers with a bemused smile.

"Well, I've had that statuette since I was twelve. Of course I know his story."

They idled in the driveway. "Where to?" she wanted to know.

"Melon Street," he answered as he felt around for a place to put his feet, feeling rather clumsy from the wine.

"Where's that?"

"Off Lily Lake."

She took off and called back, "I'll head that way. Tell me when we get close."

———————————•———————————

"Nice place," she commented while he struggled with the stubborn lock on the kitchen door.

"Yeah, it really is. Come see what Carmela's done in here."

He led her into the living room and pointed out the decorative band painted on the walls.

"She's started in on the cabinets here," he said, bringing her back to the kitchen. "She does embroidery work, too. That's what she's working on now, some shirts and stuff that she's going to sell at the fair."

They walked down the hall to her sewing room. "The light's off," he observed, peering into the dark room. "It's some special lighting, too. Manny's an electrician and put it in for her. I don't know why, really, but she's the only one who's supposed to touch the switch. But her stuff is really cool. Come over sometime when she's around and she'll show it to you. You'd dig it."

As he got to work on the dishes, she sat at the table and breathed a faint sigh. "I'd really like a place of my own. I mean, my place is my own, but I'd really like my own piece of property. My own house without some crazy old lady stalker living above me."

She got up and walked around, inspecting Carmela's sketches on the cabinets. "I do like where I live. I sure like not paying rent. It's OK to manage the properties, most of the time. Pays the bills, but it can be a total drag, too. Lowlifes trashing the place and skipping out in the middle of the night; a thousand and one tired old excuses for late rent; plumbers who don't show up when they say they will; gardeners who do a half-assed job whenever they do show up—you know, stuff like that can get to you, especially when it's all happening at once. Throw in a little criminal trespass and hey—it's lots of laughs."

He looked at her over his shoulder. She met his grin and raised him a smile. "Still, it's a good fit for me now."

Returning to his work, he caught sight of a car creeping up the driveway. It was a battered old hulk of a station wagon, a Country Squire gone seriously bad.

"Russ Pinske!" His name rang out through a bullhorn thrust through the driver's window. "We know you're in there! Come out now!"

"Friends of yours?" she asked, standing beside him now.

"I hope so."

He approached the car with trepidation. The driver lowered the bullhorn, revealing his wild-haired, snaggletoothed countenance. Guy Bogel. And riding shotgun was the always-composed and nattily attired Gary Pierce. Two men rode in the back, nondescript fellows with similar features, both wearing an expression of inscrutable introspection.

"If it ain't one of my favorite losers," Bogel greeted him, picking at a scab on his chin. "We got word you were asking about us. Tracked you down. Get in the car, we'll go for a ride."

Russell looked past him, catching Gary's eye. "Hey, Russ, how you been, man?"

Behind Guy's back, Gary circled his ears with his fingers, indicating craziness. Guy spoke up again.

"Come on, Pinske. This rig's moving. You on or not?"

"Wait," Russell said, placing a hand on the car. "I've got a friend over, and I'm right in the middle of something."

"Make it quick, man—I've got to keep this beast running."

Helen met him on the porch. "Friends of yours?" she repeated.

"Yeah, sort of. A couple guys I've been hoping to hook up with. They want me to go with them. You mind if I take off?"

"OK," she said, and started down the stairs. He slammed the door and followed her to the scooter. As she prepared to leave, she told him, "Call me sometime. We'll get together again. You know my number?"

"No, I don't."

"You have a pen? Tell me you have a pen."

He did, and she used it to write her number on the back of his hand. After she left, he walked to the waiting car. One of the guys in the back popped open his door and stood beside it. Russell slid across the torn upholstery. The guy hopped back in, shut the door behind him, and the transmission clunked into reverse. The car smelled of gasoline, swamp-water, and mothballs.

"All right. How you doin' Russ?" Gary offered his hand over the front seat.

"All right, all right," was all he could get out.

"All right," Guy chimed in as he sped out around Lily Lake. "All right. We're the All Right Gang. All right, here's what's what, Russ. You're seated between two Steves. These Steves are prepared to blindfold, gag, and hog-tie you at my command. So think real hard before you decide everything's all right."

The old wagon built up some daunting momentum as Guy opened it up on the state road north to Michigan.

"See those woods?" he asked, pointing at a clump of trees behind a dilapidated barn. "That's where we're gonna dump your body if you breathe a word of what you see or hear tonight."

The two Steves stared straight ahead. Gary rolled his eyes and wagged his tongue as Guy ranted on.

"You got to take the oath now, and swear your allegiance to our brotherhood. If you don't want to, I'll pull over right now and you can get out and you'll never see us again."

Gary continued his pantomime, encouraging Russell to agree to take Guy's cryptic oath.

"OK."

"OK. You're in. First stop, up here at the Indian gas station. You just stay put and keep quiet."

They pulled up to the cinderblock building, and Gary got out. He was the front man for the group. Smooth talking, always impeccably groomed, he put people at ease with his relaxed, pleasant demeanor. The exact opposite of Guy, whom people were right to fear. Not only was his unkempt appearance off-putting, but his eyes burned with an amoral, undisciplined intelligence. The car crept to the rear of the building. A door opened, and Gary stepped out. The Steves went into action and began loading up the back of the wagon with boxes.

"Only got menthol," Gary told Guy, who immediately went ballistic.

"What? What do you mean, he's only got menthol? That son of a bitch knows better than to pull this shit again!"

He started to get out of the car, but Gary stopped him.

"Cool out, man—it's true this time. I checked it out. He cut us a better deal this time, too, so let it ride. Don't make a scene, keep it low. We'll make our money all the same. It's cool. You just be cool."

Russell was getting nervous, watching Guy starting to freak. Back when he first met him, Guy was a young punk, living recklessly and scraping by however he could. These past four years had exacted a toll on him. He seemed hardened, jumpier, and edgier. Something was making him irritable.

Hocking a major gob out the window, he muttered, "Fucking Indian," and slouched back in his seat. Abruptly turning to Gary, he snapped, "What? You think it's funny?"

Gary kept smiling.

"Hey, man, I'm just biding my time. It's easy money—I don't know why you got to try to make it hard. Shit, what's it to you if he's only got menthol? What's it really matter? It's the same money."

"It matters that he tells me one thing, then changes the fucking deal after the fact. That's what matters—that he thinks he's in charge and I can just take it or leave it. I don't need that kind of aggravation."

Gary stared him squarely in the eye. "You are an angry man. You better find some peace, and soon, before your anger makes you do something really stupid."

Guy sneered and waved him away. "Save your sermon, son of a preacher man."

Gary was, in fact, the son of a minister who preached at the AME church in Michigan City.

"I'm just saying what you already know."

"Then you don't need to say it."

The Steves kept loading boxes. Guy sulked behind the wheel. Gary turned his attention to Russell, who was trying to make some sense of the scene he was now wrapped up in.

"What are you doing back in town, Russ? Thought we lost you a long time ago."

"While back I decided to take a road trip—came back here about a month ago. Been living out at Manny's, working in the fields, detasseling corn mainly."

Guy hissed. "What the fuck you want to do that shit work for? Ain't that why we got spicks?"

"Hey, now," Gary interjected with a meaningful nod. "Russ here's doing honest work for honest money. Something you've never even considered."

"Oh, I've considered it. I've considered it up and down and said to hell with it all, from top to bottom. I'm living off the fat of the land, that's what I'm doing—and there's plenty of fat to live off of."

"Sorrowful, meaningless, hedonistic existence," Gary scolded.

"You can get out of the car and sprout wings and fly on up to hebbin, altar boy. I'm telling it like it is."

Russell was getting uptight with the tone of the conversation and the sagging of the car as the rear end was weighed down with stolen cigarettes.

With a contemptuous snort, Guy turned to Russell. "You can say goodbye to that sorry job, man. We got you in on a sweet deal, make you some real money. This cigarette run here, this is chump change. Small potatoes. I don't even know why we're doing it. Just 'cause we always have, I guess, and we got our loyal customers. But we got something good cookin' that I'll tell you about if these assholes get a move on and finish up."

"You need to get laid," Gary abstrusely opined.

"What? Who the hell appointed you to be a royal pain in the ass? Now you're trying to tell me how to run my sex life? Get the fuck out of here."

"I'm serious, Guy. You need some tenderness, man, before you toughen up like an old callus."

"You're serious, all right, man—you're seriously bugging me tonight."

Gary had his finger on the button, and pushed it. "You been with a woman since Sharon?"

"Fuck Sharon," Guy snarled, jabbing a finger at Gary. "Fuck you, and whatever trip you're on. Just back off, man. We're gonna get this goddamn menthol shit unloaded," he jerked his thumb toward the boxes. "We're gonna clue Russ in, we're all gonna chill out and sing songs around the campfire tonight. And that means you're gonna lay off."

The Steves stowed the last of the boxes and took their places.

"Took your time, didn't you?" Guy growled as they drove away.

"Easy, man," Gary piped up. "You saw them working. They couldn't have done it any faster. You're in this business now where you think the whole world and everyone in it is out to do you harm. That's just not the way it is, man. Nobody's doing anything to you—you're doing it to yourself."

"Tell you what I'm going to do to you, man. I'm going to hit the ejector seat and send you flying."

He slammed his fist hard on the dashboard, and the emergency flashers started blinking.

"Goddamnit!" he howled, slamming the dash again in the vain hope of turning the signal off.

"Least you didn't set off the horn," Gary cajoled.

Guy answered by waving the finger in his face, then with a guttural growl he reached under the dashboard and ripped out fuses until the blinkers shut off. He threw the fuse out of the window, shouting, "Ha, ha! That'll teach you to fuck with me!"

"And I'm here—why?" Russell spoke up at last.

Guy turned to him. "You're here because I'm letting you in on a great deal, man, just 'cause I'm a nice guy. You don't know The Collector. He's this dude we met." He nudged Gary. "How would you describe The Collector?"

Gary considered before speaking. "He's a real freaky dude," he finally said. "Real freaky in an uptight sort of way, right? He lives in this funky old apartment in South Bend that's just weird. I don't know how, really, but it just has a weird feel to it, like something bad happened there or something. The guy is real fastidious about his place—everything is, like, hyper-arranged. And the guy himself tries to be real slick and tries to come off as totally together, but he's really just creepy. Whatever it is he's into, it ain't healthy."

"Anal retentive, totally," Guy said.

"Oh, yeah, totally," Gary agreed. "You see, Russ, we call this dude 'The Collector' because that's what he does, see? He's got a whole museum of drugs—collects specimens of all sorts of stuff that people take to mess themselves up. For one thing, he's got a fully stocked bar in his living room. But his big thing is these suitcases full of every sort of pill or herb or potion you can name."

"Never used nothing, either," Guy commented. "That's the really twisted part for me. He says he's never done anything but coffee and booze. And here he's got thousands of dollars of shit stashed away in these suitcases. He's got one loaded with acid: sheets of blotter with all this wild art, jars full of micro-dots and barrels, vials of liquid. Mushrooms—a ton of all kinds of mushrooms, all weighed and labeled. He's got jungle vines, leaves, funky snuff, a big wreath of peyote buttons. Suitcase full of pot and hash, ounces of all these exotic varieties; suitcase full of opium from all over the world. He's got one filled with every prescription drug you can name, and a hundred more you never knew about. I mean, the guy's The Collector, you know?"

"Oh yeah," Gary said, smiling widely. "Total freak of nature, that guy."

"So, anyway, through The Collector we get turned on to someone he got wind of, this guy in Kentucky called Skutch. Well, old Skutch has this shipment from Afghanistan—blocks of black hash. Collector turns us on to this guy, gives us money to go down and buy a sample for him. So we get together enough cash to buy a kilo, we hope, and we cruise all the way down to Kentucky, right, and we get in one weird scene."

"Totally messed up," Gary took over the narrative. "This guy Skutch, he lives down in some redneck hollow, way out where no one can hear you scream. Lives in a rusty old trailer, and there's this old school bus next to it that he's converted into some kind of furnace that was powering the place. It was just plain nasty."

"Totally screwed," Guy resumed. "Bad vibe from the get-go. We pull up, I go knock on the door. Wait a few minutes, looks like the guy's not around; then I see the shades kind of flutter, and I knock again. Then this scary looking freak swings open the door—and hell, if I'm calling someone a scary looking freak, shit—the guy was a goddamn monster."

Russell looked anxiously at the two Steves, who both stared out their respective windows.

"Old Skutch, he leans out and whispers to me, 'Are you the ones they sent for the stuff?' Just like that. And I'm, like, 'Uh, yeah, we're here for some stuff.' And that seems OK with him, 'cause he waves us all in. So we all come in, Skutch slams the door, we sit down on this moldy old couch. The place just plain stinks, and all we want is to make the deal and get out. He sits down at this table across from us, picks up this big ass glass pipe, and lights it. Takes a hit, and nods out—totally limp, all the way out."

"Damndest thing," Gary joined in, shuddering at the memory. "Not good. Not good at all."

"Yeah," Guy went on, "he was out a long time, too, couple minutes. We were beginning to think maybe the dude was dead. Then he sort of jerked awake, looks at us like he doesn't know how we got there, and runs into another room. Comes out with a loaded crossbow. I jumped out of my seat, just about shit my pants."

Gary shook his head. "And here I am, right? Down South, with this hairy Appalachian Neanderthal—kind of like Guy but worse—staring at me with a crossbow. Now that's what I call fucked up."

"Sure was," Guy carried the story along, "and I'm there with you and who else? Was it Chuck and Lester? It was Lester and someone. Anyway, we're there with hairy old Skutch who just smoked some really weird shit and is coming at us with this crossbow. So I say, 'Uh, we're here for the stuff.' And he turns to me and levels that crossbow right at me and I'm a total goner. I pissed my pants right there."

Gary laughed, slapping his knee.

"Ha ha," Guy laughed along. "You didn't smell so good yourself on the ride home."

Throughout the telling of this story they'd been swerving along a maze of country roads in the last dusky light of day.

"Know where we are, Russ?" Guy asked.

"Nope."

"Good. Anyway, Skutch has me in his sights, then he drops the crossbow and says, 'Sit down.' So I do, and he goes in another room and brings out this crate, old ammunition crate. Puts it down in front of me, opens it up. Ten kilos of black hash inside. So, I give him the money, right, and he doesn't even count it. Just throws it on the table and closes the box, pushes it at me and says, 'Take it.'"

He shot a look back at Russell, who was listening attentively while the Steves stared placidly into the darkness.

"So, I opened the box, took out a brick, closed the lid and pushed it back to him. Then he gets all crazy and picks up the crossbow again and yells, 'Don't play games! You're here to take the stuff. Take it!'"

Gary started laughing again.

"Yeah, it's funny now," Guy continued, "but at the time it was freak city. So I says to Skutch, I'm like, 'OK, you're right.' Then, I don't know why, but then I say, 'I was just testing you.' And that kind of puts him at ease somehow. He puts down that crossbow and grins, then pushes the box back at me. I put the brick back in the box, and closed the lid. He kept grinnin' this evil sort of grin and then he picked up that pipe again. Zonk—he went out, and we didn't wait for him to wake up again. Chuck—it was Chuck, I remember now—he grabbed the cash off the table. We picked up that box and shot back out of there as fast as we could."

Still laughing, Gary added, "Lester, though, that big old slob, he went right up to Skutch when he was passed out and took a crystal from the tray, some of that funky crap he was smoking."

Guy sped along, kicking up a cloud of dust on a lonely dirt road. "Hey, know where we are now, Russ?"

"Not at all."

"Yeah? Well, we're not far. So, we take off and make record time back here, right, pushing this old tank to the limit, all freaked out about Skutch coming to his senses and tracking us down. First thing we do, we go over to The Collector and try to play it cool. We go up there with one kilo, show it to him, give him his ounce or whatever it was. We don't want to tell him the whole story, 'cause he'll want his money back, right? And he's pale as hell, he's a sickly looking dude, sitting there in his smoking jacket, sort of humming to himself as he labels the stuff and puts it in his suitcase. And we're all still freaked out, all antsy, trying to keep cool. It was too weird."

Gary broke in. "Lester got out that crystal, and hands it over. Collector takes a look at it, doesn't know what it is. Checks it out with a magnifying glass, then gets a razor blade and cuts it in two. Puts one half in a test tube, gives the other half to us and tells us to smoke it sometime and let him know what it does. No one's tried it yet." He leaned across the seat, smiling suggestively.

"And that's it," Guy said with a shrug. "We've kept low the last month, all paranoid about The Collector finding out what really went down and trying to get in on our action, and thinking about Skutch out there, tracking us down. Haven't heard anything about it so far. And so we end up with about ten kilos of the world's best hashish not only for free, but with The Collector's money on top of it. It's like he paid us to get the stuff. Fuckin' A!"

They slowed to a stop. Guy turned the lights off and steered the wagon off the road, following ruts through a weedy field. The car convulsed for a full minute after he shut off the engine.

"OK, boys, you know the drill. Go sell those menthol cigarettes."

The two Steves grabbed boxes and walked into a wooded grove. They emerged on bicycles, pedaling off toward the road.

"You ever need to get around, come out here and get a bike." Gary got a flashlight out of the car and led Russell into the woods. There were a dozen bikes amongst the trees.

"We don't steal bikes," Guy explained. "That's pretty low, stealing bikes. But we do take them as payment sometimes, if they're any good. Come on, let's go."

Gary led the way with the flashlight.

"Watch your step, Russ. Sinkholes and quicksand all around here." He stopped and waved for Russell to catch up. "And here's our very own little hidey-hole."

They stood at the edge of a large sinkhole, some thirty feet in diameter and about twenty feet deep. The weeds were so thick and tall around it that one could have easily stepped right into it. Three young men sat around a smoldering fire at the bottom. One read a book, another dozed on a couch, and the third was whittling a block of wood.

"Look lively!" Guy shouted, starting down some steps that had been cut into one of the sloping sides. Russell and Gary followed. Guy made a short introduction.

"Travis. Javier. Matt. This is Russ, our new man in town. OK, you guys know your routes. We're staying here to get Russ situated."

They climbed the steps out of the hole and disappeared into the darkness.

"Welcome to Bloodstone, man! That's what we've taken to calling it. How you like it?"

Russell was at a loss, but mustered a response. "You live down here?"

"Camp out here, yeah. We found it a couple years ago, spent a lot of time fixing it up. Check it out." He walked him around the perimeter, showing him a ditch lined with gravel, with pipes sunk into the ground at regular intervals. "Drainage," he proudly informed him, then pointed to the furnishings down there. "We had to lower all this stuff down on ropes, dig?"

Down in that hole there were a couple of tents, a few easy chairs, couches, several large wooden spools, a steamer chest, cots, a pile of stuff covered with a tarp, and a store of carboys filled with water. Guy walked Russell over to the steamer chest. Inside were dry goods and medical supplies. "We got it all. We've got some tarps we can rig up on poles for shade, or when it rains real hard. But we have to figure out how to get electricity down here."

Gary leaned back in one of the armchairs, humming quietly to himself. "Settle back, Russ. Take it easy. It's good out here."

Russell sat on a couch, his eyes wide in this cave-like encampment. Guy threw a few sticks on the fire, sending sparks flying toward the clear, starry sky. A nocturnal chorus resounded around the space, a rich layering of crickets, cicadas, and frogs. In the light of the stoked fire, Russell discerned some interesting shadows along a far wall. He walked over and examined a striking series of grotesque visages that had been carved into the stone.

"Dan Sherman did that," Guy informed him while rummaging through a pile of stuff. "You know Dan?"

Russell didn't.

"Yeah, well, Dan's cool. Took off a while ago, no one seems to know where he is now. Good artist. He was out here last summer, carved all sorts of stuff in this rock. You can see it better tomorrow. These walls are all red sandstone. Soft stuff. You can carve it with a penknife."

Guy grabbed a knapsack and walked over to the couch where Russell had been sitting. "Hey, come on over, Russ. I'll turn you on to what we've been talking about."

Russell sat back down. Guy reached into the knapsack and took out a flat board with a slender nail driven through the center. He put it on the spool table and set a glass jar next to it. Then he opened a plastic bag containing a thick black slab. He cut a tiny piece off the slab, rolled it into a ball, and placed it on the point of the nail that was sticking up out of the board. He held his lighter to the little ball until it started smoking, then turned the jar upside down over it. Thick bluish smoke soon filled the jar.

"Hash under glass," Guy beamed at him. "Go ahead. Tilt the jar up a little and suck the whole thing down."

Russell didn't need to be told twice. It had been a long time since he'd gotten high, and this sure seemed like a fine time and place to get ripped. He lifted the edge of the jar and inhaled. A sweet pungency expanded into his chest. He coughed it out and was left with a clean, almost medicinal aftertaste.

As he watched Guy remove the ash from the nail and set up a hit for Gary, he found himself stepping out of the dreary fog of his preoccupations and anxieties. Guy and Gary laughed together about something, but he hadn't paid attention to what they were saying. The fire glowed brightly, and the night sounds deepened. Did he really work all day in the fields? Had he spent the afternoon with Helen? It all seemed so remote. Piecing together the day's events was a slippery business, like trying to reconstruct a half-forgotten dream.

"That's the shit, ain't it, Russ?"

"Oh yeah."

Guy nudged him. "Get up a minute."

Russell stood. Guy pushed the couch aside, then knelt and brushed the dirt with his forearm until he uncovered a piece of plywood. He removed this and hoisted a steel box out of a hole. He unlocked the box, swung open the lid, and presented the contents. Inside were black bricks wrapped in cellophane. Russell picked one up, savoring its heft and checking out the elaborate design stamped into the glossy surface.

"There it is," Guy said proudly. "Our bankroll."

"Wow," was the only response Russell could come up with.

"Yeah, 'wow,' you got that right," Guy rejoined, closing the box. He put it back in the hole and covered it up. Scooting the couch back in place, he said, "Now you know too much, Russ."

Gary broke in. "We have to start selling that stuff. Either that, or smoke it all."

"Yeah, we gotta move it," Guy said. "Gary's setting up a deal in Chicago to unload five kilos in bulk. That's a quick chunk of change, but wholesale price. We can make a lot more in the long run with smaller deals at retail around town. So what we want you to do first off is to weigh out the rest—break it down into grams and ten-gram packages. I can't sit still long enough to do it, and Gary's got better things to do, and the rest of these idiots just won't follow through. We know you good enough to know you'll manage it. Don't worry about getting paid—we'll take care of you. You in?"

Russell knew that he must have some objections to getting so deeply involved in this scheme, but none came to mind. "Yeah, I guess so," was what he wound up saying.

"Good. Now we don't have to kill you."

Guy and Gary looked at one another and started laughing. Gary leaned toward Russell and tapped his shoulder. "You're all right, Russ. Hey, man, you know where we are?"

By now Russell had completely lost track of everything.

"Come on, we'll show you."

With Gary leading the way, they climbed out of the hole. Guy turned and said, "What we need is some camouflage netting to cover the place. I know where there is some, but it's a matter of getting to it."

They followed a path into the woods and uphill to a clearing. They made their way along an old stone wall, and past a crumbling chimney. They sat on the remains of Nellie Widow's foundation. Russell looked down at his friends' house, and Lily Lake beyond, its dark surface gently rippling in the euphoric night.

"Come on, Russ. Go get your stuff and come camp out with us. It'll be cool. No more field work."

The walk through the woods and the realization that they were so close to home cleared Russell's mind enough for him to voice a concern. "I don't know. Are you serious? Live in a hole with you guys? How do you keep clean down there?"

Guy's scrawny frame shook with laughter. "Well, we piss and shit in the woods, if that's what you're worried about. Whenever I get too ripe I jump in the lake. Gary here, though, him and his fancy city ways, he has other ideas about hygiene."

"Yeah, man, I'll hook you up with Chuck Probst. You probably don't know him. He's cool. He's got a gig as a janitor at the old Rumacher Hotel—you know that place downtown? Part of the deal of him having that job is he gets an apartment there, down in the basement, right next to the laundry room. But he spends all his time with his woman at her place. It's perfect—even has a private entrance off the alley. You can get a shower there, do your laundry, crash out on a real bed, whatever. I'll hook you up with him, let him know you're with us, and you'll be in."

"So now you know where we are," Guy said. "Get your stuff and come on back. It'll be a blast—guaranteed."

The craziness of their proposition appealed to his yearning for adventure. He headed down to collect his belongings, figuring he'd take the opportunity at hand and sort through the difficulties later.

No one was home when he entered the house. That was unusual, but he didn't think much about it. What he did think about was how to word a note to those guys explaining his sudden departure. He'd be back to check in with them soon enough, but he knew they'd want to know why he'd flown the coop. Footsteps resounded down the hallway, and Manny entered the room. He approached with stooped shoulders, wiggling his fingers with hammy menace, speaking in a mock-sinister tone that came off like a cheesy Peter Lorre imitation.

"You left the door open again, Mr. Russell. Heh-heh. That's very bad. You know, any old weirdo could just walk right in here."

Russell stopped packing and stared at him, the cannabis having perceptibly slowed him down. Manny saw him gathering his things and stood up straight.

"Hey, what's up?"

"Man, I'm glad you came back before I split. I'm going to camp out with Guy and Gary. Spent the last few hours with them. They've got a camp set up right on the other side of Nellie's farm. I think I'll hang out there, maybe sort of jump-start this whole trip, see if it pans out."

Manny's first response was a hum; then he said, "Well, if that's what you want to do. Let us know how it's going."

"Oh, yeah, sure. I'll stop back by in a couple days. Where's Carmela, anyway? I want to talk to her about it."

Manny frowned. "I don't know where she is. I was hoping she'd be here. We got into it this afternoon."

"What about?"

"I don't really feel like talking about it now," Manny waved the question aside. "Can you make that fit?" He nodded at all that Russell had yet to stuff into his already-bulging pack.

"Yeah, I think so. I did it before."

"Well, come join me for a beer when you finish up."

With all his gear together, Russell took a breather on the couch. He began to feel very tired. If he sat around for too long he'd never get up, so he hoisted his pack and went to the kitchen. Manny was drinking when he got there. He sat at the table and lifted an open bottle.

"You know this beer is made by a friend of mine, Rick Smith. He turned an old warehouse down by the depot into a little brewery. They're selling it all over now—Chicago, Michigan."

Russell took a sip. His high was fading, and he hoped the beer would provide some additional mileage.

Manny leaned over the table. "Hey, did you turn off Carmela's lights?"

"No way. Uh-uh. They were off when I came home this evening."

"Damn. She must be really pissed."

Russell wondered if he should ask again about their fight. Before he could, Manny spoke up.

"Aw, hell, she can just stay pissed as far as I'm concerned. Whatever." He downed the remainder of his bottle and went for another. Russell continued to sip his. It was good beer, rich and yeasty.

"So, what's the deal with Guy and Gary and their little camp? What'd they get you into? They have to have some angle."

"A weird deal with a whole lot of hash. They're cutting me in on the profits if I weigh the stuff out for them."

Manny shook his head and took a long draught. "Hey, man, you choose who you hang out with, but I'm telling you those guys are trouble. They've been working that whole 'Peter Pan and the Lost Boys' shtick for way too long. They keep pushing their luck, and it's bound to run out. It'd be too bad if it happened when you were with them."

Smiling broadly, Russell held out his hand. Manny grasped it, and got a surprise.

"What the —"

Russell unstrapped the joy buzzer and laid it on the table. "I bought that for you and totally forgot about it—just found it when I was packing up."

"Yeah, well that's cool. Thanks. You know I've always wanted one. But I'm serious about those guys, man. You watch yourself with them." He nodded at his friend and took another long drink.

"I'll take care of myself." Russell finished his bottle and looked around. He noticed the dishes he'd left in the sink, and got up to wash them.

"Leave those, man. Don't worry about it."

"No, I'll get them done."

Manny picked up his beer. "Whatever. I'll be on the porch."

With the dishes finished, Russell hauled his gear out to the porch. Manny was smoking on the swing. It was a fine, clear summer night. "Carmela's going to miss you," Manny said after a drag. "She was joking the other night about adopting you."

"Tell her I'll be by soon. I want to try to get a handle on what they're up to out there with their camp and all. It seems pretty funky."

"Just remember what I said: Watch yourself."

Russell fished in his pocket for their house key.

"Hold on to it. You can come back whenever you want, even to just take shower or whatever"

Their windsock wriggled in the night breeze. The lake was very dark. Manny blew smoke rings.

"I better hit it now." Russell readied his pack. "It's been a long day, and I'm feeling it. Got a good mile to hike."

Manny snuffed out his cigarette and opened his arms. They hugged. He left the glow of his friends' porch and walked beneath a crescent moon to go live in a hole in the ground.

7

"Look out—here I come!" Guy rappelled down the side of the hole on a rope he had anchored above. He carried the length of rope across the pit and tossed it up to Steve, stationed at the edge. It slipped through his fingers and fell back down.

"Fools! Fools! I'm surrounded by fools!" Guy railed to heaven, then screamed up at Steve, "Hey, man, I guess you didn't understand—I threw it up there for you to catch. Think you can manage that? I mean, I don't want to push you beyond your limits."

Steve flipped him off, which was a good enough signal for another try. This time he caught it.

"Now draw it tight and stake it down, and mind you, do it right. That is, if you're capable of being more than a bumbling prick."

Steve kicked a rock over the edge. Guy dodged it and walked over to Russell, who was busy at the scales.

"You see what I have to deal with? Fools. That's what I have to deal with."

Russell stared blankly at him, then took a casual hit of hash from a pipe. He'd been down there for three days now, weighing the stuff, and while doing so had taken to smoking it, rationalizing it as being a good way to ease the transition from having a room of his own in a cozy house to living in a pit with a madman and his crew of freaky flunkies. Gary had been absent since that first night out here, and so Russell had not gained access to that apartment to shower and get some laundry done. Guy was still wearing the same clothes he'd had on since at least three days ago, and he hadn't yet felt the need to visit the lake.

"All right—this one's for the Gipper. Make me proud, boy." Guy ran another rope across the hole and flung the end up at Steve, who caught it.

"I'll be damned!" Guy bellowed. "That was almost impressive. Pretty soon you'll be ready for the Special Olympics."

Steve spat at him. Guy jumped back, grabbing his crotch as a rejoinder.

"Son of a bitch," he muttered, flopping on the couch. "What I put up with! I swear. Now if Gary'll get his prima-donna ass down here, we can get this show on the road."

With that last rope, Guy had finished constructing supports for his coveted camouflage netting. The next step was the procurement of the netting, and for that Guy was insistent upon Gary being present.

"Where's Gary been anyway?" Russell asked, throwing a ten-gram chunk on a heap of packages. "I haven't seen him since you guys brought me down here."

"Been a schoolin'," Guy drawled, slipping into the backwoods lowlife persona he adopted all too readily.

"He's going to school?"

"Yeah, and he's gettin' all uppity about it, too—readin' an' writin' an' arithmeticin'—gettin' his head filled up with notions like he's better than us. I'm gonna take that boy down a notch or two, Russ. You just watch me do it."

"Looks like you all been busy down here," Gary smiled, walking down the steps. "Bunch of spiders spinning your webs."

"Just in time as usual," Guy sneered, "the work's all done."

"Ain't that just the way?" Gary grinned and strode over to the couch. "Hey, how you doin' Russ? Man, I talked with Chuck and it's cool—you're in. Go get yourself a shower sometime. Looks like you can use it." He slid his sunglasses down the bridge of his nose and stared into Russell's red eyes. "Better lay off that stuff, man—we have to have some left to sell."

Guy screwed his face into an expression of disdain. "If your highness is ready, the Bondo-mobile awaits."

"What's with this 'highness' stuff, man? What're you snippin' on me for now?"

"You're off with your fancy book learnin', and we're down here doing all the work."

"Damned if you're working," Gary snorted. "What do you know about working? And any work you might be doing, it ain't on me."

Guy folded his arms behind his head and stretched out on the couch. Gary looked at him for a moment, expecting something more to be added, then flicked his wrist with a dismissive exhalation.

"What are you studying at school?" Russell wanted to know.

"Political science," Gary smiled. "I'm a pretty smooth operator naturally, so it fits. I could go into diplomacy, negotiations, public relations."

"You're a bedbug," Guy declared. He jumped off the couch and strutted around the fire pit, repeating emphatically: "You are a bedbug."

"What? What are you calling me a bedbug for? If anyone's a bedbug, it's you."

"Oh, that's real diplomatic, Mr. Smooth Operator," Guy smirked, then shouted, "I am the king! I am the king!"

"King of a sinkhole."

"All the same, it's mine, mine, mine!"

Gary could only shake his head.

———

After much ceremonial to-do, including ritualistic exhortations and laying on of hands on the car, they got the starter cranking and the engine of the old wagon turned over. Amid clouds of black, blue, and white smoke they roared off toward Bass Lake and Frank's home, where the netting was to be had, stored among a trove of military fetishes.

They rode out on a lonely old road in the heat of the day. Guy drove and Gary rode shotgun. Travis and Steve sat droopy-eyed and sullen in the rear. Wedged between them, Russell was feeling a little surly himself. He wished he could feel like he was on an adventure. Instead, he felt shanghaied, deprived of running water or any amenities whatsoever, now stuck in a smelly old jalopy on an errand that was of little interest to him.

"We have to be careful here, Russ. Real careful." Guy turned to him while he sped along. "Frank and I are sworn enemies. We're going in to raid his place. We're sending you up first; see if the old man's home or not. Can't tell just from his car being there—it's broke down or something. His buddy Earl's been taking him around lately."

Russell started to get nervous. He didn't like going first in any situation.

"Now, if he is there, make like you're taking a poll on a new property tax or something. And be ready to get a good stream of bile about government this and government that. He might come off like he's about to whack your ass, but he'll have his say and leave you alone. If Bob answers, that's a sure sign that Frank's not there. Raise up the clipboard, then, so we'll know the coast is clear."

Gary tossed a clipboard into Russell's lap.

"Thanks a lot," Russell sarcastically intoned. "Sending me up there to take the heat like that."

"Well, I can't send up anyone else—you're the only one he doesn't know. It's no heat, really. Just go scope the place out for us."

Russell grunted and took up the chore. His repeated knocking went unanswered, and he turned to the car with a shrug. Then the door cracked open.

"Oh, hi, Bob," Russell turned to greet him.

"I told you before I don't know where he is, and my dad gets mad. So, goodbye."

"No," Russell stopped him. "Wait. I found him. Or, he found me. He's here." He raised the clipboard.

"Oh no!" Bob proclaimed with a pitiful yelp that pained Russell, who sought to apologize.

"Hey, Bob, I'm sorry, I didn't mean to make trouble."

He protested with a pout. "But those guys are trouble."

Too late for regrets: the gang approached.

"Howdy doody, Bob Wayne Bogel," Guy tapped Bob on the arm as he brushed past him.

"Don't be like last time," Bob whined. "He got real mad then."

"And what did you do when he got mad, Bob?" Guy turned to him with a stern expression.

"Nothing. I just had to listen to it."

"Well, wise up already, poindexter. You won't have to listen to it if you're not around. Get the hell out, and you won't have to put up with it anymore."

"But I live here. He needs me here."

"What do you mean, 'I live here?' You can live anywhere. You'll always get your check, no matter where you live, so you can get your own apartment, and you can get yourself a job, and you don't have to put up with his crap any more. And as far as him needing you, all he needs from you is your check. Everything else he makes you do, he can do for himself, or he can get one of his idiot buddies to help him." He sighed and shook his head. "Damn it, Bob, just get out. I'll stand up for you, man. I'll help you do it, but you have to make the first move."

Bob shut his eyes and started swaying back and forth.

"Hey, pal, don't get all freaky—we're not going to trash the place. We're here for some very specific items this time."

Guy strode through the living room and headed to Bob's bedroom, with Bob close behind. Travis and Steve sat down in chairs by the window, keeping lookout. The rooms in the house were dark, the walls all paneled. Military regalia and taxidermy filled the place, two decorative motifs that shared a common centerpiece in the form of a massive gun safe located in what had been a formal dining room, now converted to a munitions vault. Gary and Russell followed Guy and Bob.

"How's your guinea pigs, Bob?" Guy asked in an overly loud and way-too-jolly voice. Bob kept quiet.

"Check these little beasties out," he motioned to Gary and Russell. "You feeding them too much, Bob? They're getting fat."

Guy grabbed the pair of rodents by the scruffs of their necks, one in each hand, and carried them to the kitchen.

"Don't hurt them!" Bob wailed.

"Oh, shut up—I'm not going hurt them. I'm going to get them the exercise they need." He caught Russell's eye and nodded to the counter. "Hey, man, pull out the bread board."

Russell did, and Guy put the guinea pigs down on it, circling his arms loosely around the board to ring them in.

"They have entered the gaming grid!" Guy announced, then he started chanting, "Two pigs enter, one pig leave!"

Gary clapped his hands above the stunned rodents, shouting, "Let's get it on!"

"Stop it! Stop it! Stop it!" Bob spastically swatted at all of them.

"Lay off, you wuss," Guy snarled, and then gave up the game. "Here, take your overstuffed rats back to their little playpen. They're gonna burst, the way you feed them, like weenies on a grill."

"Stop it!" Bob yelled again, picking up his pets and returning them to his room. Gary and Russell stared at each other. Guy sighed, then went to the bedroom.

"Man, I wasn't hurting them. You know I wouldn't. I was just messing around. I'm not here to get you in trouble or hurt your pets, dude. Listen to me, I can help you out."

"It's you messing around that always makes trouble," Bob asserted, stroking the quivering animals.

"Just cool out, OK, and listen?"

Bob didn't look at him or say anything. He just kept petting his guinea pigs. Gary and Russell showed up at the door. Guy looked at them; then he looked at Bob, and slumped with a pained expression.

"Hey, take a look at this thing Bob made." Gary led Russell across the room to a table that held a large, elaborate diorama of a junkyard.

"Check it out," Gary insisted, drawing Russell near. "It's a real work of art."

It was expertly crafted. The main building was meticulously constructed to appear as if it were falling apart. The small structure seemed genuinely fatigued and worn. Miniature refuse cluttered the sandy lot. Partially demolished and stripped cars were lined up before stacks of chassis and body parts waiting for the compactor, a marvelously detailed model of a grimy industrial machine, behind which were piled bales of compressed parts. The whole thing was rounded about by a hodgepodge of fences in various states of disrepair, all spliced and pieced together, complete with weedy vegetation and indiscriminate debris. The artistry was remarkable.

"Wow," Russell said. "This is really cool."

"I like junkyards," Bob explained.

Guy put his arm around him. "Man, you do really good work. You can get a job doing something with your hands, doing something you like. You know, that lady from Social Services was on his case for years about getting you a job. But he kept putting her off and putting her off, and she finally gave up." He unwrapped his arm and faced his brother. "And you know why he didn't want you out working? Because you'd get a place of your own and get a life for yourself, and there goes his booze money."

Bob started squirming and scrunched up his face. "Why do you have to be so mean all the time?"

"Hey," Guy grabbed his shoulders and locked eyes with him. "It's the way I see it. I'm just telling you the truth."

At this, Gary sputtered derisive laughter. "You're the messenger of truth?"

Guy turned to him. "Yeah. I suppose now you know better than me how I should help my own brother?"

With a long-suffering expression, Gary let it drop and said, "What are we here for? Let's get the stuff and go."

Guy squinted at him, running his tongue across his teeth.

"Yeah," he said with a crooked smile, then called his minions to the garage.

Like the rest of the house, the garage was kept very orderly. Tools and hardware were neatly organized, the workbench clean and ready. The netting was stowed against the back wall.

"Here it is, boys. Haul it away." Travis and Steve picked up the netting and carried it over to the wagon. Guy took a screwdriver from a table and walked out to the driveway. He was removing the license plate from Frank's car when Bob came over to him.

"I don't think you should do that."

"Well, Bob, you see," Guy grunted, scraping away some rust, "my plates are expired already. His are good till October. So I'm switching them. He can't keep this old heap running, so why have good tags on it? Just going to waste."

He lifted the plate off the bumper.

"But he'll know."

"You think he remembers his license number? Hell, he'd forget his own name if it wasn't tattooed on his dick. Get real."

After making the switch, Guy joined the others, who were eating sandwiches in the backyard, made with food stolen from the refrigerator. He ate some salami without bread, then went back into the garage and emerged wielding a terrible whip made of barbed wire.

"Remember this beauty?" he shouted, swinging the thing over his head. "This ain't no ordinary barbed-wire whip—this here is a goddamn cat-o'-nine-tails."

He unleashed its fury on an old maple tree, flailing at the worn trunk. "Remember when I gave those punks a lesson, Bob? Those fuckwads down the street, who kept bothering you all the time? Remember how I came after them with this hummer?" He wound the whip up and slashed leaves and small branches off of the tree. "I chased them all up and down the street, right to this tree. Remember they climbed up it, and I started dancing around underneath like this?"

He went on a rampage, whacking everything he could with his murderous weapon.

"I kept them up there a good long time, those stupid sons of bitches. They were pissing their pants. One of them started puking. Remember that?" He threw the whip on the ground and turned to Bob. "And they never messed with you again, did they? I've always looked after you, man, and I can't stand to see someone screwing you. But you got to do something about it yourself; you got to get out of here. You're getting all fat and pasty, staying inside all the time. It's creepy, like you're a veal calf or something."

Bob struggled with a lump in his throat, then managed to belt out a protest accompanied by a spray of spit. "Stop it!"

"Bah," Guy sneered, swiping his hand in front of his face. "I'm talking to a wall." He motioned to the others. "Come on, we're going to the basement."

They walked down to the partially finished basement and fanned out. Travis and Steve started a game of darts. Russell tagged along with Guy and Gary, who were headed toward a corner near the water softener. Guy reached up, ran his hand along an air duct and pulled down a pistol. He reached up again for a box of ammunition. Bob joined them.

"No shooting," he said as Guy loaded the barrel.

"Don't worry, man. Since when have I ever done anything too stupid?"

Gary broke his silence to say, "Let me count the ways."

"Could've figured you'd pipe up on that cue. Hey, make yourself useful, man, and go get the pan."

Gary cocked an eyebrow and gave Guy a meaningful look. "You thinking about playing that old game?"

"Yeah. What do you think?"

Gary smiled. "It's up to you. You're gonna hold the pan."

"It's been a long time," Guy contemplated. "Hell. Let's do it."

Gary shrugged. "Why not?"

Russell followed this exchange, then followed them both back toward the stairs. Guy picked up a hunting knife off a shelf and from halfway across the basement nailed the bull's eye on the dartboard, prompting an uncharacteristic outburst from the usually reticent Travis.

"Freak of nature! Freak occurrence! You couldn't do that again."

"Oh, sure I could. You bet. They call me 'Sure-shot'—I always hit my mark."

Travis pried the knife loose and handed it to Guy. He took it and threw it and broke a window five feet away from the dartboard.

"Way to go, Sure-shot!" Travis mocked him.

With a cry of "Shit!" Guy ran over to the broken pane. Bob grabbed his head and started rocking back and forth, emitting a high-pitched whine. Guy broke out the remaining glass with the handle of the knife, and came back to talk to Bob. He grabbed him by the shoulders and shook him.

"Ease up, man, don't go spastic. It's no big deal. It's on the side of the house—he'll never even notice. I'll be back here tomorrow or the day after, and I'll fix it, and it'll be as good as new and he'll never know."

Bob kept rocking, his head down, and mumbled, "But I have to tell him."

"Look at me, Bob. Look at me." Guy lifted Bob's head and looked him in the eye. "You don't have to tell him, Bob. You don't have to lie, but you don't have to tell him anything. He'll never know. It'll get fixed. You just forget about it now. It's not your problem. It's no big deal."

Bob sniffed and wiped some drool from the side of his mouth. "You shouldn't take that gun."

Guy squinted at him. "Why not? You want to keep it around so it'll be here when he finally snaps? He's got so much heavy metal stashed away for that, you won't be able to get down here for this. You know it's bound to happen one of these days. He's gonna flash back to Hamburger Hill, man, and you're gonna be the first Charlie he sees."

Bob started trembling. His distress moved Russell to walk over to him, his hand open in a gesture of consolation. Bob shoved him away. Guy got in his brother's face, a menacing look in his eye and in his tone.

"Afraid, Bob? You know it's true. The deed's just waiting to be done. That's what I'm saying, man—get out now while you can. It's scary, yeah, but it's not as scary as what's coming through the tunnel. You got the chance to get out now."

"You get out!" Bob erupted at Guy, then turned to the rest of them. "You all get out!"

"You heard the man," Guy shrugged. "Let's go."

On the way out, Gary stopped to get a large iron skillet from the kitchen.

The wagon grumbled to a halt behind a mound of grass clippings near the fairgrounds. Guy waited for the engine to finally conk out, then made a grandiloquent invitation: "Come, gentlemen, let us lollygag about these wooded acreages."

He picked up the iron pan and held it up like a standard as he led the way along a path through the trees. Russell sat lethargically while Travis and Steve got out. He was tired and just wanted to curl up and sleep. Guy's ranting crankiness was wearing him down pretty quickly, and his mood was darkening. Camping out with a hyperkenetic crackpot and a bunch of monosyllabic ciphers was another dead end in his attempt at adventure. He was considering packing up and moving back in with Carmela and Manny, but that seemed pretty lame. His whole approach to life was seeming increasingly lame. There must have been a time when that wasn't so, but he couldn't rightly remember.

Once out of the car, he brightened up a little in the fresh air. There was no clear reason why he should feel so dissatisfied. After all, he was doing what he'd set out to do. He was on his own, accountable to no one, free to do as he pleased. Surely this was the kind of life that would yield good stories. But his pen was dry, and the pages of his notebook remained blank. It had been a long time since he'd given any thought at all to keeping his journal. He was too busy nursing his doubts.

Russell hurried along the trail to catch up. He always liked walking in the woods, and he grudgingly credited Guy with making such expeditions possible. Guy could get things done. He could effect his plans, no matter how immoral, illegal, or otherwise offensive they might be. He had ideas about things he wanted to do, and followed through to make them happen. What Russell needed was a plan of action, a course to steer, something to believe in. Right now he was a rudderless boat.

"Hey, Russ," Gary greeted him, having fallen back behind the group. "I'm sorry about not getting back with you about Chuck and his place. I haven't been hanging out that much."

They walked along the trail a bit. Gary picked up a stone and tossed it into the bush.

"I just haven't been around that much lately," Gary went on. "This is all getting pretty old to me. You know, Guy's my friend and all, and we've had some good, crazy times, but, you know, his thing just ain't where it's at anymore. I've got way more important things to deal with. I'm going to go do something for real."

Now Guy doubled back to join them, having sent Travis and Steve on ahead. He sized up the two of them, then turned to Russell.

"You ever make opium?"

Russell responded in the negative.

"What's with you?" Guy demanded. "Every time I ask you if you know somebody or know about something, you never do. You some kind of dimwit or something?"

Dimwit though he might be, Russell could still challenge an insult. He threw up his hands and said, "What the hell? You toss all this off-the-wall stuff at me and then when I don't know what you're talking about, that means there's something wrong with me? Screw you."

Gary's hooting laughter echoed through the woods. Guy stopped dead in his tracks. Russell stopped, too, facing him uneasily. Then Guy began flailing his limbs about, his body convulsing with jerks and shakes. This grotesque display went on for a minute before Russell sought to interrupt.

"What's this, now?"

Guy continued spazzing out awhile longer before snapping out of it.

"I'm fine," he said at last, wiping the sweat from his brow. "Just doing the Bone Dance is all."

"Well, what's that supposed to mean?" Russell wanted to know. "What's the Bone Dance?"

"Nothing," Guy answered. "Just the Bone Dance, that's all. Come here, I'll show you what I was talking about."

Gary rolled his eyes and slipped off to catch up with Travis and Steve. Guy led Russell to a clearing along an irrigation canal, walking him out to a clump of plants that were starting to flower.

"Thousands of premium opium poppies out here," Guy told him, sweeping his hand all around. "Seeds came from The Collector. See this flower here?" He grabbed one of the purple blooms. "When the petals fall off, a pod starts growing. We'll come back out here and check on those pods, and when they're big enough I'll show you how to get the juice out. It's a real pain, takes forever. We'll be coming out here for a month or so, getting all the juice drop by drop. But it's worth it, 'cause the junkies around here go crazy for it. Before that hash fell from heaven, this was our main summertime deal."

Russell looked along the canal. He could spot the poppy plants, their gray-green leaves distinctive among the other weeds. Guy tapped his arm.

"Come on, they're probably at the cabin by now."

Deep in the woods stood an abandoned cabin, its sagging log walls covered in moss. Travis and Steve were engaged in throwing a hatchet at an upturned stump. Gary was nowhere to be seen.

"Check it out. This is our winter camp." Guy led Russell to the door. "We've known about this place since we were kids. Must have been built by some old homesteader. Looks like it's been here forever. Still in pretty good shape, too, really. A little breezy, maybe, but the fireplace works fine. Just throw some mud in the cracks and board up the windows and it'll be all right. Thing is, we've got to get some electricity out here, just like at Bloodstone. Diesel generator's too noisy. Got to figure something out—solar, wind, I don't know. I wish I had a portable nuclear reactor. That'd be about perfect."

"You with a nuclear reactor?" Gary stepped around the corner. "Oh, yeah, that'd be just about perfect all right." He sat on a crude bench and looked around. "Forget the electricity. What you need is water. Good, clean water in those five-gallon jugs, like they deliver to offices. You store that up for the winter before you think about anything else."

"Bah, water!" Guy grimaced, waving off the suggestion. "That water, man, that stuff's not good for you. Besides, who needs plain old everyday water when you've got the water of life!"

He rushed to the woodpile and dug around in it, bringing out a nearly full bottle of Scotch. He popped the cork and downed a good gulp, then yodeled in delight and handed the bottle to Steve.

"Pass that liquor around, boys. Good for what ails you."

Steve gulped a good dose; then Travis took a long swig. It came to Russell, who drank as much as the others. Gary downed a double shot and handed the bottle to Guy. He tilted it back and slammed it down.

"Who's got that pipe?" he demanded. "I haven't smoked my fair share yet."

The pipe was handed over, and he lit up. He inhaled deeply, passed the pipe to Steve and exhaled in Gary's face.

"So what's up with those Chicago guys and the big deal? That happening anytime soon, Mr. Negotiator?"

Gary waved the cloud away. "It'll happen when it happens. Pretty soon, yeah. I talked to these guys, see, who have to talk to their people, who are putting up the cash. They're going to get back to me when they got it together. It's in the works. Just chill."

"I've been chilling over a month now, goddammit! I want some action. I want to see results from you, you son of a bitch."

Gary rose from the bench. "You can pull that hard-ass bullshit with your retard brother, but don't try it with me."

Guy picked up the iron pan and swung it over his head a few times, then brought it to his chest and held it tight. "Let's go," he said, handing Gary the gun. Gary took it, then gulped another slug of booze. They walked to a clearing. Guy stopped and clutched the pan. Gary continued in a straight line, then turned around.

"Was it twenty-five paces, or thirty?" he asked

"Twenty-seven and a half."

Travis, Steve, and Russell clustered together. Birds chirped in the trees. A few fluffy clouds meandered in the clear sky. Guy tensed his whole body and shouted, "Do it!"

Gary lowered the pistol and fired. The bullet hit the pan with a dull thud and ricocheted into the thicket. Russell screamed. Travis and Steve sent up a rowdy cheer.

"Yee-haw!" Guy whooped, running over to Russell. "You want to try it, man?" He tried to hand off the pan. Russell bolted, backing away from him.

"Get away from me, you crazy fucker. Go get shot somewhere else."

Guy grinned and rushed at Gary. He stopped suddenly and let out a whoop. Gary shot at him again. This time the deflected bullet whizzed past Russell's head. He convulsed in terror, much to the merriment of his companions.

"Jesus Christ!" he proclaimed, scrambling to take cover inside the cabin.

"Come on out here, you yella-belly," Guy jeered. "It's only a .22."

"Only a .22?" Russell shouted back. "You go get shot at all you want, but leave me out of it."

The sport lasted for four more shots, each round successfully stopped by Guy's deft deployment of the pan shield. Gary walked up to

Guy, and they stood toe to toe, staring each other in the eye. Travis and Steve exchanged a significant look. Russell watched from the window. Gary cracked up and started laughing. Guy broke into another version of the Bone Dance, then whooped again and grabbed the whiskey. He ran his hand through his long stringy hair and sucked a good belt from the bottle, then strode over to Travis and Steve.

"Adrenaline rush, man, big time. Holy shit. Gotta try it sometime."

"Not if you're shooting," Travis replied, taking the bottle.

"No, no, man, you don't get it—you choose your own guy. Like Steve here, or the other Steve. See, Gary and me, we can face each other like that. You find someone to face down." The bottle got passed back to Guy. He took another drink and turned to Russell. "And Russ here, when he grows some balls, maybe he can face his shadow."

Never too quick on the draw, Russell at least had presence of mind enough to flip him off. Gary laughed and practiced gun tricks. Guy paced around. Travis and Steve drank their share of the liquor. The bottle came to Russell, but he refused. His head was light enough already. Sunset lit the sky above, and darkness crept through the trees. Guy wiped his mouth on his forearm after another drink.

"Time for a good pack-squawk," he announced. Everyone but Russell seemed to know what that meant.

"You're going to like it," Guy told him with a disquieting connivance in his voice.

"There's something killing sheep on farms around here," Travis spoke up. "You hear about it?"

No one had.

"Yeah, well, it's ripping their heads off—only sheep, I guess—on a couple of farms out by Union Mills, down around there. Eating only parts of them, too, innards I guess, but it tears their heads clean off. Don't have any good tracks, either."

This caught Gary's attention. He put the gun down and came over to where they were talking and joined in with his story.

"I read something a while back about something over in the Philippines that was ripping the heads off animals—sheep, goats, even cows. Whatever it was, it didn't eat any of them, but they were all completely drained of blood. They called it the Philippine Vampire. Had villages all freaked out for, like, a year. They tried to trap it, but no one ever saw it. Then it just stopped coming around, like it just disappeared."

"Sort of reminds me of the Kankakee Swamp Monster," Guy got a gleam in his eye as the twilight sky deepened and the crickets began in earnest. "Something I heard about when I was a kid. This one was a chicken killer, killing this farmer's chickens. In the morning he'd find a few of his chickens splattered all over the coop, so he waited up one night to find out what was going on. It came just before dawn, and he said it was taller than the chicken coop door, and it had to stoop to get in. That's when the farmer gave it both barrels, when it was bent over like that. The thing screamed and ran off through the cornfield. Next day they found some long red hairs and dried blood, but then lost the track. Nothing else, until a week or so later some kids were swimming in the river, and they see this big, shaggy, ape-like thing come limping out of the woods. They said it was stretching out its arms like it was asking for help or something. Of course they took off running. People came out to see, but they couldn't find it."

He chuckled and shrugged. "Who knows? It's one weird-ass world we're living in, that's for sure. You want to know how I'm gonna die? I already know, man. Spontaneous combustion. I'll just be sitting here rapping with you all like this, then—whoosh—up in flames, just a little puddle of grease left behind, and a pair of smokin' shoes."

"Oh, you wish," Gary said with a grin, ever eager to burst Guy's bubble. "You think you're just so great and extraordinary that you're going to die this great, extraordinary death. Hell, you're going to die with shit in your pants like everyone else."

"Too bad we're out of bullets," Guy sneered.

Russell filled a break in the conversation by bringing up a subject that was problematic for him, asking, "Hey, what about the cops, anyway?"

"Look at him now," Guy laughed. "Now the coward's afraid of getting busted!"

"No, no I'm not at all, and that's just it—where are the cops? I mean, you've got all this stuff going on, all your schemes and the hash and that field of poppies and everything else. Why haven't you been busted?"

"Because we're cool, man, that's why. The Barney Fifes they got around here couldn't find their own asses with both their hands." He got up and stretched. "Speaking of the fuzz, let's go see if that fool's been by yet."

They traipsed through the dark woods and came to a clearing where they could see a shed across the road. They waited in silence, watching the moonlit roof, then Gary spoke.

"Maybe he's already been here."

"No," Guy said. "I don't think so."

Just then a patrol car cruised slowly up the road and circled around the building. It stopped for a moment, then moved along. Guy smiled.

"That's one reason we've never been busted," he told Russell. "They have their little routines that they follow. Predictable as hell. Always know where they're going to be and when." He paused, then added, "In case you haven't noticed, I don't have a routine."

Guy gave the signal and they descended on the shed.

"This here's where the pound keeps dogs before they kill 'em. We're gonna give 'em something to live for tonight. I got to callin' it pack-squawk!"

With that, he started whacking the corrugated metal walls with a large branch.

"Wake up, losers! Wake up and howl for your lives, because there is no tomorrow!"

The dogs dutifully began to bay, and Guy and crew retreated. On their way back through the woods, Guy stopped and cocked his ear to the distant wailing of the hounds. He smiled.

"God, I love that sound."

8

A shower had never felt so good. Russell had ridden to town on one of the bikes and helped himself to Chuck's apartment. He'd shaved for the first time in a week and was luxuriating in a long, soothing deluge. He washed his hair twice, intending to make the barbershop his next stop. Having fully indulged in the miracle of running water, he stepped out and grabbed a towel. As he stood preening before the mirror, he was caught unawares by the rightful tenant of the apartment, Chuck Probst, a sturdy guy who could easily have mopped the floor with him.

"Who the hell are you?" he demanded. "How'd you get in here? What do you think you're doing?"

Russell clutched a towel to himself and stammered, "Are you Chuck? I'm Russ Pinske."

"That means nothing to me. What are you doing in here? How'd you get in?"

"Gary Pierce told me where the key was. He said he'd talked to you about it, and you said it was OK."

"Oh he did, huh? Jesus H Christ. You open the door to one of those guys and the whole goddamn army comes in after them. You go tell Gary, and Guy, too, to cut this crap out. Where was the key?"

"Taped to that boiler out there."

"You have it on you?"

"In my pocket, yeah," he said, reaching for his trousers.

"All right—you take it back and tell them I'm changing the locks. I've already had a dozen of his slimeballs through here at all hours, whenever they please. I can't afford any more trouble from those guys."

He shook his fist in the air and paced around, mumbling to himself, then turned back to Russell and told him, "Just get dressed and get out of here, dude. I can't deal with this right now."

Russell had already packed his toiletries and hastily finished dressing while Chuck sat on the couch, holding his head. On his way to the door, Russell apologized for intruding. Chuck looked up at him with bloodshot eyes.

"Hey, I'm sure you're cool and all, but I've been up all night and I have to show up for work in four hours, and I really wasn't expecting to come home and find someone in my bathroom." He waved his hand and sighed wearily, "So, just, later on."

The barbershop was only a couple of blocks away, but Russell rode there anyway, not wanting to have to come back for the bike and risk running into Chuck again. It was another hot day in Door Prairie. Moving through the thick heat was a sweat-breaking chore. The noontime sun was trapped in muggy air. Cars spewed their exhaust into the mix. People walked sluggishly, sapped of energy.

Smitty's Barbershop was housed in a graceful old building across the street from the Masonic Temple. It had been there forever. Back when Russell was a young boy, it was Howard's, and it was where his grandfather regularly went. Russell had received his first haircut there, a traumatic affair for him since he was a squirmy child and Howard was not a patient man. Howard went on to his reward many years ago, and Smitty stepped in right afterward.

With a slight nod Smitty casually acknowledged Russell's entrance while he continued lathering his current client, a bald man who was in for a shave. Two old gents were sitting in the shop, so he settled in for a long wait, taking a seat beneath a display of small scissors that bore the warning: 'Plucking nose hair can be fatal!'

"He got a gold-dollar as reward," one of them was telling the other. "Took that gold-dollar and he turned it into a hundred, and with that he started the family business."

"Well I'll be," stated the other old guy. "Used to be you could get by with your wits and elbow grease. I don't know what's happening out there now." He gestured out the window to the world at large. "Seems like everyone's got some get-rich-quick scheme these days, trying to get something for nothing."

The shop hadn't changed at all. Its walls were the same faded blue they'd always been. The windows were spotless, even the transom above the door. Shelves offered goods for sale: pomade and brilliantine, combs and brushes, mustache wax and shaving soap. Russell stared at the hexagonal floor tiles, arranging them in patterns in his mind. A shadow crossed the floor, drawing his eyes to a young woman walking by in a light summer dress. Sex was what he needed. It had been way too long since he'd been laid. If he went on the make, he would have a purpose and could ignore for a while his true aimlessness.

"Speaking of getting rich quick, Smitty, you ever find anything out there with that metal detector?"

"You mean other than rusty nails and keys?" he answered, shaving his customer. "Yeah, I find some things. Last week I found some old buttons out by Kessler School. Fellow down at that antique store on Monroe tells me they're from cavalry uniforms from the French-Indian War."

He finished the shave and repositioned the chair.

"Lot of old battlefields around here," the man in the chair added.

Smitty nodded and cleared his throat. He wiped the man's face with aftershave and removed the apron, snapping it smartly.

"Aren't I handsome?" The man admired himself in the mirror.

"Don't get carried away," one of the old men told him.

"You're next, young fella," Smitty addressed Russell, who indicated that the other two were there first.

"They don't need haircuts," said Smitty gruffly. "Not much I can do for them anyway with what they've got left. No, they're just here to shoot the breeze and scare off my customers."

Russell sat in the chair. Smitty wrapped a paper collar around his neck, then smoothed the apron. He scrutinized Russell.

"Looks like you fell in with a bad crowd," he commented. "Well, we'll see if we can't get you fixed up."

He washed his hands, picked up his shears, and set to work.

Russell was surrounded on three sides by mirrors, so he watched Smitty mow his crop of unruly hair. Light bounced off the mirrors and filled the room, illuminating jars of ointments and liniments lined on the shelves. A calendar of classic cars hung on the wall, this month featuring a Studebaker. Russell's grandfather had worked for Studebaker for years, up until the day they closed.

"Police say the murder of a woman found dead in her apartment earlier this week is linked to three other recent slayings in the area," one man read from the newspaper. He looked at his friend. "Serial killer in Michigan City. What do you say about that?"

"I'm innocent of all charges," came the reply.

Smitty joined in. "Jury's still out on you, Sam."

He rubbed some hot lather on Russell's neck, dabbing a smudge on each temple as well. A straight razor was pulled from a jar of green fluid, quickly rinsed and casually set against his flesh. With practiced strokes, Smitty quickly scraped him clean. He lowered the chair, brushed and toweled him, unwrapped the paper collar and removed the apron.

"Looking a far sight better than before," Smitty boasted, giving Russell's neck another swipe with the brush.

He'd been buzz-cut, Russell had, and it was good. "Oh yeah," he affirmed, looking in the mirror and running his hand over his scalp. He paid for Smitty's service, keeping in mind the advice of his grandfather, who told him to always tip the barber. Two bucks seemed about right, and it was acknowledged with a nod.

The fragrance of the shop followed him on his walk downtown, amid the dust and debris from renovations being perpetrated along Lincoln Way. There was an inherent sadness in this place, in the cracked sidewalks and faded buildings and expressionless people with stories dying to be told. Maybe it wasn't sadness, really, but resignation, a surrendering to life's hardships and human failings. He was accompanied by his own shortcomings and disappointments as he approached the door to Helen's workplace.

"No, she's not here," said the white-haired man behind the counter, whom Russell presumed to be Wayne Edwards, proprietor of the shop. "She wanted to take some time off, so she did. She said she wouldn't be back until next week sometime, I think. I can't remember when. Maybe Wednesday."

With that, Russell got back on the bike and headed out to Helen's. He rode around Long Lake, enjoying the breeze coming across the water, then cruised through the shade of the trees in the park before emerging near her place. His knocks went unanswered. He walked around back, and found her scooter there. Through the windows of the garage, he could see her car was gone. He turned to walk to his bike away and caught a movement in the window on the second floor. A curtain up there was quickly drawn. He rode away smiling, thinking about Myrtle spying on him.

It was too bad Helen wasn't home. Not only had he been wanting to see her, but he'd hoped she could give him a ride out to Stillwater to see Carl and Ellie. Last week he had stopped over at Carmela and Manny's, and from there had called out to Stillwater, hoping they could all get together. It didn't happen. Russell got the impression that they didn't hang out with each other too often anymore. He told Carl that he would come visit in the next few days. A few days had already passed, and it wasn't until now that he'd gotten his act together enough to venture out that way. If it wasn't so hot he might consider riding the twenty miles out there. But the roads weren't good for bicycling, and the heat was just too oppressive. He rode back to Bloodstone.

"He said what?" Guy snarled.

Russell repeated what Chuck had said, handing over the key to the apartment. Guy snatched the key and threw it out of the pit and into the brush.

"I don't give a flying fuck about his key, or his little hissy fits. And I don't need a key to get into his place, anyway. He wants to cut himself off, good for him." He leaned in and told Russell, "The guy's a stone-cold junkie is what he is. I know. I sell him all his opium, and any pills I get he pops. And I know that he knows that I sell him his junk for cheap. He'll be singing a different tune next time he needs me to hook him up." He sputtered a derisive dismissal and flopped back on the raggedy old couch.

Russell settled into an armchair and sat quietly. Both Steves were down in the hole today, each reading comic books. Gary and the other denizens were off doing their things elsewhere.

"You want to go to Stillwater?" Guy exclaimed when Russell asked for a ride. "What's out at frickin' Stillwater, man?"

Russell told him he wanted to visit Carl Paulette, which Guy thought was a riot.

"He lives out there now, huh? And you want me to take you out to his place? I tell you, we're not exactly chummy anymore, Russ." He proceeded to explain why.

"You remember when we were living up above the Red Rooster? Back when Carl was working the bar there? Well, right before we were getting ready to move out, there was this shipment of booze left out in the alley, and it was just too tempting. We helped ourselves to a couple of cases, and they got on Carl for it 'cause he was supposed to make sure all the stuff got put away. He knew we were behind it, but he didn't rat us out. They couldn't nail him for it, but they rode him hard, looking for an excuse to can him 'cause they were pissed with him anyway. So when he comes in, like, ten minutes late or something they fire him on the spot. He came up and bitched us out big time. Then we all ended up getting totally shit-faced, and he was cool then, but once you get on that guy's bad side you stay on that guy's bad side."

He rose from the couch, stretched and yawned. "I don't want to cross paths with him again at all, and I bet he's not too keen to see me, either. So I'll take you out there, but I'm just dropping you off. You're on your own after that."

It was all right by Russell, since he didn't want Guy or any of them coming along anyway. The Steves were rousted, and they all climbed out of the pit. On the way to the car, Guy ran his hand over Russell's head and said, "Hey, buzzy, when'd you get the haircut?"

"This morning."

"Well, it's about time. You were starting to look like a dirty hippie."

Russell laughed to hear this coming from Guy, who was beginning to look disturbingly like Charlie Manson on the ranch. The usual hullabaloo was raised to get the car started, and they roared off. Guy headed north, the opposite direction of Stillwater.

＊

"How many bottle rockets in a pack?" Guy asked the man at the fireworks stand, just across the state line in Michigan.

"Twenty to a pack," he said, fanning himself with a newspaper.

"All right, then. Let's have twenty packs. What do you think, boys? Four hundred bottle rockets last us a little while?"

One of them shrugged.

"Gotta have Roman candles. Take twenty of those, too, what the hell. OK, I'll buy this stuff. You guys want anything else, you buy it yourselves."

One of the Steves got a mess of firecrackers, the other a bunch of smokebombs. Russell hadn't yet gotten any money from Guy for weighing the hash, work that was still far from finished, so he was mindful of his budget as he checked out the combustible goodies. He chose an item contained in a box that depicted a smiling fireball, whose only English words labeled it, "Jolly Ha Ha."

"Jolly Ha Ha?" Guy asked Russell as they climbed back in the car.

"Yeah, I like the box."

"Take it out, let's see it."

It was a black sphere, about the size of a tangerine with a wick sticking out of it.

"Looks like a cartoon bomb."

"Wha-wha-what's it do, anyways?" Guy asked in an affected stutter.

"I don't know," Russell answered. "The writing's all in Chinese, except for the name."

"Guess we'll find out," was the consensus of the Steves as they pulled away, once again traveling away from Stillwater.

"Where did you want to go again?" Guy asked, driving past dairy farms on a two-lane highway.

"Stillwater. Back that way." Russell jerked his thumb behind him, to the southeast.

"I know, man. I'm just messing with you. I want to take you out here first, show you something."

Heat rose in shimmering waves off the sticky asphalt. One of the Steves fired a bottle rocket into a field.

"That was an unauthorized discharge, Rambo," Guy warned him. "Keep a lid on it, all of you. I don't need any trouble in Michigan. I've got at least two outstanding warrants here that I know about." He made his voice gravelly like an old-time gangster and growled, "So youz mugz be on the lookout for the fuzz, see?"

Pulling onto a dirt road, he slowed the car to a crawl.

"Let me know if you see any farm equipment operating out here," he announced. "Put down your picture books and be on the lookout."

They crept along until they came to rutted tractor tracks that ran along an irrigation canal between two cornfields. The car continued until it was concealed by a clump of trees.

Guy and Russell got out. The Steves stayed behind as lookouts. Guy gave them instructions.

"Give the signal if you see any hayseeds. I don't think they're out here now, but they could be. We won't be long, but keep an eye out."

"Stay low, Russ," Guy warned as they crawled along. "Back when we started this operation they weren't farming these fields. Past couple of years they have been, though, and they don't cotton to trespassers."

Along a ditch secluded by woods, Guy showed Russell a marijuana plant. Having seen one, he looked around and spotted hundreds. "Seeds came from The Collector, like the poppies. Been out here three, four years now, all sorts of varieties bred into one kick-ass ultra-kind. It might grow in a ditch, but it's no ditch weed. Especially since about a month from now we'll come out here and yank all the males we can find, so we'll have big female plants. We can't get them all, and there'll still be some seeds, and that's all right, 'cause they'll grow back next spring. We started with this one field. Now we've got a lot more. The stuff knows how to take over. Guess that's why they call it 'weed.' I call it 'money.'"

They walked along the ditch, Guy pointing out some of the bigger plants.

"This was my first project, still the best cash crop by far. It's kept me going for years, and that's OK as far as I'm concerned. Last year I got shot at in one of the other fields, though, so I've got to play it extra cool now."

Russell was at a loss. Guy's schemes were beyond him. He accepted them as he learned about them, and was continually surprised by the scope and brazenness of his operations. Guy had his own way of getting by, and Russell could only watch him go to it.

"So when we get those poppies all processed we'll start tending to this stuff and pulling males. Buds are ripe in September, October."

As they stood talking, the low rumbling of farm equipment came to their ears.

"Shit!" Guy exclaimed in a harsh whisper. "Quick, crawl back through the weeds."

They got to the car and Guy started chewing out the Steves while he drove down the path.

"We didn't see it," one of them protested.

"And why didn't you see it? Because you had your noses in your Jughead Digests? This ain't no picnic. It ain't no joke. And it sure as hell ain't no comic book. If I get nailed 'cause of one of you clowns, I will whack your scrawny asses. That you can count on."

They got back to the dirt road, and Guy continued to harangue them until he noticed a county sheriff's car coming up behind them.

"Oh, damn." He tensely admonished them all to behave calmly and concocted a cover story.

"We were at the dunes. We decided to take a shortcut home, sort of got lost and ended up out on this road. Anybody have anything on them?"

Russell had a pipe filled with hash.

"Stuff it down your shorts and sit tight. Everyone just act cool. Act like you don't even know there's a cop on our tail. No worries, man." He looked in the rear view mirror at the Steves and told them through a forced smile, "If we get pulled over, you both are so dead."

The sheriff followed the wagon until they came to the main highway. Guy signaled a right turn, using the indicator light that sometimes worked. He made the turn and got up to speed. The sheriff crossed the highway, and disappeared among the cornfields. Guy laughed and bellowed to the occupants of the backseat.

"That was a good one. I should make you two walk from here, you know that?"

They got a little closer to Stillwater, then took a turn, and ended up around Hudson Lake.

"We're too close to good old J. C.," Guy explained. "I've been meaning to get out here and talk with him. He's an old man now, been farming all his life. Been a junkie forever, too, since a combine accident in the sixties. He grew his own poppies until he got paranoid and cut it out."

Guy drove on while Russell regretted having asked him for a ride.

"I learned from him how to do it, and he's my best customer. Totally safe. We barter. He gets his opium; I get meat. Last year I had a locker full of beef. This year I'm getting some smoked and cured stuff: hams and bacon and jerky that I can pack in the snow out at the cabin. I'm just going to hole up out there all winter."

They cruised up the drive and stopped at an old farmhouse whose bleached siding was scaled with layers of flaking paint.

"I'll go see if he's in there. You stay here. He's real particular about the company he keeps, and he doesn't like people he doesn't know. I'll try to be quick about it."

Russell knew Guy well enough to know that he was rarely quick about anything, and if this J. C. fellow was at home, he was going to be waiting out here for a while. He regretted not riding his bike. At this rate, he could have gotten there faster if he'd walked. The car was out in the open in the heat of the day, and it reeked. The odor of the unwashed Steves complemented the stench of swine that permeated the air. Russell was in a bad way. He was far off track and needed to get away from Guy and his craziness. He needed to get back in touch with his friends, who would help him figure out why he was here, and what he was going to do to with himself.

One Steve was entranced by his comic book. The other was passed out. What terrible company to be stranded with on a godforsaken pig farm. He got out of the car and sought refuge beneath a leafy old chestnut tree. All he wanted was a ride to Stillwater. Instead, he'd bought fireworks with money he couldn't afford to spend, trespassed to see a field of pot that was of no interest to him, wracked his nerves over a close encounter with the law while in the company of a known felon, and now he was stuck out on the dismal land of a stranger. All of his life was so much like this single day. He gave himself over to fruitless wandering and squandered his resources. He'd been a pinball for years, ricocheting and reacting without any volition. His lack of direction and discipline were threatening to overwhelm him and get him permanently lost.

He was thirsty. He went in search of a spigot or pump. Even in the shade the climate was unbearable.

"Pinske! Hey, Pinske, you son of a bitch, you want a ride or what?"

Russell came around the corner from where he had found a hose. Guy stood by the car, droopy-eyed and slack-jawed.

"You drive," he slowly intoned, handing the keys over.

Now at the wheel, able to speed off to Stillwater posthaste, Russell got nervous. There was a lot to be nervous about. He knew the general direction he needed to go, but he didn't know the best route to take. Either the gas gauge was broken, or the tank was empty. He didn't have a driver's license, and he was about to transport a wanted criminal and two of his lowlife underlings. Guy groaned and exclaimed, "Oh God, I've gotta puke. Pull over."

Russell had not yet started the car. Guy stumbled out the door and gagged in the bushes, then crawled back in.

"I can't remember the last time I smoked that much opium," he slurred, looking really out of it. Russell asked him how to get to Stillwater from here.

"Fuck Stillwater," was his reply. "Just drive."

So Russell got the wagon going and headed toward Door Prairie, thinking he could find his way once he got near. He drove through a landscape of corn and sorghum fields, interspersed with lakes and wood-lands. The sky was bright, and the glare from the roadway seared his eyes. He squinted, and aimed the car close to where he wanted to go.

"Where are we?" Guy demanded, waking up as the car slowed down.

"At Carl's. I'm getting out."

"All right. Stop here. How close are we?"

"This is his driveway, I think. I'm pretty sure this the address he gave me."

Guy hunkered down. "Back up," he said. "Call me paranoid, but I just don't want him to see me."

Russell sighed and put the car in reverse. Guy moved over to the driver's seat and pulled away, saying, "See you at Bloodstone, dude."

Russell wished he'd never see Guy again, but knew he would have to.

———————•———————

The house was a ranch-style construction with a couple of additions tacked on. Russell walked up the driveway to the main door. He rang the bell and waited. It was late in the afternoon, and the day was baked through with the summer's heat. Stillwater was a tiny community that had sprung up around the intersection of two train lines. There wasn't ever much out here by way of a town. Their house was on a rural route, surrounded by sheep pastures and alfalfa fields. He leaned against the wall, realizing that he might be stuck here for a long time. He knocked. As he was considering his options, the door opened.

"Yes?" said a woman he'd never seen before. "Can I help you?"

"I was looking for Ellie Sellers. I thought this was her place."

"Are you one of the fathers? You're supposed to use the other door."

"One of the fathers?" he asked. "Is this Ellie and Carl's? I thought this was their house number. Do you know them?"

She smiled and asked him to come in, then began to walk through the house. He followed. "It's pick-up time, and I thought you were here to take home a child. I'm Sarah," she introduced herself with a wave. "I help Eleanor out a few times a week. You call her Ellie?"

"Yeah. That's what she called herself when I met her. I'm Russell. Or Russ, I guess, with her." They came to a room where Ellie was playing with two girls. She looked up as they entered. He was delighted to see her eyes brighten when she saw him. "Hey there," she smiled. "There you are—we've been wanting to see you."

She stepped around the girls and came to hug him. Sarah took charge of the kids so they could visit.

"You're looking good," Russell told her, speaking the truth. She was a warm, attentive person with a mischievous streak that he had always found intriguing.

"I'm glad you're here, Russ. Carl's going to flip. We were both bummed when we couldn't make it a couple weeks ago, but we had something to do."

She turned away and looked at the kids with a weary smile. They were playing a game that involved making loud animal noises. Sarah mostly left them alone and went about picking up toys. Ellie surveyed the scene and yawned.

"Oh, I'm tired. I'm so ready for them to go." She consulted her wristwatch. "They should be picked up by five-thirty. Carl's usually home around six-thirty. You hungry?"

He was, and she asked for his help.

"Could you take out the kitchen garbage? It's not full, but it has to be changed before I can use the kitchen for household cooking. Tie up the bag and take it to the big brown container in the garage."

He was glad to help her, eager to do so. He had a deep affection for her, and he never tired of reminding Carl that he had seen her first.

After taking out the garbage, he met up with her in the kitchen. She took a bowl of chicken parts out of the refrigerator. With a sly look in her eyes, she said in a playful tone: "Some chicken's gonna get fried tonight."

He raised his eyebrows and nodded. She put the bowl on the counter and washed her hands.

"So, I've got to go help Sarah until the kids get picked up. If you want something to do, you could peel potatoes for me. That would be great. When you're done, put them in this OK?" She pointed to a kettle on the stove, then handed him a peeler and the potatoes. "It's nice out on the patio in the afternoon, cooler than it is in here. And, hey—save the peels for compost, OK?"

He carried the potatoes to the patio. It was shady back there, and the bench he sat on caught a good breeze. He breathed deeply and peeled potatoes, glad to be here. His friends meant a lot to him, and they made him feel like he meant a lot to them. Four years had gone by since they'd seen one another, and they hadn't talked in nearly a year, but they had no trouble picking up where they'd left off. He liked being that comfortable.

Leaves sparkled in the golden afternoon. A jet trail smeared the sky. Gnats swarmed in a sunbeam. The surrounding woods were already alive with crickets and cicadas. Ellie stepped out onto the patio, stretched and yawned, then sat next to him.

"The kids are gone," she said. "Sarah's finishing up now." She reclined in her chair and looked at him. "How are you, Russ? How have you been?"

He shrugged. "I'm weird. Life's been weird. How are you?"

She closed her eyes and sighed. A train approached, sounding its whistle. He peeled the last potato. She appeared to be asleep. When the train faded to a distant rumble, she opened her eyes and slowly rose.

"There's lemonade and ice water in the refrigerator," she told him. "Help yourself if you want. I'm going to change."

He took the potatoes to the kitchen and returned to the patio with a glass of lemonade. Shadows lengthened. Insects grew louder. Ellie returned, wearing shorts and looking refreshed.

"Nice out here now," she said. "It was a real scorcher earlier. Storm hit over in Wanatah, really cooled things off."

"Yeah, sure. How long you guys been out here now?"

"About three years. Yeah, it's been pretty much perfect. Things have worked out OK. I've got ten full-time kids, and a lot of drop-ins. I'm hoping I can go back to school this fall to get certified to teach kindergarten. That's what I really want to do, eventually."

After a quiet moment she announced she was going to the kitchen. She switched on the radio and started washing dishes. His offer to help was declined, so he sat at the table, listened to the Top Forty, and drank lemonade. Ellie seemed distracted, preoccupied, maybe even a little irritable. It occurred to him that maybe he had come at a bad time.

"Carl's home," she said, turning off the water and wiping her hands on a dish towel. "I just heard his car door."

Russell hadn't heard anything, and was about to say so when Carl walked in and threw a briefcase onto the kitchen counter. He caught sight of Russell as he moved toward Ellie.

"Whoa," he said, turning to Russell with a growing smile.

They hugged, then broke the embrace and looked at one another. They were both the same height, but cast from different molds. Russell was rather scrawny, while Carl was a fireplug. They met in grade school and fell into an immediate friendship. When they discovered they were born six days apart in the same hospital, they decided they were long lost brothers. Their fraternal feelings thus established, their roots became entwined.

"How many years?" Carl asked.

"Carmela and Manny's wedding." Carl shot a look at Ellie, then turned back to his friend. "Four years. Where did four years go?" He shrugged wearily. "Want a beer?"

Russell sure did, and Carl brought him one. They sat at the kitchen table. Ellie touched Carl's shoulder and said, "I haven't told him."

Carl looked at her, smiled, then turned to his friend.

"We're married."

Russell's expression made them both laugh.

"Really?" was all he could think to say.

They held up their fingers to show their rings. Ellie winked and said, "I was counting on you not noticing."

"Remember a couple of weeks ago when we couldn't see you?" Carl asked. "Well, that's why. Just us and two witnesses and the justice of the peace. Real low-key, you know."

Russell congratulated them and said, "I always just sort of thought we'd be best man at each other's weddings. I would have liked to have been a witness at least."

Ellie laughed. "You and our parents and everyone else. My mom and dad are totally ticked off. They want a big to-do, and they're trying to get us to have what they call a 'real wedding' in their church and make a big deal about it. But I don't know."

Carl chimed in. "And my parents are ragging on me. I'm their only son, I should have a proper wedding, blah, blah, blah. I swear I don't know where that comes from. We never did church. My mom's a divorced Catholic, for one thing. And my dad—hell, look up 'heathen' in the dictionary and there's his picture. And they want a church wedding? Why?

I've got nothing against it, but these people haven't gone to church all my life, and now it's important for the ceremony? I just don't get it."

Ellie shrugged. "It's all for them, you know? I mean, we're already legally married, so it would be like putting on a show or something."

"Of course, there would be presents," Carl said.

Ellie snorted a little laugh. "We already have two toasters."

"I'm not against redundancy in appliances," he replied.

Russell asked if Carmela and Manny knew.

"No, we don't really talk with them too much anymore. We used to run into them all the time in town, but since we moved out here, we don't see them much."

Carl and Ellie exchanged a significant look, then he said, "There's something else that no one knows. We're going to have a baby."

Russell shot out of his seat, spilling his beer. He grabbed for the rolling bottle, but it fell off the table. Carl laughed and got a towel. Russell turned to Ellie with an incredulous look.

"You're going to have a baby?"

She smiled and nodded.

Russell bounced with excitement and hugged them both.

"We haven't told anyone else yet," Carl said. "My parents already know about the baby, but we're going to wait and let Ellie's folks get used to the idea that we're married first. They'll know about the baby soon enough, and we really don't want to get into this business of, 'Oh, so you had to get married.' You know?"

Russell was overcome with joy and asked if he could call Carmela and Manny. They weren't home, so he left a message for them to call back.

Ellie got up and said, "I'm going to get moving on dinner."

"Need any help?" Carl offered.

"Russ already helped a lot. You two can go gab all you want."

Carl brought Russell another bottle of beer. "Try to hold on to it, OK?"

They went out to the patio and settled in.

"This is good." Russell sipped his beer and contemplated the new status of his friends as a married couple and expectant parents. He began to laugh.

"You're married! You're going to be a father!"

"Yep."

"Well, hell, man—what's that like?"

"It's not like anything. It's all happened so fast that I don't even know. I don't think it's really sunk in yet. So, ask me in a month. I'll probably be freaking out in earnest by then."

"Goddamn," was all Russell could say as he took a drink. He was pleased and excited, thrown for a loop. Getting married and having a baby. Now, that was doing something. Thinking about it, Russell felt acutely aware of how unformed he was. He looked at Carl, who was leaning back in his chair and staring into the deepening shadows. Just beyond the edge of the patio a thistle grew in gravel, its spiked stalk supporting a defiant purple bloom. The sun was going down.

"How are your mom and dad?" Russell thought to ask. He had long been intrigued by the stories Carl told of his parents. They were stories filled with verbal abuse, physical abuse, and substance abuse, but set in a context of real connection and intimacy. The chaos and uproar of his family was the outcome of all the members being deeply involved in each other's lives. In contrast, the members of Russell's family had all disengaged from one another, had atomized. Carl's people had a fiery center of gravity while Russell's people were scattered to the wind.

"Oh, those foxes are happy in the henhouse," he replied, referring to the fact that his parents now owned a bar. When the owner of their hangout for thirty-odd years retired, they scraped together all they had to take over the business.

"Yeah, they practically live there," he continued. "They call me to help out every now and then. Even pay me sometimes. They're pretty much drinking and smoking themselves to death. My dad's up to four packs of Pall Malls a day. I tried to tell him that's nuts, but he gets real hot when anyone tries to tell him what to do."

"That's too bad," Russell said.

Carl took a drink. "It is what it is. When I stopped smoking he called me a quitter. What can you do?" He shrugged. "They haven't said much about the baby business. This will be their first grandkid. I guess they're still in shock, kind of like me."

The shadows deepened, and fireflies appeared. Carl put down his empty bottle and looked at his friend.

"How long have you been in town?"

"Oh, boy, about six weeks now I think. Something like that."

"Can I ask why?"

Russell laughed. "You could, but I couldn't tell you." He finished his beer and told the story of his planned big adventure, and how once he arrived in Door Prairie he started to have doubts about the endeavor and sort of lost his gumption. It didn't help that now he was living at Bloodstone, a lifestyle that robbed him of any remaining smidgen of ambition that he might otherwise have had.

"You're hanging out with Guy Bogel? I don't need to tell you to watch yourself with him, do I? He fucked me over more than once at the bar." He thought about it a little, then said, "Actually, maybe he did me a favor. I needed to get out of there anyway; he just gave me the kick out the door. One thing about him, though—you can't trust that he'll act in his own best interest. So watch out."

Ellie called them to dinner. Her table was spread with a feast of chicken and baked beans, mashed potatoes, coleslaw, and cornbread. Russell hadn't eaten a real meal in weeks, and he helped himself heartily. The phone rang, and Carl nearly jumped out of his seat.

"What's with you?" Ellie asked as he made his way to answer the call.

"Nothing. Just excited is all." He picked up the receiver and carried it out of the room. Russell chowed down. Ellie kept an eye on her husband as he talked in the hallway.

"That was Manny," he said, returning to the table. "I told him the news. They're coming out."

"You told them the news about what—the wedding or the baby?" Ellie wanted to know.

"Both. What the hell. Russ knows, and he can't keep a secret." He winked at his friend. They both knew it was true.

———

Carmela and Manny drove through town in silence. They'd been living stiffly for a couple of weeks, ever since their fight over the housing development planned for Nellie Widow's farm. The issue still hung between them, unaddressed. Both of them were good at avoiding conflict, so when they stumbled into contentious territory they would back off and shy away from each other. It was a tactic that kept the union peaceable, but left the individuals perturbed.

Manny maneuvered his beloved Imp down the drag, swinging past his mother's and his aunt's on his way out of town. They came to a stop at the last light before it was open road to Sillwater. It didn't feel right to be so nervous around his wife. He wanted to feel close to her, and when there was distance between them, he got uptight. As they waited, a woman walked in front of them.

"Look at that," Manny nudged Carmela. She looked around.

"What am I looking at?"

"That woman there. See her face? She's cross-eyed."

"So?"

"So, I've been seeing way too many cross-eyed people lately. Her, and there's this guy I see downtown all the time, and there's this other guy who works in the supply shop. Last week I was at the bank and the teller was cross-eyed. I made sure to double-check my receipt. That's too many cross-eyed people, if you ask me. I mean, can't they do something about that these days? That seems like something they can fix, you know?"

She shrugged and turned away from him.

He drove on, a scowl curling the corners of his mouth. So much for his attempt at conversation. He wanted to pull over and tell her to just get over it. But he couldn't. She needed a good talking to, but if she wanted to give him the cold shoulder, he could play that game too. The more he drove, the more irritable he got. This whole trip out here was annoying. He and Carl had always been on unsteady footing with one another, and as far as he knew Ellie and Carmela hadn't even talked in a long time. But Carmela insisted that they go pay a visit, so here they were. He drove on, getting surlier by the mile.

Carmela was depressed. Her hopes of seeing Nellie Widow's farm preserved as a park were dim. She'd gotten nowhere with the mayor. It was all the doing of the city council, she was told, and the mayor could only voice his opinion. Since he didn't have an opinion on the matter, he couldn't help her with anything at all. She tried talking to someone she knew who worked on the newspaper, but was told the story held little interest. Old houses were getting torn down, historic places were being paved over, local businesses were folding under national chains, and no one seemed to care. There had to be something she could do to preserve what she loved about this town.

She glanced at Manny. There was no doubt he was devoted to her. That she knew for certain, and she could count on him. But sometimes living with him was like living in slow motion. He could bore her silly, and he could also bug the hell out of her. Lately it was almost like he was intent on being unpleasant. If he would make an effort to understand where she was coming from, that would be one thing. But he always had to be right. It was as if her concerns were of no importance—like he just didn't care what was going on with her.

They approached Stillwater, and she grew anxious about seeing Ellie again. All through school they had been inseparable, and up until a couple of years ago they'd remained close. Ellie had cried on her shoulder repeatedly about Carl's various transgressions, and Carmela had repeatedly told her to dump the bum. Then something changed after they moved to Stillwater, and Ellie seemed determined to make it work with him. Carmela's advice was no longer sought. Living in different towns and living different lives, they just sort of stopped doing much together.

Now Ellie was going to have a baby. The more Carmela thought about it, the closer she came to tears. She had a whole chest full of baby clothes that she'd made for her own hoped-for children. She was feeling desperate. It was another instance of Manny being clueless about what was important to her. His lackadaisical attitude about starting a family was infuriating. She felt certain that Ellie hadn't planned this pregnancy, and the thought of that made her even sadder. There would be the baby shower, too. She'd sew a cute little outfit or two and make nice and mask her envy and return to an empty house. The tears came suddenly.

Manny saw her and slowed down. "What's the matter?"

"Nothing." She waved him off. "Nothing. Keep driving."

He knew it had to be something. He was used to her being moody, but he had almost never seen her cry. The only time he could remember was when her grandmother died. It had something to do with having kids, he knew that, but he didn't know what he could do about it. He drove on while she stifled her sobs.

"You OK? You sure you want to go in?" he asked as the car idled in the driveway. She turned to him, her chin trembling.

"I love you, Manny."

They hugged, then she wiped her eyes and motioned toward the house. "Let's go in."

Russell was overjoyed, his sentimental heart fluttering to be with all these people together again. Carmela greeted him with a little peck on the cheek. Manny pointed at him without saying a word, on his way to greeting Carl.

"Hey, pappy, how's it hanging?"

He gave him a one-armed hug and sized up Ellie.

"You're looking fine these days, Mamma," he greeted her. She rolled her eyes. He laughed a little self-satisfied laugh as Carmela and Ellie walked together to the living room.

"There go the womenfolk," Manny drawled. "And here we are, us menfolk."

He lit a cigarette. Carl gestured toward the patio.

"What? Don't you smoke in the house anymore?"

"Not since I quit. Hey, you want a beer?"

Manny settled into a lawn chair. "You quit? No kidding. When?"

"Almost a year ago."

"Oh yeah? How long's it been since I saw you last?"

Carl made to go get the beers. "I don't know. A long time, I guess."

"I guess so."

Manny turned to Russell, who had sat down beside him. "I saw Arturo the other day. He said you just up and disappeared on him. What's going on?"

Russell cringed. Manny could be such a pill. "Yeah, I quit. I really wasn't into it, and now I've got better money coming in."

"You mean with Guy and his gang? More money, maybe, but I wouldn't say better. Arturo's an upright kind of guy. You should have given him notice at least. He said he still has money for you. I told him I'd tell you if I ever saw you again. You know, maybe you don't care one way or the other, but I have to live here, and deal with people here. And if word gets around that I'm vouching for flakes, that comes back at me."

Waving an understanding hand, Russell said, "I'll talk to him," never intending to follow through. That whole job had been Manny's doing. Russell didn't want anything to do with detasseling corn, either then or now. Carl returned with a six-pack.

"Ah, summertime." Manny popped the top off his bottle and raised it. "To Daddy Carl—who woulda thunk it?"

"Not me," said Carl from the shadows at the far end of the patio.

"Well, me either." Manny took a long drink. "What's it like to know you're going to have a kid? I mean, I'd be like—well, I don't even know what I'd be like."

Carl laughed and jumped out of his chair. He took a miniature tape recorder from out of his pocket and played back Manny's last comment. "That's a keeper," he said with a grin.

"What?" Manny demanded. "You were taping me?"

"Yes, I was. It had to be done. See, I got this little tape recorder a while ago," Carl explained. "I carry it around and trawl for sounds. Just a little hobby, I guess. When I get a good little bit I add it to this tape I've been putting together." He got up. "I'll go get it."

Manny looked at Russell. They shrugged in unison. Crickets and cicadas loomed large in the night. Carl returned with a boom box.

"Here's a little of what I've got." He smiled suggestively as he played a portion of the tape for them. They first heard a chain saw, then the sound of something heavy thumping on a hard floor, accompanied by a man screaming, "Oh, no you don't!" Next came the unmistakable sound of an automobile collision, followed by the bawling of an infant, the shattering of glass, and someone loudly whooping.

Carl stopped the tape and added Manny to the mix:

"I mean, I'd be, like—well, I don't even know what I'd be like."

Carl laughed, his dark eyes dancing.

"That's pretty weird," Manny said.

"Uh-huh," Carl acknowledged. "Just the way I like it."

Heeding the call of the weird, Russell reached into his pocket and withdrew his loaded hash pipe.

"Hey, Carl, you still smoke hash?"

Carl's face lit up at the offer. "Do bears still shit in the woods?"

Russell considered this rejoinder, hesitating long enough for Carl to prod him.

"Fire it up!"

Manny stood. "Hey, I don't want to be antisocial or anything, but I have to make sure I'm nowhere near that. I can't even have a trace of it showing up in my pee."

He lit another cigarette and watched while they passed the pipe and got high. Carl expressed his appreciation for the smoke.

"Is that what Guy's got you into?" Manny asked, finishing his beer.

"Yeah."

"Can you get me some of this?" Carl was eager to know.

"I'll give you as much as you want."

Manny looked Russell in the eye as he extinguished his cigarette, the suggestion of a smirk on his thin lips.

———————

Carmela and Ellie scratched away at the surface of things. After all, they hadn't seen each other in over a year, and no matter how far back they went, they were both aware that they were drifting apart as friends. It was just the way it was. Ellie had shown off the room that would become the nursery and described plans for organization and decoration. Carmela had thrown in more than her two cents' worth. She was a fount of opinions on all things pertaining to pregnancy, childbirth, parenting, and life management. Ellie was reminded of how strident Carmela could be, how full of herself she was. Here she was, pregnant with her first child, and Carmela hadn't even congratulated her. She was asking a lot of questions, but using them as platforms to come off as some sort of motherhood guru.

They sat on the couch. Carmela held a glass of wine. Ellie propped her bare feet on the coffee table, checking the condition of the polish on her toes. Carmela had always been this way, and Ellie had always encouraged her. She saw Carmela as a more powerful personality, and was content to follow her lead. While she listened to her go on, she was reminded of a scolding she got from her mother in high school: 'That Carmela is a bubblehead, and she's turning you into a regular fun girl. And those boys you run around with are a bunch of weirdoes.' At the time she thought her mother was ridiculous and got the idea of forming a band with the name Bubblehead, Fun Girl, and the Weirdoes. Now she could better appreciate her mother's perspective.

Still, in all, they were and remained trusted friends. What was different was that they used to be confidantes. Now that level of intimacy simply wasn't there. Carmela dealt with that by coming on even stronger than usual. Ellie preferred to remain pleasantly passive.

"Well, that's all going to work out just great, isn't it?" Carmela was saying. "You've got everything all set up. I'm just so excited for you. I'm sure it's going to be wonderful. I'll have to get you those books I was talking about. I suppose your sister's going to have a shower for you? I'll have to talk to her."

Russell walked into the room rather clumsily and plopped down next to Carmela, throwing his arm around her.

"Hey there, Russ, my boy," she greeted him jauntily. "Make yourself comfortable."

He rested his head on her shoulders and she laughed. "I believe you've been drinking, Mr. Pinske."

"I've been celebrating," he informed her. "What a great night to celebrate. Remember the last time we were all together? It was at your wedding." He remembered that night, and added, "If Victor were here, it would be a regular reunion."

Carmela squinted at him. "You're drunk."

He laughed and leaned toward Ellie. "I'm just so happy for you guys."

She smiled, then paused before asking him, "Have you heard from Victor at all lately? I see his mom around a lot, and I usually hear what he's up to from her, but she says she hasn't heard from him since January."

"I haven't talked to him since he left boot camp at Great Lakes. Last I knew he was stationed in Virginia, but that was a couple of years ago."

As he talked with them on this sweet summer night, his inebriation sharpened his desire for female companionship. He asked Ellie if he could use her phone.

"Sure. You know where it is in the kitchen? There's one in the bedroom, too, if you want."

"Who are you calling?" Carmela asked, then sipped her wine, looking at him over the rim of the glass.

"I've been trying to get together with Helen. I went over to her place this morning, but she wasn't around."

She raised her glass. He went to make his call, and he heard her giggling behind him.

"Hey, you're home," he greeted Helen when she answered.

"Am I?" she wryly replied.

"I came by your work and your house today. I was hoping to see you sometime."

He heard her fumbling around with something. After a pause she said, "I've been out and about. I just got home a little while ago. Do you want to come over?"

He explained that he was at Stillwater and shared the good news of the night with her. "Oh, that's nice," she said, her voice strained through a half-suppressed yawn.

There was more shuffling on her end during another pause, then she said, "I should let you go. I'm famished. All I've eaten today is a grapefruit. I've got to make some dinner and there's a pile of papers on my desk that need tending to. Come by sometime, though—I'll be around all week."

He walked down the hall, feeling better than he had in a long time. This night was a good one, and he knew it. They were all in the living room when he returned. Carl and Ellie were entwined on the couch. Manny sat in an armchair, gnawing on a chicken leg. Carmela pointed to Russell as he entered the room.

"Russ wants to go out there, don't you?"

He shrugged. "Sure."

"Oh, he doesn't even know what we're talking about."

It was true. He didn't.

"Come on, it'll be fun," Carmela insisted, kicking her husband. "Don't be a fuddy-duddy."

Manny sucked the joint-end of the bone and grinned. "Fuddy-duddy, eh?" He wiped his mouth with the back of his hand. "It's just a waste of gas. What's out there, anyway? Nothing but some stupid houses."

"No, it's a whole freaky scene. Russ would love it." She turned to him. "Tell him you want to go to Viking's Hollow."

"I want to go to Viking's Hollow," Russell repeated, then added, "What is Viking's Hollow?"

"A bunch of stupid little houses about ten miles from here that we found once," Manny answered, then belched.

Carmela finished her wine and winked at Russell. "It's a strange little enclave out in the middle of nowhere. You've just got to go there."

"I'd like to check it out," Carl said, nudging Ellie. "How about you?"

"I'm game."

"Oh, all right." Manny got up, wrapping the bones in a paper napkin. "But let me take a leak first. Great chicken, by the way, Ellie."

He tossed his garbage and used the toilet. His wife was a real trip. She could be his dearest friend one day and a stranger the next. Sometimes, like tonight, she would be a totally different person with him than she was with other people. Now she was being vivacious and outgoing and spontaneous, when just a few hours ago she was distant and mopey, even crying in the car for some unknown reason. Who she would be on the way home, he could not tell. He washed his hands and splashed water on his face. Life with her was like living in a hall of mirrors. He could never be certain where they were in relation to one another, or what facet of herself would be revealed next.

Everyone was outside, standing around The Imp. Carl ran his hand along the dent in the rear fender, and asked about it.

"Don't get me started," Manny snarled, cranking the ignition. "Some old bat rammed me, and it turns out she doesn't have insurance. I have a pretty high deductible, so I'm going to get screwed unless I sue her. And that's going to be a major hassle. The whole thing has been one big pain in the ass."

They drove with all the windows rolled down, the country night rushing through the old car. The gently rolling hills were pocked with ponds and swamps, whose essence filled the sultry air.

"Are you sure this is the way?" Carmela asked.

"Yes, I'm sure this is the way," Manny answered sharply. "I found the place, remember? I know exactly where we are. Just up the road there's a one-lane bridge across some ravine or something with a funky name."

"You sound like an old married couple," Carl said.

Carmela turned around to tell them, "We are an old married couple."

They approached the bridge. "Mencher's Ditch," Manny said, reading the sign. "That's it—Mencher's Ditch."

"I wonder who Mencher was," Ellie wondered. "And why did they name a ditch after him?"

Carl scratched his chin and mused, "What would you have to do to get a ditch named after you?"

Manny slowed, almost coming to a complete stop in his search for an unmarked road. He found it, and they went downhill through a grove of pine trees. A beat-up Pinto was parked beside a hand-painted sign that read, "Viking's Hollow."

"Don't see too many Pintos around," Carmela observed.

"I think it's the official car of Viking's Hollow," Manny told her, then pointed ahead. "This place freaks me out."

He pulled up across from a small, dark house surrounded by an exceedingly tall chain-link fence.

"That's a twelve-foot fence," he said. "That's crazy. What are they try-ing to keep out?"

"Or keep in?" Carmela suggested.

"Yeah, you're right—put some razor wire up there and you got a prison fence."

"Maybe whoever lives there is a werewolf, and locks himself inside when there's a full moon," Russell speculated.

"That's a thought," Manny said, driving on to the next house.

"On your left you will see what appears to be a concrete igloo," Carmela announced in her best tour guide voice. Indeed, a structure re-sembling a concrete igloo stood in someone's front yard.

"That could be the entrance to an underground bunker," Carl said.

Manny nodded. "Could be."

"Here's my favorite," Carmela told them as they approached the next house, which was surrounded by topiary bushes.

"I just love topiary."

The next house they came to sported an obelisk out front; then they cruised by three houses in a row that looked like they had been built on similar plans at the same time. Each had a placard above the front door, identifying them as Shangri-La, Xanadu, and Kismet.

"Go knock on the door, Russ," Carmela dared him. "Go up and ask if you can visit Shangri-La."

Manny stepped on it and pulled quickly away. "He would, too. But not tonight. We came here to check the place out, not mess with it."

They were on their way back to the main road when Manny slammed on the brakes to avoid hitting a raccoon with a missing hind leg that had hobbled onto the road. The creature turned to face the car and let out a sinister hiss.

"Hiss at me, will you?" Manny shouted, then blasted the car's very loud horn. "Take that, gimpy!"

The animal shuffled off into the bushes. Carmela patted him on the back in mock commendation.

"You told him, dear."

Carl laughed. "That, my friends, was not just any old three-legged hissing raccoon—that was the Spirit of Viking's Hollow."

9

Russell heard Helen's wind chimes as he rode up the street to her house. A fair breeze was blowing on this unseasonably cool day, more like spring than summer. He dismounted and leaned the bike against a tree, then took time to compose himself, not wanting to show up at her place all sweaty and out of breath. Having cooled off a bit, he began walking the bike along the sidewalk.

He was feeling good. Since the debacle at Chuck's, he'd been availing himself of Carmela and Manny's place more frequently, splitting his time between there and Bloodstone. Yesterday he spent the whole day with them. He helped Carmela with errands, cooked them all dinner, then spent the night. Sometime during the evening, when they were all on the couch watching TV, Carmela proposed throwing a party.

Manny was dead set against the idea. They went back and forth about it, off and on for hours. Carmela's argument was that they had never had a housewarming party. Manny argued that that was because he didn't want to have one. He knew the kind of parties she liked to throw, and he knew she would invite everyone and their cousins. People he didn't know would wander through his house. Things could get broken. Things could be stolen.

The upshot of it was that Carmela would have her party. Manny reiterated several times in many ways that he would take whatever measures he deemed necessary to secure his property. Carmela kept assuring him that everything would be OK. Russell sensed that if he hadn't been present, the exchange would not have been as cordial as it was. The outcome would likely have been the same, though. Manny would protest any idea of hers, sometimes seemingly reflexively, but he always went along with whatever she wanted.

Russell walked slowly in the lengthening afternoon shadows. He was here to ask Helen to that party and was mulling over how to go about it. There was no real reason for him to believe she would be interested, except for the fact that they had met at a party, and he knew she was an outgoing person. His hope was to persuade her that they could have some fun mingling with what would surely be a strange crowd.

That summer they spent together years ago had been a good one. They became friends by establishing a mutual perspective, and through that lens they viewed their individual preoccupations. There had been some moments when he felt like there might be something more than friendship between them, but he didn't imagine that she thought of him as anything more than a friend.

But then again, she could be hard to read. Maybe things could be different now that the gap in their worldly experience had narrowed a little. The age difference didn't seem as significant as it had when he was a teenager. But surely she had many better prospects than him. These thoughts would normally put the kibosh on any notions of his, but he was in high spirits. He really just wanted to hang out with her and see what flowed from there. She seemed to enjoy his company, so all of that was well and good. They'd get reacquainted and have a bit of fun.

He leaned his bike against the side of the house and walked up the porch stairs. Her glass baubles shone and her chimes tinkled. That tuna can with the cigar in it was still on the railing, but now it was filled with butts. He knocked once, and the door opened immediately. She held a phone to her ear and waved him inside as she continued her conversation.

"I understand that. Yes, I hear what you're saying, but it's what you said ten days ago and it's still not done. I need to know exactly when you're going to do it."

She rolled her eyes and motioned for him to sit.

"Come on, Larry, it's four towel racks—that's all I'm asking—four towel racks."

He eased onto the couch. Pacing the room, she shook her head in disbelief and said, "I'm sure I could do it myself, but I thought I hired you to do it. If you want the job, OK. If not, just say so and I'll find someone else. All that matters to me is that it gets done."

She stopped pacing and turned a scornful countenance to the phone.

"OK, on Monday these good people are going to have a place to hang their towels. Monday. This coming Monday. Not next Tuesday."

As her interlocutor spoke, she held the receiver away from her ear and gave it the finger, hanging up without further comment. He watched her huff a bit, thinking about telling her she was cute when she was pissed.

"And here you are," she turned to him. "The vanishing vagabond with your 'now I'm here, now I'm gone' routine." She slumped into an armchair. "Maybe you can redeem yourself by keeping me from going totally misanthropic. Or maybe you'll be what finally turns me against humanity."

He gulped. "Yikes. That's putting me on the spot."

"You have to play the hand you're dealt, bub."

Sunset colors burnished her gold hair as she leaned toward the window.

"Sun's behind the trees," she said. "Good time for leftover champagne, what do you say?"

She pulled a bottle out of the refrigerator and filled a couple of juice glasses. "I opened this up last night. Better get to it while she's still got some fizz left in her."

He offered a toast. "To humanity—love it or lump it."

They drank to that.

"Heard from Myrtle that you were snooping around here a while back," she said, setting her glass on the counter.

"That was the day I called," he told her, and took another drink.

"When was that?"

He sat on a tall stool. "I called from my friends' place. Remember? I told you about them getting married and having a baby."

"Oh yeah. I was really out of it that night. I'd just gotten back from three days of driving around." She snorted a little laugh, opened the refrigerator, and rummaged inside it.

"Want some pizza from two nights ago, too?"

She handed him a piece and took one herself, commenting on their fare with a smile.

"Leftover pizza and champagne."

"God bless America," he said, raising his glass again. They toasted the sentiment and ate their slices.

She took a bite and looked at him, noticing a dab of sauce on his chin. What was he doing here? What did he want? Whatever it was, she was sure he couldn't name it. She'd known many an odd duck in her time, and he was among the oddest. Although he came across as perpetually bemused, there was a sense about him that he knew who he was and was on a path uniquely his own. She understood his desire to take off and leave everything behind. The best times she'd had recently were when she was out and no one knew where she was, no one could reach her, everyone had to make do without her. Now he was at an age and in a position to cut loose. She admired his determination to do so but worried that he would remain adrift and become one more shiftless loser like so many she had known. Right now, though, she was interested in what he was up to, and felt like sharing some things with him.

"So, I spent a few days driving around," she began. "I was looking for fabric for a quilt that I had a dream about. It was one of those intense dreams that leaves you thinking, you know? I saw a pattern, and it was something I just knew I could do. I saw the colors, everything. It was very vivid, and I thought about it for days. Then about a month later, I had another dream about it."

She leaned toward him and removed the pizza sauce from his chin with her thumb.

"I was working on it in the winter," she continued. "Outside it was snowing. And I felt deeply, profoundly happy. I woke up with that happy feeling, very peaceful, and that's totally unusual for me. That's when I decided I had to go look for the material I needed. It was just one of those dreams I couldn't ignore, you know?"

He knew.

She finished her pizza and wiped her mouth with the back of her hand. "Come on, I'll show you."

They walked past the bathroom and continued down the hallway to a part of her place he'd never been before. The small room they entered was cluttered with boxes and miscellany.

"Here's the cloth." She took folded bundles out of a box and displayed them. "It took a lot longer to find than I thought. I looked over bolts and bolts of stuff, and nothing was close to what I had in mind. I finally ended up in northern Michigan. My aunt's a member of the Spinning and Weaving Guild in Cheboygan, and they make beautiful traditional textiles, all hand woven. Sure enough, their stuff was perfect."

He ran his hands over the fabric. It was fine material, with delicate floral and paisley patterns in purple, blue, and burgundy.

"I finished one block while it was still fresh in my memory. Now I can use this as a pattern."

She showed him a square with a starburst design in the middle.

"My plan is to alternate colors and rotate the angles of the stars so that the whole adds up to one large star in the center surrounded by smaller stars all around." She trailed off, knowing she wasn't doing a good job describing her vision. Actually, the more she talked to him about it, the less clear it was to her.

"I should draw a diagram of this sometime, then I can show you what I mean."

He examined her sample, and ran his hands again over the stacks of cloth.

"Carmela would love this," he began, hoping to segue into an invitation to the party. "You'd like her stuff, too. She's going to have a booth at the fair this year."

Helen nodded silently, then replaced the cloth in the box. Russell thought to bring up the party, but hesitated.

"This will be the first quilt I've done on my own. I've worked on a few over the years with some of my mother's friends and some aunts, but that was a long time ago."

She moved the box to a shelf by the window, then cupped her hands around the glass and looked out.

"Good and dusky. Want to go be seditious?"

He had no idea what she meant but followed her anyway. She opened the door to her bedroom and rummaged through a closet. He was surprised at how messy these back rooms were. The rest of her apartment was so tidy, and he had always considered her to be a very together, organized person. She slipped on a pair of tennis shoes, and they went out the back door to the garage. She handed him a pair of long-handled pruning shears, then grabbed a canvas bag.

"Let's go," she said as she glanced upstairs. "Myrtle might spot you and think you're abducting me."

He mocked a prod to her ribs with the shears and growled, "Get going, you."

They went around the side of the house, and she began gathering wildflowers, telling him to pick some, too. They carried their bouquets down the street and stopped at the house on the corner. It was a house he knew well from growing up here, but one he'd completely forgotten about. It was a modest old place that used to be surrounded by a lovely garden in bloom from spring through fall. What he remembered most was a large wooden stand by the porch that held fresh flowers from whatever blooms were in season. A colorful sign read, "Cut Flowers—Freewill Offering."

Tonight the house was dark, the garden was weedy, and the weathered, old display stand was empty. The sign was still legible, but badly faded. Helen put her flowers in one of the tin vases, then took Russell's handful and filled another.

"You know this place?" She stood back and looked at her arrangements.

"Oh yeah, I remember this house."

"Do you know Evelyn personally?"

He didn't.

"I made friends with her when I was a little girl. I came here to get some flowers for my mom when she was sick, and that's when I met her. I used to come by all the time, and she'd give me treats, and she was just very sweet to me. About three years ago she lost both her husband and her son. Her husband was killed in a car accident in the spring, and by Christmas her son was gone too. An aggressive type of leukemia. He was only forty."

She began to walk away. The streetlights flickered on.

"I never got to know her husband at all. He mostly kept to himself. I did know her son, Alex. He was a sign painter. Such a shame, he was really talented. His work is all over the town. Ever notice the window on Wayne's shop? Check it out sometime. Sign painting is quite a craft, and he was great at it. Evelyn never recovered from that loss. I don't presume to know how anyone could."

She shook her head and led him onto a dark side street. He wondered about her life, and all the things she got up to. She knew so many people and had so many stories. Her experience and interests were wide and varied, and he knew he hadn't heard a fraction of all she had to say. He wanted to know what motivated her, how she came to be the person she was. She continued talking about Evelyn.

"The first year she spent totally obsessed with her garden. She wouldn't leave it, wouldn't go anywhere or do anything else but garden. She even slept out there sometimes. Then she just gave up on it, and everything else, too, I think. She lived with one of her sisters for a while, then came back to her house and took to staying inside all the time. Almost never goes out, certainly never tends to the yard anymore. I stop by every week or so to visit with her, and I go out to the garden and do what I can, but I can't maintain it without her. And unless she wants to care for it, I shouldn't, really. It's hers, after all, and if she wants to let it go then it should go, I guess. I do make bouquets when I have flowers, and people put money in the box, but she's never said a word to me about it."

She stopped and pointed to a tree.

"This is why we're here."

She drew his attention to the trees lining this side of the street. They were all smooth, with slender trunks. On the other side of the street towered mature, old trees.

"They had to tear up the sewer line here. Should've seen it. Big cast-iron pipe that had been in the ground for one hundred three years. They replaced it with concrete tubes they fitted together. I took some good pictures—you can see them if you want. But they had to rip out all the big old maples on this side. They replaced them with saplings, but they haven't maintained them at all since then. And now is the time in their growth when good pruning is crucial."

They walked along while she pointed to individual trees and discussed her pruning strategy.

"I've gotten as far as here," she said, and dropped her bag on the ground. "I came out here to tend to them one afternoon and the police showed up and asked what I was doing. I explained, and I was certain I was charming enough to make them understand, but I almost got ticketed for vandalism. Assholes. Anyway, now I come at night. These trees need care."

She opened the bag and instructed him.

"You see, we want them to grow up, not out. These lower limbs have to go now, and those above them have to have their downward-growing branches removed. If we leave them, the tree will grow laterally faster than it grows vertically, and these lower ones will eventually have to be sawn off. By then it will get scarred and end up all lopsided."

He went around the tree with her, chopping wherever she indicated. They cut up the debris and stuffed it in the bag, then she took another look around.

"See that, where the one branch is growing over the other? The bottom one's got to go. Can you reach it?"

He tried, but couldn't. As he puzzled how to get at it, she wrapped her arms around his waist and he gave a start.

"Ticklish?" She laughed, then grabbed him again and hoisted him up so he could cut the branch. It was a big one and fell to the ground with a thud. She scanned the street and quickly got it stuffed in the bag. They walked away and she high-fived him.

"A good deed well done."

On the way back to her place, she shivered and put the bag down.

"Middle of summer and I just got a chill." She hugged herself and shook her arms. "My grandmother would say someone just walked across my grave."

He wished he had a jacket to lend her, or some chivalrous act to perform. He took the bag, put the shears in it, and slung it over his shoulder.

"Thank you." She smiled and linked her arm in his. They walked under a streetlight and she began to laugh.

"Look at your head," she said, stopping and pointing to his shadow. "Look how square your skull is—it's like a can."

"A big can of creamed corn," he suggested.

She laughed and flicked his ear. "A can of creamed corn with a couple of knobs."

"And what's yours like?" he asked. "It's round, that's for sure."

"I'd say it resembles a muskmelon," she concluded, then bounced her curls. "A muskmelon with tendrils."

They moved on, and she gave his arm a little squeeze.

"It's good to be with you, Russ. You're always game."

Her voice was deep and sweet, qualities amplified in the darkness. She leaned on him when they turned the corner.

"It's funny," she said. "I don't really miss people when they're away from me. But when I see someone again after it's been a while, I realize all at once how much I missed them. I've missed you."

A train came by. They were close enough to smell it, to feel its heat, and for a minute all they could hear were the steel wheels rolling along. He was happy to be here. He had missed her without really knowing it, and she had just expressed his own feelings. When the train rattled into the distance, they crossed the tracks and walked near the fairgrounds. He asked her if she planned to go to the fair.

"Probably when they run the demolition derby. I always like to see that. But I usually make myself some money on an empty lot my parents own down the road. Parking on the grounds costs five dollars. We charge two. I have friends help me out, and we all split it at the end. It's fun—I get to hang out with my friends, meet some interesting people, and make easy money."

They walked up the drive to her place and threw the contents of the bag on a mound of leaf litter behind the garage. She noted that Myrtle's windows were dark. Back in her house, he made use of her bathroom. He washed his face and wished he'd shaved. He wanted to remain with her, to luxuriate in her presence. She met him in the hallway.

"It's been really good to see you, Russ. I'm going to get ready to go out now." She walked to her bedroom. "There's a lecture tonight on landscape photography. I'm going with my friend, Ian. He's a professional photographer, has a studio in Valparaiso. Are you interested in photography? Come along if you want."

She piled some clothes on the bed, then removed her shoes.

"No," he said. "I mean, yes, I like photography, but no, I don't want to tag along."

"You wouldn't be 'tagging along,'" she said, removing her earrings and placing them in a tray on her dresser. "You're good company."

He nodded politely, feeling foolish for having thought she would have nothing better to do than to hang out with him.

"Yeah, but I should check in with Carmela."

"So, you're staying with them? At that house we went to?"

"Sometimes, but I'm also camping out with these guys. They have this site set up."

"They live 'off the grid,' eh? That could be interesting."

"Sort of, except it's mostly been a drag. I mean, I'm feeling like I'm treading water, wasting time."

She punched him lightly on the arm and said, "Hey, we can talk about that sometime, OK? Call me, and we'll get together again."

It was clear that it was time for him to leave. He hesitated just a moment, then asked if she'd like to come to the party with him.

"A party?" She shrugged. "Sure. What kind of party?"

"A Carmela house party. She knows how to do one. Well, you remember her wedding—that was a good time, wasn't it?"

She agreed to meet him there next Saturday night, and shut the door behind her. He left with a peculiar feeling, her wind chimes ringing in his ears as he rode into the night. She was coming to the party, and that elated him. He wondered if this Ian was her boyfriend or something. She'd never mentioned any boyfriend, but then why would she? Maybe he just craved the sort of connection he was reading into their evening, but he got himself all wound up thinking about her. He felt like he'd been startled awake and was fuzzy about what reality he was partaking in. More confused than usual, he rode around the lake, not relishing the thought of going to Bloodstone but not wanting to lean on Carmela and Manny too much.

Something whizzed by his ear, then exploded in a shower of sparks. Another, then another, and the roar of a speeding vehicle behind him. His bike hit the gravel and he went tumbling with it into a ditch. The vehicle screeched to a halt, then slammed into reverse. He realized that being in a ditch was not the best place to be and took what cover he could find behind some weeds.

"Cease fire, cease fire," a bullhorn blared. "Come on up, Pinske—we've got you nailed dead to rights."

He walked his bike up to the smelly old station wagon.

"You fools made me wipe out—I could've gotten seriously hurt."

Guy laughed and repeated his statement in a mocking tone, then added, "Come on, lighten up. We're burning through our stockpile. Get in."

He looked at the car. The Steves placidly stared at him. Travis was passed out in the cargo hold.

"What about the bike?" he asked.

"What about it? Ditch it—we've got plenty. It'll make some bum's day when he finds it."

"But I like this bike."

Again Guy repeated him in a whiny voice, then told him to hide it and come back for it later. Russell went along, partly because he had nothing better to do, partly because he needed a diversion, and partly because fireworks held so much allure for him. They roared off into the dark countryside.

"Let's see if we can wake Travis up from his coma," Guy suggested. "He's been asleep for at least two days, after a weeklong bender. He might be brain dead now. I never had much use for him as an animal, but I sure don't need him on my hands as a vegetable. So let's give him a chance to wake up before we dump him in the woods."

They slowed to a halt out near where the party barn used to stand.

"Remember burning that down?" Guy asked the Steves. They chuckled.

Russell looked at him. He hadn't known Guy was responsible for that, but wasn't surprised. Guy shrugged.

"Somebody had to do it." He turned to the Steves. "Set it up, boys. Make it good."

One Steve grabbed a coffee can, the other several packs of bottle rockets. They filled the can with rockets, set it on its side, then proceeded to twist the fuses together so they would all fire at once. They lit the bundle, opened the tailgate, and sat down beside the prostrate Travis. Guy counted to three, then put the car in gear and drove slowly away as the rockets began to go off. They surrounded the car and lit up the night, some coming through the open windows, bouncing off the dashboard and seats, exploding all around. Guy shouted, "Incoming! Incoming!"

The Steves shrieked, Russell ducked, Guy howled, and Travis' shirt caught on fire. That woke him up. He jumped, whacked his head on the ceiling, and fell back down.

"It lives!" Guy shouted as a rocket exploded on the rearview mirror. Travis moaned and patted his smoldering shirt. He then leaned out the car and vomited.

"It pukes!" Guy cheered.

The fusillade ended, and the car coasted to a stop. Stars filled the moonless night.

"Watch this." Guy pulled a can of lighter fluid from under the driver's seat and poured some on his shoes. Then he lit them and ran, shouting, "Feets, don't fail me now!" He got some distance before the flames died down.

"That's a good stunt. Old one, but still a good one."

He took the can of lighter fluid and drew a pentagram on the pavement with it, stood in the center, set it on fire and cackled like a maniac possessed. The Steves set off Roman candles. Russell leaned against the wagon and watched. Travis hung his head over the tailgate and moaned.

"Hey, Pinske—you left that Jolly Ha Ha in the car," Guy said, walking toward him. "It's in the glove box. Fire that bad boy up."

Russell had forgotten about it, and was glad to have something to add to the show. He got it out and set it on the ground. The Steves gathered round as Russell knelt to light it. The wick sparked, then sputtered and went out. Guy paused a moment before going to inspect it. One of the Steves tossed a firecracker behind his back when he leaned over it, causing him to spring back so quickly that he fell.

"Funny, funny, funny," he said, wiping the seat of his pants. "Regular yuk a minute with you clowns."

Guy relit Jolly Ha Ha's short fuse and stood back. The thing began to tremble, then a jet of green flame shot out of it. It hissed and began to roll toward Guy, emitting an ominous whine. The Steves ducked behind the car. Russell ran. Guy jogged in reverse, skirting the rolling explosive. It suddenly began to smoke, then leapt at Guy, who turned and ran. It gave off a loud whistle and shot over his head, landed a few feet in front of him, then started rolling back toward him. He stopped as it gave a long hiss and exploded with a bright white bang.

"Son of a bitch! It went right for me, you see that? Goddamn guided missile with my name on it. What the hell was that, Pinske?"

Russell shrugged. "Jolly Ha Ha."

"Everyone's a comedian," Guy said, kicking the burnt remains of the murderous munition. He turned to them. "Anybody got anything left? Light 'em if you got 'em."

The Steves fired a few stray bottle rockets, lit the last of the Roman candles, filled the air with smoke bombs and set off packs of firecrackers. Guy poked Travis and got a moan, then slapped his face. "Come on, man, sit up or I'm leaving you."

"Fuck off."

"OK, good enough. You'll live."

Guy got back behind the wheel. The Steves folded up the tailgate and climbed in the backseat, leaving the semiconscious Travis curled up in the rear. Guy got the engine cranking, pushing it faster and faster. The wagon began to shake.

"Gotta blast the carbon out of the beast," he yelled. The vehicle sounded stressed and strained. It was dark, and the speedometer was broken, so Russell couldn't tell how fast they were going, but he knew it was way too fast. He could clearly see the headlines of tomorrow's paper, the photos of the mangled wreckage. The engine gave a series of reports as loud as any of the fireworks, and acrid smoke leaked through the vents.

"Thar she blows!" Guy shouted, and eased off the accelerator. "Old gal likes to be put through her paces. She'll run smooth for a while now."

He whipped the still speeding car into a U-turn, causing Travis to fly across the floor and hit a wheel well. He shouted a string of slurred obscenities.

"I can't hear a word you're saying," Guy shouted back, then announced, "We're going to Lester's. I hate to do it, but I've put it off too long."

The Steves slumped. Guy turned to Russell. "You don't know Lester." He snorted. "No one knows Lester. Lester doesn't know Lester. Unfortunately, I've known him since about the second grade, and I have to look after him. No one else ever really has. If it wasn't for me, he'd be dead long ago. The world would little note or long regret his passing, to be sure, but I feel obliged to do what I can to help him. I don't know why, especially since I mostly can't stand him." He shrugged. "What can I say?"

They entered town and crept along the back streets and alleyways to the train depot, where they parked. Guy tried to roust Travis, but to no avail. He got a flashlight from the car and waved Russell and the Steves down a cobblestone alley. The Steves opened two steel doors behind a warehouse. Guy shone the light into the cellar, and led the way down a musty brick passageway.

"Ever been down here, Russ?"

He hadn't.

"Most people don't know that there are a lot of underground storage vaults behind these buildings. Back in Prohibition days they started building tunnels between them to move the moonshine around." He swiped away cobwebs and led them through a narrow corridor. "We're on the way to the Red Rooster now. That place was built in 1840, always been a tavern. It was meant to be a den of iniquity, and by God it's been one. Bootleggers walked through here back when it was a speakeasy. Perfect location, really, straight shot off the railroad to the basement. Pretty slick. Have to hand it to the old-time gangsters. Imagine them down here in pinstripe suits and fedoras, toting Tommy guns."

They reached the end of the tunnel and came to a wooden door. Guy tried to open it, but it was locked.

"Goddamn Lester, I told him to take this lock off."

He handed the flashlight to Russell, then got a pick out of his pocket and worked the lock open. He took back the flashlight and they headed up the back stairs of the tavern.

"What are we doing here?" Russell asked.

"Hooking up with Lester. Where you been?"

"Nobody lives up here anymore. I came up here when I was looking for you guys when I first came to town. It's totally abandoned."

Guy laughed. "Yeah, it's supposed to be. The place has been substandard forever, filled with vermin, real firetrap. City got around to giving the landlord a shitload of violations a few years back. Instead of fixing the place up he kicked us all out. Bums still come around to flop once in a while, but old Lester never did move out. Got a permanent settlement up on three."

They walked down the dark hallway, kicking trash aside.

"Lester Owen!" Guy bellowed. "Smells like a goddamn zoo in here."

A form stirred under a raggedy blanket in the far corner of the room.

"Lester, I'd call you an animal, but animals have more respect for themselves than you do. You're worse than any pig by far."

Lester sat up and yawned, rubbing his eyes. He was a big man, fat and pasty. He had large watery eyes, a red lump of a nose, and a drooping mouth that was permanently open.

"What day is it?" he asked.

Guy snorted. "What do you care?"

Lester yawned again and shrugged.

"At least toss your pisspot out the window," Guy said with a wrinkled nose as he stood near a bucket by Lester's mattress.

"I do when it gets full," Lester drawled.

"Oh, God, how do you stand the stink?"

Lester shrugged again. "I don't know."

Guy tore at his hair with a look like he was about to fly into a rage, then bit his tongue and said quietly, "Did you sell those cigarettes?"

"Uh huh."

Lester got an envelope from under the mattress and handed it over. Guy took some of the money out of the envelope and gave it to Lester, then stuffed the remainder in his pocket.

"Buy yourself a fucking bar of soap. Christ almighty you're a mess."

Lester scratched his hairy chest. A rat scuttled through the debris.

"You eaten today?"

Lester shook his head no.

"Come on, let's get some food."

They went back the way they came, Guy reminding Lester on the way to remove the lock on the door. When they got to the car, Travis was gone.

"Where the hell did he stumble off to?" Guy scanned the surroundings.

"That guy's a mess," he said, getting into the car. "Let him die in some gutter. Good riddance."

The car backfired and lurched forward.

"Whoa, big girl," Guy patted the dashboard, then winked at Russell. "She's all riled up."

They got out on the main drag and headed through town.

"Is that Eugene Naegler?" Guy asked, spotting someone on the street.

"Looks like him," said one of the Steves.

"What's that little prick doing wandering around?" Guy asked, pulling a U-turn. "Haven't seen him around in a long time. I forget how he found us, but he was slumming around with us for a while and taking notes. He thinks he's a writer" He swatted Russell. "This guy's a real prick. Considers himself a genius and wants everyone else to think so, too."

He cruised slowly behind a young man with dark shiny hair dressed in a black knit shirt, black slacks and sandals.

"Behold the jackanapes," Guy sneered.

He pulled the car to the curb.

"Hey Naegler," he shouted. The guy stopped, stooped to see into the window, and smiled.

"Why, Guy Bogel!" he exclaimed in a clipped, nasal tone. "I'll be! Thought they'd have put you away long ago."

Guy scratched his chin. "Oh, they've tried, but this old cat has a few lives left."

"So I see," he replied, looking over the car and its other occupants.

"Get in," Guy told him. "We'll give you some more material for that great American novel you're not writing."

He approached the car. "A little jaunt with you fellows might be just the ticket. I was out for my evening constitutional anyway."

Guy ran his tongue over his teeth. "I'm sure you were."

He got in and the car jerked into traffic.

"Is this equipped with safety belts?" he asked, groping for a strap.

Guy turned and gave him a blank look. Lester belched. They turned onto a side street and Guy spied an old woman pushing a shopping cart along the sidewalk.

"Look at that." He clucked his tongue and shook his head. "Disgraceful."

"You shall always have the poor among you," Naegler sententiously stated. "There but for the grace of God go we."

"I don't care if she's poor," Guy snapped. "She stole that shopping cart. Those things ain't cheap. If I were any meaner I'd take it away from her. This is just the sort of thing I'm talking about." He raised his voice and pointed at Russell as though they had been discussing some weighty matter, which they hadn't. "You let the little things slide—you let the broken windows stay broken, you let the old ladies steal shopping carts—and soon enough you have the likes of us loitering around your neighborhoods."

Naegler wrinkled his brow and started to say something before he was abruptly cut off by Guy, saying, "Is this guy a genius or what?" Guy poked Lester, who appeared to be in some sort of stupor, a bit of drool dribbling down one of his chins.

"I rest my case," he declared.

They pulled up by the dumpster behind the kitchen of the restaurant where Russell and Gloria had parted ways.

"Go see if Osborn's in there," he ordered a Steve, who went into the kitchen and soon came back accompanied by a gangly cook with a beak-like nose and bulging Adam's apple. He greeted Guy.

"What can I do you for, chief?"

Guy snapped his fingers. "Let's make it easy. Six cheeseburgers. How much you want for that?"

The cook scratched his head under his paper hat and said, "Let's say, three grams of that good hash?"

"I'll give you five and you bring us out some onion rings and root beers, OK?"

"You the man," he said with a casual salute, then loped back to the kitchen.

"So," Naegler spoke up. "Exchanging narcotics for food, eh?"

"God you're observant," Guy gushed, then flashed a look in the rear view mirror. "Hey, boys, I bet Naegler here would love to know all about a dollar bill."

They lit up at the suggestion, both producing a dollar from their pockets and ranting at once. One went on incoherently about how serial numbers are linked to historical events; the other was obsessed with the alien messages encoded in the engraving on the border. When they got to the Masonic symbolism of the Great Seal, Guy broke in.

"Novus Ordo Seclorum," he chanted. "A new order for the ages.'" He raised a finger and in a stentorian tone proclaimed: "Gentlemen, I submit to you we are on the brink of a new age, an age of chaos. And I say, bring it on!"

Russell laughed. Naegler stared at him with a dumbfounded look, his neck curling out of his shirt like a turtle's from a shell. Guy howled like a dog with a bellyache. Their food came, the exchange was made, and they took off.

"Well this is truly nice of you," Naegler said by way of thanks when he was handed his sack.

"Oh, the pleasure's all mine," Guy assured him.

They cruised through town and chowed on the burgers. The food perked Lester up, who shoveled it in.

"This is good," he said between gulps.

Guy nodded and patted him on the shoulder.

"Hey, I know a good melon patch," Lester told him.

"Oh yeah? How far is it?"

"Depends how fast you go," Lester answered, sucking his greasy fingers.

Guy stared at him. "That is the most brilliant thing you've ever said."

They made their way out to a dark and lonely corner of the county.

"How'd you find this place, Lester? What were you doing out here?"

"I don't remember."

"Then how did you remember how to get here?"

Lester shrugged. Guy rolled his eyes.

"OK, big guy, go get us a good one."

Lester lumbered out of the car and crashed through the field into the darkness.

"Lester loves his watermelons," Guy told them.

He returned, panting and sweating, with a good thirty-pounder.

"Holy moley, Lester, that is a big-ass melon!"

He grinned gleefully and nodded his head.

"There's a buck knife in the back somewhere, start slicing it up. Whack off a good hunk for me."

They sat around eating melon on the side of the road, Guy and Lester getting in a seed-spitting contest. Between rounds, Lester turned to him and said, "You remember Skutch?"

"Skutch the Barbarian who almost killed me with a crossbow? No, I don't know who you're talking about."

Lester screwed up his face and began, "Well, remember we took that long trip that one time to go get some stuff?"

"Of course I remember Skutch, you numskull!" Guy interrupted, giving him a curious look. "What about him?"

"Oh, he's dead."

Guy put down his piece of melon. "Dead? How do you know?"

"That friend of yours, you know, that Collector guy, he told me. He came up and said he had to find you." He chortled and spit out a seed. "He got a bloody nose talking to me."

Guy's eyes widened. "What else did he say?"

Lester shrugged. "He just told me Skutch was dead and said you knew why. Said he had to find out where you were quick. Kept asking where you were. Couldn't tell him 'cause I don't know."

"Good. That's good. You don't know where I am. That's true. Remember that. Now, if anyone asks you if you've seen me, you have to say no, OK? You don't know where I am, and you haven't seen me."

Lester placidly chewed melon while Guy began to tremble.

"Why didn't you tell me about this before now, Lester? Why didn't you tell me? Why am I just now hearing about this?"

"I don't know. I just remembered it."

Everyone looked at Guy. Naegler's voice pierced the silence.

"What's all this business?"

Guy's face flushed. He pointed at Naegler and shouted "Out!"

Naegler recoiled. "What do you mean?"

"Out!" Guy shouted louder. "You—out!"

"Certainly not," Naegler asserted. "If you want to be rid of me, take me back to town."

Guy stormed to the rear door, flung it open and grabbed him by the shoulders.

"Get your hands off me!"

"Or what? You'll wet yourself?"

Guy pulled him out of the car, dragged him across the road and threw him into the ditch. Lester spit a seed and bragged about how far it went.

"Get in, Lester," Guy barked. He crawled into the rear with the melon. Naegler started climbing out of the ditch and yelled futilely as Guy started the car. The Steves tossed their soda cans at him.

"Stop it!" Guy scolded them. "This is serious, you fuck-ups, and you're in it as seriously as I am."

They sped to town on empty country roads. Guy turned to Russell with a grave look.

"I'm burned."

———◆———

Lester got out in front of the Red Rooster, and Guy emphatically admonished him to remain ignorant of his whereabouts.

"You don't know where I am. Remember that. That's the truth. You don't know, and you haven't seen me, OK?"

"I'm not stupid," Lester said, holding the remainder of the melon under his arm.

"I know you're not," Guy assured him with a desperate edge in his tone. "I know you're not, it's just real important, OK?"

With a last round of reminders, Lester hauled his melon up to his lair and they headed off to the Rumacher Hotel.

Chuck Probst was not pleased by his company, but he'd been expecting them. He ushered them into his apartment with many furtive looks all around. He bolted the door and tersely addressed Guy.

"The Collector's been leaning on everyone he knows to find out where you are. Somebody could be watching this place. I don't know how heavy they think I am, but I'm out, you got it? I'm out. I am out of this totally."

"The hell you are," Guy told him. "You were there, we're here, you're in it."

Chuck put up his hands. "Not any more. This is it. I told him the truth. I don't know where you are. It's good for you that no one seems to know. He said someone'll be coming around to follow up, see if I've seen you or heard from you. I'll keep saying no, but that's all I'm doing for you. I got nothing to do with you from here on."

"You tell me everything you know and I'm gone for good and I'll be happy to never see your ugly ass again."

Chuck sighed. "This is it, OK? What he told me is that whoever it is that's running this, they used Skutch's shack there as a warehouse, right? So Skutch is all fucked up, hands the stash over to us thinking we're the boss. Real boss shows up, Skutch doesn't know where the shit went. Bam—execution style. Somehow, from someone, they learn about The Collector, and how he has this new sample of their goods. They want to know where he got it, and he wants to rat you out."

The next stop was Gary's parents' house in Michigan City.

"Go and get him out here, Russ. You're the only one they wouldn't recognize. Say you're in one of his classes and you want to ask him something. They think he's so precious they'll buy that."

To his relief, Gary opened the door.

"Russ? What are you doing here? What's up?"

Gary's father appeared at the far end of the hallway.

"Who's calling at this hour, son?"

"A friend from school," he answered, stepping onto the porch and scooting Russell toward the steps. "We have to talk about a class project."

Russell led him to the car. Guy briefed him on what he'd learned and demanded his help.

"You got to get that deal set up. Whatever it takes, get it set up. We should have this unloaded already, but you've been dragging your heels. Get that deal set up."

Gary scowled, started to say something, then paused and said, "I'll make the calls tomorrow. I'll come out and tell you where and when. We'll get it moved, and then I suggest you get moving."

"You're in it as deep as I am, motherfucker, and they're gonna find you soon enough."

Gary shook his head. "You're the only ones who know I'm here. As far as anyone else is concerned I'm with you guys, wherever you are. Unless you give me up, they'll think I'm off with you. Cisco Kid and Pancho, right? We'll sell it and be done with it and then I'm done, Guy. I just can't hang with you anymore. I'm onto something else now. One last deal, then adios."

He got out of the car and went back to his house. They returned to Bloodstone in silence.

10

"Got enough booze?" Russell asked, loading a keg of beer into the trunk of the Imp, alongside a case of liquor.

"Probably," Carmela said. "I don't want to run out. Besides, anything left over can be put to good use."

They had asked Russell to get a good deal from Guy, and he told them about the trouble he was in, after which he had to listen to numerous variations of Manny saying, "I told you so." Russell hadn't been back to Bloodstone since that night, although a lot of his stuff was still out there. Guy also owed him money for weighing some of the produce, but he didn't hold out much hope of getting paid. He didn't know what was happening with Guy's situation, and he really didn't want to get involved in whatever was going down. At this point he'd be happy with the recovery of his belongings.

He was glad to have spent the past week or so with Carmela and Manny. He'd made himself useful around their house in preparing for this shindig, and they'd been appreciative: Carmela for his help in cleaning and Manny for helping with the preparation of horseshoe pits in the backyard that he'd always wanted. Carmela had scoffed at the horseshoe project, telling him that if he wanted to play, he could go to her parents' house. She also pointed out that he didn't have anyone to play with. He was determined find some players tonight, and maybe get a tournament organized.

Russell slammed the trunk and got in beside her.

"How many people did you invite?" he asked. She shrugged as she adjusted her sunglasses and pulled into traffic.

"I don't really know, just everyone. Hey, you remember Lydia Perigrue?"

He rolled his eyes. "Is she coming?"

She laughed. "Well, sure. What? You thought I wouldn't invite her?"

"But she's so, so—pesky."

"Oh, give her a break. She just doesn't have a lot of inhibitions."

"She ought to get some."

Carmela slid her sunglasses down the bridge of her nose and looked at him with an amused assessment. Manny was out back practicing horseshoes when they returned.

"Damn, I'm good," he told them. Carmela kissed him quickly.

"Of course you are, dear." She looked around the yard. "I thought you were going to cut the grass."

"I got half of it done. I'll let Russ take the other half."

"I'll cut anyone's grass anytime," he said.

"You're a good man," Manny called out to him.

Russell got the mower going and attacked the lawn while they sorted the refreshments. He felt good doing it. Ordinarily he wouldn't be so excited, but he was looking forward to Helen's company this evening. He'd called her last night to make sure she was still coming, and they'd had a good, long, rambling conversation. She was so easy for him to talk to. Her candor and matter-of-fact attitude grounded him.

Manny came out of the house with a couple of beers as Russell was finishing. They cracked them open, and Manny offered to school him in the ways of horseshoes.

"There are those who flip," he began his instruction, tossing a shoe end over end. "There are those who spin," he continued, likewise demonstrating. "Me, I'm a straightforward, deadringer kind of guy." He threw the shoe and almost nailed the post, but not quite.

"Give it a try." He handed a shoe to Russell, whose first toss landed right beside Manny's.

"Yeah, that's it. You're on my team."

Carmela came out. She was barefoot, wearing shorts and a tank top. Russell was struck by how much she resembled her mother, with her high cheekbones and large, dark eyes.

"What a beautiful day," she said, sitting in a lawn chair and looking skyward. A few clouds puffed across the blue in a gentle breeze. She worked her toes through the freshly mown grass.

"Yep," Manny replied, fixing his eyes on his target. Russell just smiled. She closed her eyes and yawned.

"I think we're all ready. I'm going to have a lie-down before the festivities begin." She sat up as Manny retrieved his tossed shoe. He looked at her and said, "I'm not far behind you," then focused for another toss. Once he was certain she was back inside, he looked at Russell with eyebrows raised. He dropped the horseshoe and his voice.

"Do me a favor, man, and make yourself scarce for a while. You know?"

"Sure, sure. I'm out of here," Russell assured him, even though he keenly felt the need for a good nap. Manny faked a punch, then went inside the house. Russell considered trying to catch some sleep on the lawn, but opted to take a walk to the lake.

The road was dusty and hot. The lake murmured in the breeze, the heaving lilies flashing like sequins. He sat a long while and watched a heron take flight. When he returned to the house, they were out lounging on the porch. He passed them wordlessly and went to sleep in their guest room.

Carmela and Manny were talking at the kitchen table when Nestor gave a perfunctory knock and walked through the open door with Cheryl, Luis's girlfriend. He had a bottle of tequila in one hand and a six-pack of nonalcoholic beer in the other.

"Hey there," Carmela greeted them, then looked beyond the doorway as though expecting someone else to follow. "I thought Luis wasn't coming."

"He's not," said Nestor, handing Manny the tequila. "That's for you guys," he told him, then set his near-beer on the counter. "And that's for me."

"Luis is working late," Cheryl said in a quiet voice with a demure smile, her eyes briefly catching Carmela's then darting away. Nestor grinned.

"So, I says to her, I says, 'Why stay at home darning socks when there's a perfectly good party to go to?' That's what I says all right."

Carmela gave her brother a look that he returned with a wink.

"We the first ones here, sis?"

Manny thanked him for the liquor and put it next to the other bottles on the kitchen table. Nestor and Cheryl made themselves at home in the living room. Carmela walked past them, and stepped out the side door to the porch. Manny invited Nestor to pitch some horseshoes.

"OK," he shrugged, and glanced at Cheryl.

"Ever play horseshoes?" he asked her. By way of response, she pulled a pair of sunglasses out of a pocket of her denim jumper and slipped them on.

Out in the yard, Cheryl eased onto a lawn chair while Manny walked Nestor out on the grass. Nestor picked up a horseshoe, stared at the post, then ran and flung himself headlong, holding the horseshoe in front of him. He slid several yards before coming to a halt. Manny stared at him. Cheryl unfolded a paper fan and started waving it in front of her face. Nestor stood up, wiping grass clippings from his clothes.

"You're all green now," Cheryl said flatly as she slowly fanned herself. "Those stains will never come out."

"I am the Green Man," Nestor boomed, doing a little jig and shaking himself like a wet dog.

Carmela came around the corner of the house, walking purposefully.

"Has anyone seen the cat?" she asked the assembled company.

"She chowed down this morning and puked in the hallway," Manny informed her, then turned to Nestor. "Come on, let's play."

He pitched his shoe and cringed when he missed his mark. Nestor mocked a dropkick with his horseshoe, grabbed his foot and started hopping around, whooping loudly. Manny picked up a horseshoe and held it as Nestor concluded his display.

"So, you don't want to play."

"Oh, I'm playing all right, just not quite right. Hey, Manny, I'm just goofing you. Tell me the rules. I'll play straight with you. For real."

Carmela came back and called out to her husband to help find the cat. Manny could tell she was anxious and agitated, exactly the state he never wanted her to be in, particularly when their home was soon to be full of people. He went with her to search the house. Cheryl lifted her sunglasses and addressed Nestor, who was juggling horseshoes.

"Cat's gone missin," she told him.

He grunted, concentrating on keeping the shoes in midair.

Carmela opened the door to the guest room, startling Russell awake. He hadn't seen the cat recently, but volunteered to look for her. They scoured the house and were about to go back outside when Manny called up from the basement.

"Found her!"

They went downstairs where the cat lay on a shelf, acknowledging them with a mien of discontent.

"I don't know how she got down here. The door was locked. She was behind this toolbox." Manny picked up the box to show them where it had been on the shelf. "She got back behind it somehow. I just happened to see her mangy tail sticking out."

Carmela was relieved to have found her, and gave her a few strokes, which the cat tolerated without altering its attitude of perturbation.

"All right, so now we can have a party," Manny announced.

When they went back to the yard, they found Nestor and Cheryl engaged in a heated contest of horseshoes.

"You should take her on," Nestor called out to Manny. "She's a killer."

Cheryl walked to the side of the house, turned on the spigot and drank from the hose.

"We have glasses, and a faucet inside," Carmela informed her.

"I'm OK," she replied beneath the wide brim of her hat.

———————

Manny was having a good time with a bunch of guys from work, some of whom he'd known for many years. Russell had sort of been hanging out with them, but didn't get their in-jokes or their gossip. He wished he could speak Spanish, or at least some decent Spanglish, because most of the conversations were unintelligible to him. He never got a punch line or denouement, and always felt a beat behind. There were a lot of people here now, and Russell wandered around, unable to find someplace to settle. Nestor was sitting with Cheryl and his old bandmates, recounting their exploits and exchanging what passed for witticisms among them. Russell sat with them until he finished his beer, then went out to the porch. He kept a lookout for Artruro or some of the other field-workers, hoping to avoid them if they showed up.

People were milling about on the porch and front lawn, under the trees and among the haphazardly parked vehicles. A couple reclined on the porch swing. Russell sat alone on the railing, then stood when he saw

Helen's car. She parked on the street and walked up the driveway, checking out the gathering as she made her way to the porch. She was dressed for summer in white Capris, sandals, and a pink blouse. Russell met her on the stairs. She looked good to him, and he told her so. She smiled.

"Show me around this shack," she said.

They walked the length of the porch. She noticed the yellow bug light and asked, "Do you remember those mosquito coils, the citronella things you burn?"

He certainly did. They talked about their glow on summer nights, and the smell of their smoke.

"Who knows what sort of nasty by-products those things put out," he commented.

She shrugged. "Whatever it was, we both absorbed our share of it."

He took her inside and showed her around, ending up at Carmela's sewing room. Carmela was in there with a group of women who worked for her parents at the dry cleaners. Carmela saw them and waved them in. The conversation was in Spanish, which Helen spoke quite well. Russell sat in a chair and watched her. He was enjoying himself now.

Helen looked over the items Carmela was displaying and complimented her on the designs. As Helen fingered some linens, she thought of the quilt she'd started. A couple weeks ago she'd driven all over Michigan in search of material, but now felt absolutely no desire whatsoever to do anything with it. She didn't know why, but it had become a matter of complete indifference to her.

They left the seamstresses and drifted to the living room, where they took a place at the couch near Nestor and his friends. Nestor greeted Russell by saying, "That's the look right there, man. Russ—that look you have—I just recognized it. I love seeing people driving around at night with their lights off, looking like they're in control, all cool and everything, and they're driving around with their lights off. That's what you look like—like you're driving with your lights off."

Russell responded with a raised eyebrow. Helen looked at him, then at Nestor.

"And who are you?" she asked.

He straightened his posture and proclaimed, "I am Nestor, here with these Lords of Misrule, Mike and Jim. We used to be The One-Eyed Kings, you know, a damn fine band playing in the land of the blind. This is Cheryl, Dame of the Disillusioned. And you apparently know Russ there, who I now dub Duke of the Duped. And who are you?"

Helen introduced herself.

"And what brings you here tonight, Helen? What's your pleasure?"

"I need some confusion."

Nestor beamed his approval. "Helen, Countess of Confusion. Someone get this woman a drink."

———— •• ————

Carl and Ellie had joined the party, and Helen was catching up with them on some mutual acquaintances they had through Carl's sister, Pam.

"You know, I almost took Pam up on a gig she told me about this summer, down around Rensselaer," Helen said. "I could have been a counselor at a 'nutritional camp.' That's what they call the fat farm these days, 'nutritional camp.' Fat farm to me."

Carmela came over, having heard this part of the conversation.

"Fat farm," she chimed in. "That's a good one—'fat farm.' I like the sound of that."

When the topic turned to Ellie's pregnancy, Helen offered the services of a friend of hers with the recommendation, "She's a super midwife."

Ellie laughed. "Super Midwife? I hope she shows up in a spandex suit and a cape."

Carmela wondered what powers she would have.

"She can boil water just by looking at it, and has an endless supply of clean sheets," Russell said.

Carl shook his head. "Why the boiling water and clean sheets? You always hear that in childbirth. What is that?"

"It gives the men something to do and keeps them out of the way," Helen told him, then licked the salted rim of her margarita glass.

"How nineteenth century," Carl commented.

"Those things help prevent the 'blood poisoning,' too. That was big back then."

Carmela thought this was a hoot. She was keen on nineteenth-century ailments and remedies. She daintily brought the back of her hand to her forehead and made as if to faint.

"I am overcome with the vapors," she melodramatically moaned.

"Looks more like the grippe to me," Russell said.

Ellie shook her head. "I'm afraid it's the consumption," she gravely diagnosed.

"Bleed her with leeches," Carl demanded.

"No, no," Helen insisted. "A tincture of laudanum."

"I'll be happy just to get rid of these rickets," Ellie complained.

"Yeah," said her husband. "This scurvy is killing me."

Russell clutched his chest and cried, "Apoplexy!" and collapsed in Helen's lap. She fanned his face and offered her glass of spirits to his lips.

"Since we're in the nineteenth century," she said to Carmela, "you've got a little piece of local history in your backyard, up there at the old widow's farm. I remember when I was nine or ten, me and my little friends decided we were going to have a séance out there one night. So we start doing what we thought people did at séances, and I don't know—the wind blew or something and I just freaked. I'd ridden my bike out there, but I didn't even think about getting on it—I just ran and ran, all the way home, clear across town. It was that kind of scared like only a kid can get, you know?"

Carmela listened to her, sighed, and told about her disappointment over the land being turned into a housing development.

"You've got to talk with Goot Elmberger," Helen said.

Carmela snorted a little laugh at the suggestion. "Who or what is Goot Elmberger?"

"My parents are friends with his parents. They're old-school bohemian types, named him Gautama, you know, after the Buddha? Anyway, he goes by Goot and he's real active in historic preservation in the area. Started a group called PIP—People Involved in Preservation. I'll get you his number. You definitely want him on the case."

Manny came over, whispered something to Carmela, and they left the room. Helen asked for directions to the bathroom and went off to it.

"Are you done in here?" Manny asked Carmela, standing in the doorway of her sewing room.

"I don't know. Why?"

"Well, there's no lock on this door, and with the lights on it's like an invitation for someone to steal your stuff. You've got lots of money wrapped up in these projects, you know."

To avoid an argument, she put up her hands and said, "OK, let's turn off the lights and close the door, and if you see anyone walking off with stacks of linen, you stop them."

She went back to the living room. He turned off the light and shut the door. Then, considering the special nature of the expensive ballasts he'd installed for her, he got some duct tape to cover the light switch so no casual passerby could turn the lights back on. Helen came by and saw what he was doing. He looked at her, smiled, thought for a moment to explain himself, then decided not to and walked away.

———————

Neil Zook drove wordlessly. He was laconic and expressionless, a demeanor befitting a man in the company of the flamboyantly effusive Lydia Perigrue. She was louder than usual tonight, matching pitch with their drunken and shirtless backcountry companion, Todd McManus, who was sprawled in the rear seat, worn out by his own blue streak of gibberish.

"Where's the party, baby?" she said, tossing a cigarette out the window and lighting another. "I thought we were going to a party."

"Yeah, where's the party, baby?" Todd slurred.

Neil said nothing, just drove straight ahead, then slowed down and entered the parking lot of the municipal golf course. He turned off his lights and drove onto the fairway, going from hole to hole. A night watchman came after them on foot, trying to steady his flashlight on the license plate. Neil turned the car around and switched the lights on bright, and absently steered straight at him. The guard stood his ground until it was clear the car wasn't going to stop. He scrambled out of the way as it roared past. Neil skidded down a slope, spun a donut on the lush green turf, and sped away.

Lydia and Todd burst into the party whooping and hollering.

"OK, we're here—the party can start," she shouted, then went straight over to accost someone she recognized from somewhere. Neil disappeared into the crowd. Todd nosed out the keg and filled a cup. He walked around the house and ended up in the kitchen, where he noticed Carmela's paintings on the cabinets. It intrigued his drunken eyes enough that he pulled a chair over to stand on in order to better appreciate it. Manny came right over. Todd noticed him and said, "Hey, you know whose house this is?"

"Yeah," Manny replied. "Mine."

"Oh, hey, cool. You do this?" Todd pointed to the artwork.

"My wife did."

"It's really cool. Lots of detail." He resumed his examination of the cabinets.

Manny stared at him. "Maybe you can get off the chair now. Did you just wander in here or what?"

"I came with Lydia," he said.

"I see. Well, the cups aren't free."

Todd returned the chair to the table, took off one of his cowboy boots, and fished around in it. He pulled out a two-dollar bill and handed it over, then staggered back into the crowd while putting his boot back on.

Lydia made her way over to Russell, Helen, Carl, and Ellie. She approached them, saying, "Hey, it's you guys."

Their conversation interrupted, they all turned to her. She latched on to Ellie.

"I remember you. You and Carmela were always together. But God, I can't remember your name."

"Ellie."

Lydia gulped her drink, smiled and blinked. "Ellie. How silly of me. How are you, girl?"

Giving her a sideways look and a coy grin, Ellie said, "Fine, Lydia, fine. What are you up to?"

"Oh, you know. Rock and roll and whatnot."

Nestor called out, "Hey, Lydia."

She turned around. "Hey yourself. I'm mad at you."

He cocked his head. "Why?"

"The last time I saw you, you said I should wear a fruit hat."

"Well, what's wrong with that?" Nestor shrugged. "Not everyone can pull off that Chiquita Banana Chick look."

"Well, the way you said it was mean," she said, draining her glass.

"Oh, I didn't mean to be mean. Really. I mean it. You'd look good in one of those."

She huffed.

"Tell you what," he said, "I'll get one and wear it first."

"It'd suit you better." She turned around and pointed at Carl and Russell. "I remember you guys. You're—"

"Carl."

"Right. And—don't tell me—Rodney? Ruben? Something like that."

"Russell."

"I knew it started with an *R*. See? I remember." She gave his shoulder a little swat. "You always look so serious."

Before he could reply, she turned to Helen and asked, "You know these guys?"

Helen put her arm around Russell. "Yeah, Russ and I are old friends."

"We're all old friends!" Lydia shouted, then raised her empty glass to her lips and stared into it.

"God, I need another."

After Lydia walked away, Helen asked, "Who was that mooncalf?"

Ellie rolled her eyes. "Lydia Perigrue. Part of Carmela's fan base."

Helen tugged Russell's sleeve.

"It's all rock and roll and whatnot, Ruben," she said to him.

Luis had decided to join the party. He walked through the house, loosening his tie and looking for someone he knew. It wasn't long until he came across Carmela.

"Hey, sis," he greeted her.

"Well, hey there. I thought you weren't coming tonight."

"Oh, I wrapped it up early. Figured the world wouldn't come to an end if I left some work on my desk till Monday."

They went to the kitchen, and Carmela mixed him his favorite, a gin and tonic.

"Have you seen Cheryl?" he asked. "I went by her place and she wasn't there. We'd talked about coming, so I figured maybe she'd be here."

Carmela handed him his drink. "They were in the living room last I knew."

"They?"

"Yeah, she showed up with Nestor."

He went to the living room but didn't see them. He did see Manny, and joined him and his friends from work. As they stood chatting, the windows started to rattle, then the walls began to shake. Manny stormed through the house, shouting, "Hold tight everyone. Someone's where they're not supposed to be."

He raced downstairs, where Todd McManus's scrawny frame was being tossed around by The Wiggler.

"Hey, this is great!" he shouted above the din of the contraption.

Manny ripped the cord out of the wall. "How'd you get down here?"

Todd slumped against the big rubber belt and pointed to the top of the stairs. "That door up there."

"What? Did you pick the lock?"

"Didn't have to. It was open." He stepped off The Wiggler and nodded toward the shelves. "I think that cat over there is dying or something."

Manny went over to check on the cat, who gave him a malevolent look and growled. Carmela came down the stairs, drink in hand.

"Someone found The Wiggler, eh? We could charge for rides."

Manny called her over to look at the cat. She put her drink down and started frantically waving her hands.

"Oh my God—she's having her kittens!"

She ran upstairs. The first people she saw were Russell and Helen, who had come to see what the fuss was about.

"You know anything about cats giving birth?" Carmela asked Helen.

Flummoxed by the odd question, Helen simply answered, "Sí."

Carmela grabbed her arm and took her downstairs. Russell followed. They went over to the cat, who was purring very loudly. Carmela began to pet her.

"She probably doesn't want to be touched now," Helen said. "She needs her space. She can do this on her own."

"Oh dear," Carmela fretted. "Where's Super Midwife when you need her?"

"It's OK," Helen reassured her. "Cats have been doing this for umpteen million years. We'll just watch and make sure they don't get tangled up or anything."

Carmela was stressing out. Helen watched her pace and fidget, then suggested a task.

"One thing she'll need is a safe, warm place where she can feel protected. A big box with a towel or something."

"A box. Right. I'll go get a box."

Russell and Helen stood together, looking at the cat. Then they looked at each other.

"Having fun?" he asked her.

"This is kind of cool," she answered. "Could you go make me another margarita?"

He was glad to. He retrieved her glass from the living room and told Carl and Ellie about the cat. Carmela carried a large box through the kitchen as Russell was refreshing the drink.

"Woman on a mission," Todd commented with a leer.

Russell brushed past him and followed her down the stairs. She put the box on the floor and started wringing her hands. Russell handed Helen her drink. The cat gave birth to the first of six kittens. Carmela squealed at the sight. Helen asked her for some rubber gloves, which she ran to get.

Helen watched her go off. "She's a little high strung, isn't she?"

"She can get like that sometimes."

"I'm glad you asked me here." She sipped her drink. "I'm having a good time."

He was happy to hear that. "I'm glad you're glad. I've been thinking about you a lot, and I've been wanting to see you."

"Yeah?"

"Yeah."

"Well, it's good to be with you," she said, leaning her body into his a little.

———————— ◆ ————————

Luis had finished his second drink and was thinking he might have another, just to be sociable. He'd only really come here to hook up with Cheryl, but she had apparently taken off. He thought he might hang around for a while longer, then go over to her place, but more importantly he had to piss something bad. The bathroom seemed perpetually occupied, so he decided he'd take advantage of the darkness out back. He started to unzip his pants as he walked around the far side of the garage and was startled to come across two people rolling in the grass.

"Oh, I'm sorry," he stammered, embarrassed. Then he realized his brother was getting it on with his girlfriend.

"What the fuck!" he erupted.

Nestor sprang up. Cheryl fell back on the grass and emitted a low, piteous moan.

"Take it easy, brother. Keep calm," Nestor said, keeping plenty of distance.

"Tell me to calm down? I don't care if you are my brother. I don't care if you are a lunatic. I'm going to kick the living shit out of you."

Nestor hesitated just a moment, then turned and ran.

"Get back here!"

Luis chased his brother to the horseshoe pits, where he picked up a shoe and hurled it with murderous intent. It whizzed past a stunned Nestor, who cringed when he saw him pick up another.

"Whoa, brother. Whoa, whoa."

"Don't whoa-whoa me," he bellowed and flung the shoe. It whacked the side of the house with a horrible thud. Manny stomped down the stairs, demanding to know what was going on.

"I'm going to kill his punk ass!" Luis grabbed another horseshoe. Nestor ran to the front of the house. Manny tried to hold Luis back, but he broke free and ran after Nestor, who was scrambling to take cover behind a tree. Luis let the shoe fly and it shattered the reflecting ball. Cheryl ran to her car. She started the engine and turned on her lights. Nestor sprinted over and dove in the open passenger door. They peeled out. Luis stood paralyzed in a posture of rage, his veins bulging on tensed muscles. Manny came over to him, arms raised.

"OK. OK. It's over."

Luis marched to his car, groping in his pocket for his keys, which he dropped. Manny approached him.

"Don't do anything stupid," he said.

"Too late!" Luis screamed. He scooped up his keys and roared off down the road, leaving Manny and assorted guests standing around, not knowing what to say or do.

A pickup truck stopped in front of the house. Victor Van Donkersloop got out, closed the door, and leaned back in through the window to say a few words to the driver. The truck drove off. He walked up the driveway, looked at everyone standing around, looked at the shattered glass ball, and then turned to Manny.

"Did I miss something?" he asked.

"Just attempted fratricide," Carl quipped.

Manny made sure everyone knew Victor was in the house. Victor wasn't too comfortable with that and tried to tone him down. But Manny was slightly drunk, more than slightly freaked out by his brothers-in-law, and overjoyed to see his old buddy. It had been a long time since Victor had been back on leave.

"How long's it been? Two years? Three? More than that? Last I knew you were in Okinawa or someplace."

"Japan. Yeah. Hey, if I'd known you were having a party, I would've come some other time."

Manny was dumbfounded. "What? Why? Since when don't you like parties?"

"Well no, it's just—" Victor started, then waved a hand and began again. "I had to hitch into town. My car's out of gas. The gauge doesn't work. I thought I could make it. You know."

"Oh, OK." Manny tried to think of the best way he could help. "You could use my car, but I've got to stay here. Things have been going crazy."

"Yeah. Looks like it."

Helen and Russell were leaning against a wall. She whispered in his ear, "Who's the guy with the alien cranium? Some sort of celebrity in your circle?"

He was tickled by her phrenological description of Victor, whose skull was decidedly outsized, a feature accentuated by his military crew cut.

"Victor Van Donkersloop," he said, and laughed once he said it. So did she. "He went off to the Navy, and no one's seen him in a long time."

Russell caught his eye, and Victor walked over.

"Didn't think I'd run into you," Victor said.

They stood apart and gave each other the looks that old friends give when they meet after many years. Russell introduced Helen. Carl came over and offered to take Victor to his car.

"You're driving?" Victor asked.

"Sure, I even have a gas can. Let's do it. Who's coming with?"

Helen had her arm loosely around Russell's waist. They shrugged in unison.

"Yeah, OK, let's go."

Through scores of revelers they made their way to Carl's car.

"So, where are we going?" Carl asked as he unlocked the doors. Victor took a moment to get his bearings, then pointed over his shoulder. "East?"

"You don't know?"

"No, I know I'm east of town, but I'm turned around down here. Is that east?"

"Close enough. We'll get some gas, then you can tell me where to go."

"Milepost 18," Victor said, getting in the car.

"Right. Milepost 18. East of town. We'll get there."

As they drove away, Carl shook his fist at the rock pile in the corner of the yard.

"One of these days I'm coming out here and tear that apart rock by rock, and then there won't be any damned pile of rocks there anymore, ever again. Ha ha!" He went off on his little tirade, then excused himself. "Something about it—I don't know what—just every time I see it I want to destroy it."

They got gas in the car and in the spare can, then Victor led them to where he thought his car was. His vague sense of direction got even more confused when Carl pulled out his hash pipe.

"Can you smoke?" Carl asked as Victor took the pipe and sucked down a bowlful. "I mean, don't they piss test you all the time, especially after leave?"

Victor waved off the question as he exhaled.

"You are on leave, right? You didn't get kicked out or anything, did you?"

"It doesn't matter. I'm here for a few days; we can talk about it later."

He passed the pipe back to Carl, who offered it to the backseat passengers. Russell didn't know if Helen would approve, but she accepted it, saying, "Just what the doctor ordered."

As they made their joking way through the night, Helen told them about seeing Manny taping over the light switch.

"Is that the sort of thing he's known to do?"

"Doesn't surprise me," Carl said.

"What was going on when I showed up?" Victor asked. Carl told what he had witnessed of the blowup and speculated that the fallout would not be good.

"I know I wouldn't want to be on Luis's shit-list. That dude's intense, you know? And he's built like a truck. And that temper? Holey moley—forget about it."

They managed to find Victor's vehicle, a rusty old Renault Le Car out on a dark stretch of country highway.

"This is what you're driving?" Carl laughed.

"Runs OK. When it's got gas in it, that is." Victor got out and proceeded to fill the tank.

"Ooh," Helen softly moaned as she leaned her head out the window. Russell was concerned.

"What is it? Are you OK?"

She pointed to thin wisps of fog fingering the trees of the dark quiet woods. They all looked.

"Ooh."

———————

By the time they returned Manny had already called the cops on his own party in order to roust Lydia Perigrue and her ilk, the hangers-on who would not leave. It was one thing to have her on the floor of the porch offering all takers the opportunity to slurp rum out of her navel; it was quite another to have someone vomit on her. The place was a shambles.

He picked up the last of the broken glass and put it in a bag with other trash. Carmela's lack of concern about her brothers disturbed him. He expected her to be trying to intervene somehow, but she didn't seem to care at all. In fact, she seemed to be dismissing it as trivial. It was fine by him to avoid involvement in this sort of family drama, but he wouldn't mind at least an apology for the broken ball. A replacement would be nice, too, but his hopes for that were slim. He carried the bag to the back of the house and slipped on the soaked grass. The horseshoe pits were a muddy mire. He groaned, put the bag in the garbage can, and stepped across the spongy lawn to turn off the water.

Ellie was glad to see them come back, hoping she could now go home and get some sleep. She'd spent too much of this night half-listening to Carmela go on about baby shower this and midwife that. It took too much energy to pretend to be interested in the opinions of a woman from whom she was feeling more and more distanced. She was waiting for Carl to pick up on the fact that she was ready to go, but he was oblivious as usual. Victor sat down beside her. She hadn't greeted him earlier, so she smiled and leaned toward him.

"How are ya, sailor?"

"Pretty good," he casually replied, and took a long drink from a bottle of beer.

Manny came into the room shaking his head. "Some fool left the hose running. Whole side of the house is flooded. What's a guy to do?" he rhetorically asked while he slid into his favorite chair.

"How long you in town for?" Ellie asked Victor.

"A few days."

"You staying with your mom?"

"She doesn't know I'm coming."

Manny sat up. "She doesn't know? Well, stay here tonight. You can give her a call tomorrow." Carmela came back from checking on the cat and her kittens.

"Victor's staying here tonight," Manny told his wife.

She stopped short, then yawned and said, "OK. You and Russ can work out who gets the guest room."

"This couch is fine," Victor said, stretching out. "Feels real good, actually."

"How are the kittens?" Helen asked Carmela.

"Oh, it's just so sweet to see," she cooed, then put her hand on Helen's shoulder. "And thanks. I knew it was going to happen any day, and I should have had everything ready. I'm glad you had a level head."

Helen looked at Russell. "You think my head is level?"

He shrugged noncommittally. "It's pretty roundish."

"Would you drive me home?" she asked. "I think you're less impaired than I am at this particular moment."

He wasn't so sure about that, but was delighted to chauffeur her anywhere she wanted to go. They all bid Helen goodnight and cautioned Russell to drive carefully. She handed him the keys to her old Volvo. It occurred to him then that he'd have to find a way back. But he'd figure something out. He was wide awake, energized by the evening's events. That bike he'd ditched wasn't too far from her place. He'd find it if he could, and if he couldn't, he'd walk. Right now he just wanted to make sure she got safely home.

"Pump it a couple of times," she advised him before he turned the key in the ignition. He did so, and it fired up. She clasped his shoulder.

"Right the first time. It can be tricky."

He backed out of the driveway and started toward her place.

"Take the long way," she said. "Go around the lake. It's pretty when it's so dark."

They accordingly circled the lake, still and black in the quiet night.

"I like your friends," she told him. "They make me laugh. God, I need to laugh. Make me laugh. Tell me a joke."

Put on the spot, his brain temporarily froze, then mercifully a joke came to mind.

"A priest, a rabbi, and a minister walk into a bar, and the bartender says, 'What is this, some kind of joke?'"

Her laughter gained him access to other jokes he didn't even know he had committed to memory. He had a thousand of them and told her one after another as she giddily guided his driving on a roundabout route back to her place.

"Come in," she said, her voice heavy from laughing.

They entered from the side door. She switched on a light in the living room, then went to the kitchen and returned with two snifters of brandy. She took a sip and leaned her forehead on his.

"Keep me laughing," she said, and kissed him.

When he opened his eyes she looked deeply into them. He thought to say, "Hey, you know, you've been drinking and smoking and all, so maybe there's some rule being broken here."

She took his glass from his hand and put it on the table.

"I make the rules," she let him know.

11

Russell awoke with eyes blinking, trying to make sense of his strange surroundings. He slowly faded into the reality of Helen's place. Sunlight streamed through thin cream curtains and played on the soft lemon wash of her walls. A bumblebee bumped against the screen. The sound of a distant lawnmower drifted on the summer-scented breeze. His clothes lay in a heap on the floor. He sat up and put them on. They smelled like last night's party. He splashed some water on his face in the bathroom, then went to the kitchen. She was sipping coffee and reading the paper in a tank top and boxer shorts. Her hair was wet. She smiled and gave him a look that he couldn't interpret.

"Well there you are," she said.

"Here I am."

"Would you like to take a shower? I'll put on a fresh pot of coffee."

In the shower he was confronted with a bewildering array of bath products: a dozen bottles of shampoo and conditioner in various formulas and fragrances, soaps of all sizes and colors and scents, oatmeal exfoliant, royal jelly cold cream, cucumber moisturizing lotion. It was a bit much.

He dried off with a thick towel and looked at his clothes. He hated to dress in dirty clothing. The socks in particular were off-putting. But there was no choice, so he put them back on. He ran his hand through his hair, then slapped his face to help wake up. He'd really like to go back to Carmela and Manny's to sleep a lot longer, but he didn't know what Helen expected of him now.

She was making pancakes when he returned to the kitchen. She smiled that smile again and handed him a cup of coffee. He wasn't particularly hungry, but it was nice of her to make breakfast, so he ate some of her pancakes and drank her weak but bitter coffee. Things were different between them, but he couldn't make out how.

"Have any plans for today?" she asked.

He couldn't come up with any and knew he'd be spending some time with her.

"Well, you can come run some errands with me if you'd like. Those errands need their exercise, you know."

The first stop was her post-office box, which was full.

"I should have checked this days ago," she said, sifting through the envelopes. "Oh well. OK. Here's something I need to make sure happens first thing tomorrow." She checked her watch and stuffed her mail in a large canvas bag, saying, "Let's go see if Larry's sober enough to take this in."

He hung his arm out the open window as they cruised through town. Church bells chimed down quiet streets in neighborhoods where lifetimes of Sundays were lived. He was a little hung over and a little confused, moving in unfamiliar territory. Spending time with her was always kind of strange, but until now it had never felt awkward. Sometimes she could be exhausting, especially when she was in one of her hyper moods. She seemed intent on running around today. He settled back as comfortably as he could on the cracked upholstery, wishing he had his sunglasses, but glad that she wasn't making him ride on that scooter of hers. She'd stopped riding it for a while, after having to push-start it one too many times. They pulled up in front of a small house in the deep shade of huge trees and overgrown bushes. She turned to him.

"Why don't you stay here? This guy's a real trip. He's been my parents' handyman forever. He's usually too far gone to be of any real use, but they love hardship cases."

She got out and went up to the porch. Then he lost sight of her behind the wild shrubbery. He waited a long time and began to wonder what he was doing here. If he was good at anything it was going along for the ride, but he hadn't expected things to take this particular turn. She walked down the stairs, running her hand through her hair. He sat up as she approached. Once in the car, she tilted the rear-view mirror and looked at herself, messing with her hair some more. She pumped the accelerator and cranked the motor.

"I don't know why that man is still alive," she said, nodding back toward Larry's house. "I swear the human body can take a lot. I mean, I've known him all my life and I've never seen him when he wasn't drunk or on his way there. He used to be functional, but now for all intents and purposes he's dead already. He's just too stupid to know it."

She was always dishing on people he didn't know. Meeting Myrtle had been a rare glimpse into her world, a place apparently populated with a weird assortment of people. Apart from her family, there were acquaintances and friends, some of whom she spoke about almost reverently, others she was mystified by. Still another class of characters seemed to exist only to vex her. He usually liked listening to her stories, although he found them hard to follow her when she went on and on, as she often did.

They parked in front of a nondescript white house surrounded by tall brown grass. She knocked on the door. There was no answer, so she returned to the car and leaned in his window.

"Can you hand me a pen and my notepad from the glove compartment, my dear?"

He did and she kissed him, then ran back to the house. He watched her go and sighed. Things were different all right. Almost surreal, in fact. Maybe sometime today she'd tell him that last night was a dreadful mistake and they must forget all about it. That would clarify things. Maybe they should forget all about it, even to the point of never mentioning it. He'd just like to know what she wanted from him now.

She squeezed his knee before starting the car. "I like you, Russ. You're easy to be with. Usually I'd be doing this alone, and I mostly prefer being alone. I don't usually want someone around for long, but you're a good companion."

She had told him many times before that she liked his company, but he heard it in a new way. The tone she used, the looks she gave, were all different somehow.

"Let's head out to the County Home," she suggested, heading that way. "Jim's the maintenance man out there now. If Larry's too far gone, Jim'll cover for him."

They went to the County Home, a stately campus of old brick buildings. She had spoken to him often about the years she lived here when her father was the director. Although Russell had passed by countless times, this was the first time he'd been on the grounds.

"I don't see his car. I seriously doubt if he's here today. I'll have to give him a call later. But I like coming out here anyway." She drove to what she identified as the director's house, her childhood home.

"Bernie and Twila run the show now." She looked at him and turned off the car.

"Bernie and Twila?"

"Yeah. Want to see if they'll let us take a look? It's a great old house."

A large woman with a sagging, tired face answered the door. Helen greeted her and introduced Russell.

"We were driving by and thought we'd visit with Jim, but it doesn't look like he's here."

"No, but he'll be in tomorrow first thing. He's painting over in the south wing. We had some water damage there a while back. That roof never has been right since they built it."

"Well, I wonder if I could ask you something. You see, Russ is just in town for a little while, and I've told him a lot about this place. Could I show him around real quick, if it wouldn't put you out too much?"

She waved them in, then placed her hand on the small of her back and slowly led them through the entryway.

"Bernie's at mass," she told them. "I got hip problems these days, dear. I'm not doing so good. I was just listening to the radio, that program where people call in to advertise stuff they have to sell. I'm keeping my ears open for a new refrigerator for Molly. Her old one's on the fritz. So, you show him whatever you want. I've got to sit down."

Left on their own, they went wandering through the place. It was a charming house built in an era of gracious spaces. The design provided rooms for a private residence, public areas for entertaining, and a business office. She took him upstairs to her old room, now empty and covered with a thin layer of dust. Downstairs she walked through the office to the library, where they looked at a wall of photographs of people who had run the place over the years. There was a sepia print of the director of the original orphanage, a man wearing a high collar and sporting severe muttonchops. They walked the length of the wall, looking at the faces of people who had worked here when it was a tuberculosis sanitarium and an insane asylum before it became the home of those with no other means.

"From loony bin to poorhouse," as Helen put it, pointing to a photo of a building under construction. "That's the south wing there, with the crummy roof. It was built as a separate ward for opium addicts. Apparently there were quite a few junkies at the turn of the century. I've seen lots of old ads for cures, some involving cocaine. Nice, eh?"

"It probably worked for a while," he mused, "until they needed to build the cocaine ward."

"No, by then the cocaine ward was the jail. What used to be thought of as a spiritual or moral weakness became a criminal offense. That's a big cultural shift, and a recent one."

He thought about that as he looked at another set of faces staring out from a bygone world.

"You can't look like that anymore," he observed, pointing at the photo of a young doctor and wife in the twenties. "I mean, I could cut my hair like that and put on the clothes, and you could, too, but we'd look like we were posing, because we would be. It wouldn't look the same at all—there's something that gives it away. I don't know what it is. It's the context of the times, or something. I mean, the look in their eyes—they're seeing things in a different context than we are. And that shows."

She stood beside him and looked at the photo. The woman wore her hair in a bob and had a come-hither look in her eyes.

"I've been thinking of cutting my hair," she told him, running her hand through her curly blonde locks. "What do you think?"

He didn't know what to say. He really liked the way she looked right now, but she'd look good with short hair, too. To say so, however, might imply that she could improve her looks, an implication he did not want to make. To have no opinion, though, might imply indifference; and he wanted her to know he was not in the slightest way indifferent to her appearance. He attempted to skate around her question by saying, "You can do whatever you want with your hair and you'll always look good."

She didn't like that response and pressed him. "Yes, but what's your opinion?"

He was wise enough to rely on honesty when all other options had been tried. "I've only ever seen you with your hair like this." He brushed the back of his hand against her hair, then took a step back. "What length are you talking?"

"Short, to show off my ears." She pulled her hair back and showed them off.

"Well, that would be a big change. If you want a big change, go do it."

They stood together for a silent moment, then the grandfather clock in the hallway chimed twelve noon.

"Let's go." She nodded toward the door. "If we're here when Bernie gets back, we'll be stuck all afternoon."

On the way out she went to speak to Twila while he stood in the entranceway. She came back and hooked her arm in his while they walked to the car. Another car pulled onto the campus as they drove out. Helen waved to the other driver, who didn't acknowledge her.

"That was Bernie," she said. "We got out just in time." She high-fived him and shook her head. "I was talking with Twila there, and, boy, is she in bad shape. She used to be a nurse, and that's what gets me. I know a lot of nurses who have atrocious habits—poor diet, smoking, pill popping." She shook her head again and wagged a scolding finger at him. "You'd think they'd know better."

He shrugged. Whenever she went off like this, he didn't know what response, if any, she was looking for. Why should he care if Twila's poor habits had caught up with her? What could it possibly mean to him?

They drove across the summer landscape on a country road somewhere way out of town. She said she had things to do, and she seemed to know where she was going. He didn't really care, now that he was committed to spending the day with her. He felt like a foreigner being taken on a tour by a strange woman who was trying to show him what life was like here. She stopped the car on the side of the road by a weathered brick building.

"Check it out," she said, getting out of the car.

They walked through the abandoned one-room schoolhouse. It had been gutted by vandals and nested in by vermin. Shards of broken slate lay scattered on the floor, among debris blown in through the shattered windows.

She stood by the door and swept her hand along the horizon. "See any houses?"

There was nothing to be seen but plowed fields, meadows, and woodlands.

"This is pretty much what it used to look like back when this place was built. This is probably centrally located to the old farms that used to be here. Imagine kids trudging for miles to get here. People had what you call character back then. Had to."

She put her hand on one of the worn walls. "It's touching to think about these people making a go of it here, building this sturdy place for their children to get an education." Her eyes surveyed the deserted interior. "I'm surprised no one's plowed this under yet."

On the way back to the car he recoiled at the sight of a snake darting through the dry grass.

"What's the matter?" she teased him. "Don't tell me you're afraid of a little garter snake."

He shook his head and walked toward her car.

"But snakes are our friends. If it wasn't for them, we'd be up to our eyeballs in bugs and rodents."

"Oh, I know," he said, a little exasperated at having to have this conversation. "I appreciate their role in the ecosystem and all, but I just don't want to get near one."

"I used to catch them all the time when I was a kid. It's good sport." She punched his arm. "Come on, let's find one and cure you of that phobia."

He denied having a phobia and waved her off. "Go on alone, serpent lady."

They got back to the car and she drove to a small town consisting of two blocks of shops, a church, and a granary. They parked in front of a pale pink stucco building with a large sign that read, "Sanitary Lunch" in bold sans-serif lettering.

"Ever been here?" she asked.

"I have no idea where we are," he replied.

She took the keys out of the ignition and opened her door. "You grew up around here, right?"

"Yeah, but there are all these little places I don't know anything about."

"Well, welcome to the Sanitary Lunch, where they make potato chips to order. Let's get some to go."

A bald man in an apron sat at a table, reading the paper and smoking a cigarette. A woman sat with him, leafing through a magazine. He looked up when they came in, put out his cigarette and stepped behind the counter. He wiped his hands on his apron and asked them what they wanted. She ordered a pound of chips, which the man set to frying.

Russell checked out the place. He guessed it dated from the thirties and hadn't changed much since then. The walls wore a faded Depression-era green. A dusty blackboard listed the sandwiches offered. The chrome surround on the counter was dented and tarnished in places. In a corner there were shelves stocked with basic dry goods, candy, and tobacco. She paid for the chips, and he bought a couple of sodas.

"Oh, man, these are so good," she said, crunching a hot handful before starting the car. He agreed they were delicious. They snacked on chips and soda while speculating on the history of the Sanitary Lunch and how it managed to remain in business.

The afternoon rolled by while they drove through township after township all over the county. He didn't know what errands she'd had in mind before, but she seemed to have forgotten them and was just out for a drive. The fact that he didn't have anything better to do was slightly distressing. This whole summer he'd just been along for one ride or another, and he couldn't see that any of it amounted to much. Once again he felt like he'd embarked on a pointless trip and was utterly unable to discern any good direction to take. Now there was the complication of his having gotten maybe too involved here with her. Would she expect him to spend days with her like this, running phantom errands and sightseeing while listening to tales of people whose lives he knew nothing about?

They were on a country road, crossing gentle hills marked with rural residences. She turned at an intersection, and they drove through a wooded area on a route that followed a stream to a small lake surrounded by handsome little houses.

"Don't tell me," she said. "You've never been here."

Of course he hadn't. As they slowly cruised along, she told him about where they were.

"These are the Stonybrook Model Residences. I have a whole history back home about this. They were built by this utopian dreamer-type in the twenties who wanted to build affordable, nice homes in country settings. He placed all sorts of demands on the team of architects he hired. Like, all the homes had to have equal amounts of land, no fences of any kind allowed, and no trees could be cut down or moved. A whole bunch of rules. So these guys got to work to outdo each other with the budget they had, and they built some wonderful, clever houses."

She slowed down to admire the view of the lake and the homes nestled around it.

"I mean, just look at it—the wide-open yards, the huge old trees, pretty little cottages—picture perfect. His plan was that this would be a model, and once everyone saw how great it was he'd build little communities like this all over the place. Of course, then the stock market crashed and he was ruined. But he got these lovely homes built."

She parked the car in front of one such lovely home that was for sale.

"My parents own this now," she told him, getting out of the car. "But they're putting it up for sale. They bought it cheap ages ago and have been renting it out to a woman who got too old to live alone anymore. I've been trying to tell them they should keep it. It's in great shape, and they could really hike the rent, but it's too far out of town for them now. They want to have all their properties in the city limits."

She led him up to the porch, where she took hold of a large lock hanging on the front door.

"I know the combination," she said with a sly look as she unlocked it. They went inside.

He stepped into a space that emanated warmth. Soft light through mahogany windows fell on smooth walls and rich oak floors. The place was filled with an essence of serene livability. It was not particularly large, but it felt spacious. She drew his attention to nice details like the filigreed copper heat registers, the built-in shelves and ornamental woodwork.

"These walls are solid," she said, tapping one. "I love old plaster lathe construction. You can just feel it's built to last."

She took him upstairs and opened the door to a small room with walls painted a dusky lavender. It was a plain space, common enough, but when he stepped inside there was something about it that prompted him to proclaim, "Oh, wow, déjà vu—I know this room."

She whipped around, eyes wide. "That's weird. That's really weird. The first time I walked in here I went, 'whoa, I've been here before.'"

They looked at each other, separated by a rectangular patch of yellow light on the floor. He stepped toward her and kissed her. She leaned against a wall and they kissed until they were interrupted by a loud rapping on the front door that rang through the empty house.

"I shouldn't have parked in front."

She sighed, then went downstairs. He lingered for a moment in this simple room, made strange by their strange connection.

She was talking to a man interested in buying the property, explaining that she was the owner's daughter. They walked to the kitchen, where there were flyers about the house and business cards of the realtor. She then proceeded to give him a tour, going over some of the same things she'd talked to Russell about.

"Are you sure you're not the realtor?" he asked. "You know enough about the place you should be."

"Oh, no," she shook her head. "No, I don't think so."

After he left she took another walk around and spoke in a wistful tone. "I'd love to be able to buy this place, or even just rent it from my parents. I can just see myself living here. But they're set on selling it."

The sun was below the horizon as they drove away, turning the sky the colors of a ripe peach. This model enclave made Russell think of another, odder group of dwellings. He tried to describe Viking's Hollow to her.

She shook her head. "There's no such place."

"Really, there is," he protested. "It's out by Stillwater."

"Where do you think we are now?"

He shrugged. It turned out they were near Stillwater. He tried to remember the general direction they had taken that night, but it was dark then, as it was now, and no landmarks were familiar to him. They drove all over, but never did find it.

Back at her place, they sat on the porch eating tuna sandwiches and the last of the potato chips, washed down with some of the leftover champagne from one of the half-empty bottles she always seemed to have in her refrigerator. They talked above the crickets and watched fireflies. He swatted a mosquito.

"That's the first one tonight. There aren't too many out, are there?"

"There usually aren't too many here. They're real thick down at the lake, but they don't seem to like my place too much. I don't have any evidence for it, but I think the wildflowers help keep them down. Maybe just because I never have to water."

He listened to her go on about mosquitoes and wildflowers and thought about the evolution of their friendship. From a chance meeting at a party to a summer of hanging out, then the crazy time at Carmela and Manny's wedding, followed by a long period of silence, and now another summer with a twist. Upon reflection, he realized that he was now about the age she was when they met. What changes six years had brought. And here they were at the end of another day, another drop of life finding its random but inevitable course to the ocean of experience.

She poked him in the ribs and whispered, "Here she comes."

He looked in the direction she indicated and saw a tall woman with short hair and a prominent nose approaching with long, loping strides. When she got near the porch, Helen raised her hand slightly and gave a small wave. At this the woman took off in a trot down the dark street. Helen shook her head.

"I see her from time to time, and whenever I acknowledge her she runs away like that. I call her Sally. I don't know if you can see it, but I think there's something of the giraffe about her."

She smoothed her hair and he was moved to say, "You have beautiful hands."

Responding with a sideways look, she sipped her semi-flat champagne.

"So, Russ, what are you doing here?"

He reeled a bit at the thought of answering such a question. Leave it to her to ask it.

"I don't know what the hell I'm doing," he told her quite frankly. "I've been messing around for a couple of months now. Like today, it's been a lot of fun, but I don't know where it fits in with the grand scheme I had, because I've lost sight of what it is I set out to do in the first place. So I'm just hanging, and that makes me antsy. But I don't really feel like moving on, either." At this point he threw up his hands and proclaimed, "So, basically, I'm trying to figure out what I'm doing here."

Her phone rang. She turned to look in the window, then dismissed it with a shrug.

"Let it ring," she said.

They sat wordlessly while freight cars rumbled by on the tracks, then she turned to him.

"Would you know what you're looking for if you came across it?"

"Well, that's just it," he said excitedly. "I don't even know what it is I'm looking for, let alone how to recognize it."

She gave him a skeptical look. "Really? I find that hard to believe. Come on. What were you looking for when you quit everything and came up here? Name it."

He closed his eyes and took a deep breath. "A story. I want to have a good story to tell, something more than just becoming a cook and working in a restaurant. A real story, a bigger one."

She nodded contemplatively. "I think your story is all around you," she said. "You just have to begin telling it."

12

"Come on, come on, don't play games with me," Guy growled, grinding his teeth and drumming the steering wheel. He was grimier, smellier, and more on edge than he'd ever been. Since Lester's revelation last week he hadn't gotten any sleep at all, or if he had it had been fitful, punctuated by his startling awake and grasping for his gun. He was just about at his wit's end now, waiting at a parking lot in Michigan City for Gary to show up so they could finally unload this cursed hash and he could get the hell out of Dodge.

Gary spooked Guy by approaching from the rear, and in doing so brought upon himself a barrage of abuse.

"This scene is too tense to be cute," Guy snarled through his clenched yellow teeth.

"Man, you look like shit," Gary said, sliding onto the bench seat beside him. He waved his hand in front of his nose. "Phew, get this heap moving. It's funky in here."

Grousing to himself, Guy got the rattling heap of a station wagon going and headed toward Door Prairie.

"Where are you going?" Gary asked.

"Bloodstone. Where do you think?"

"Why are you going out there? We're supposed to be in Cicero in an hour."

Guy turned to him, his bloodshot eyes filled with barely contained fury. "Well I've been waiting for you here in goddamn Michigan City for over an hour already. You think I'm going to drive around with that stuff for a minute longer than I have to? I don't think you fully understand, dude, but this is serious. Serious, serious, serious."

"Oh, I know it's serious all right." Gary shook his head, an expression of weary resignation on his face. "Now, when are you going to admit how really serious it is? When are you going to see this just isn't working anymore, Guy?"

"Spare me the sermon. We have a job to do."

"Yeah, and we're doing it, but you're going to hear what I have to say about it."

Guy held up his hand and flapped his fingers in Gary's face. "Talk to the hand, talk to the hand," he sneered.

"Come on, Guy. I don't have to do this, you know. I could walk away right now. But I'm not going to, because you're my oldest friend. We've been through a hell of a lot together. I'm helping you out this one last time, but I wouldn't be a friend to you if I didn't tell you it's time to stop. You can't keep on doing this kind of thing and get away with it forever. You've had a real good run, but you're heading for a dead end."

"After today you won't have to worry about me, man."

Gary gave a little snort of derisive laughter. "Oh, I'm not going to be worrying about you at all. But you better start worrying about yourself."

"Well then leave me to it, all right? And leave me alone."

Guy drove on the dirt path by Bloodstone and parked the car in the woods. They trudged to the sinkhole, Gary complaining along the way that Guy's paranoia was making them late and possibly blowing the deal. Guy responded by telling Gary to blow him. They got to the hole and Guy woke the sleeping Steves by beaming them with sizable stones.

"Just what is wrong with you idiots? You're supposed to be guarding the place, and you're here getting your beauty sleep? What if I was one of the dudes who's looking for us? I sure wouldn't be chucking rocks at you."

What little patience he had was stretched way too thin. The frazzled Steves quickly procured the remaining seven blocks of hash that had not been packaged into smaller units. Gary stopped them as they climbed out of the pit.

"Whoa, what's this? How many you got there? Why seven?"

Guy looked at him as though he were a complete stranger. "Because we're unloading the shit." He jabbed a finger at Gary's sternum. "That's why you're here."

Gary batted the finger away. "Well, the deal I set up is for five kilos."

"We've got to unload all this, pronto," Guy hissed, waving frantically at the goods.

"Well, you should have told me, 'cause last I knew, the deal was for five, so that's all they're bringing money for. You want to give them seven for the price of five, I'm sure they'll take it."

Guy brusquely gestured the Steves back down. "Fuck it—go stash two of them and be quick about it."

The old station wagon roared through the darkening countryside toward the Illinois state line. Gary grew impatient with Guy's erratic route.

"You want to get there on time, stop playing John Dillinger on the back roads and get on the highway already."

"We could have been there and back if you had been on time in the first place. Hell, if I knew these guys, I'd have gotten rid of this stuff months ago instead of sitting on it, waiting for you to get it together."

Gary shook his head and let it go, not wanting to continue an inane argument. There was really nothing left to say anyway. It was too bad things had degenerated to this state, but upon reflection he saw that it was inevitable.

He and Guy had been thrown together in childhood, when his family moved to Guy's neighborhood. They formed a friendship that misfits are likely to form when they encounter one another. Gary was the only black kid in the elementary school where Guy and Bob had already been marginalized because of their dubious home life. Bob's retardation and Guy's uncouth behavior pushed them completely out of the mainstream. They ran around with a few other outcasts and quickly formed a little group that kept pretty tight through the transition to middle school.

When Gary was in eighth grade, his father was called to be the pastor of the AME church in Michigan City. After the move they lost touch for years, until they ran into each other at a party on the beach. That was the summer between Gary's sophomore and junior years of high school. Guy had long since dropped out of school and had set up shop above the Red Rooster Inn with his scraggly band of petty, opportunistic criminals. Gary was in a phase of adolescent rebellion, and reveled in the lurid doings of his old friend. In order to ingratiate himself into the scene, he cultivated underworld connections to set up deals bigger than Guy could concoct. Thus he became the big shot of the gang, Guy's right-hand man.

He had his fun with it for years, living a secret, dangerous life behind his good-student, preacher's-son facade. He gradually learned that wasn't a facade, though, and the fun he was having with Guy was really a farce. He grew into the realization that he wanted to be respectable, to find a way to use his talents for a good cause. For years now his lingering affection for Guy had kept him from making a clean break. Guy had been his only friend through many lonely childhood years, and it was painful for Gary to see him heading for certain ruin. But with this one last deal, he'd send him off and turn his back on him for good. He'd grown up, after all, and it was clear that Guy wasn't about to.

They prowled the seedy streets of Cicero, among dreary rows of houses and businesses shut behind steel gates. They were looking for a warehouse that Gary had an address for, but they were unfamiliar with the city. It wasn't the kind of neighborhood where Guy was going to ask for directions, so he drove around systematically, block by block, until he chanced upon the street. They searched awhile before they found the place, a dreary brick building with soot-covered windows by some railroad tracks.

Guy parked across the street. Gary got out, and one of the Steves handed him the backpack filled with the goods. He walked to the first door he saw and found it locked. He looked back at the car and shrugged, then walked to the rear of the building and disappeared inside it.

There was dead silence in the car, except for Guy's incessant drumming on the steering wheel. They waited a seeming eternity, Guy getting more fidgety with each passing second. He didn't like that it was taking so long.

"You go in, you get the money, you give them the stuff, you get the hell out," he muttered. "It doesn't need to take this long."

He wasn't feeling good at all. His bloodshot eyes darted about, looking for clues to confirm or dispel his suspicions.

"Something's not right here," he told the Steves. "Keep your eyes open."

A flash lit up a dark window on the second floor, accompanied by a muffled pop.

"Oh shit!" Guy exclaimed, then fumbled for the gun he'd stashed under his seat.

"Duck!" he yelled, and they all went down as a car flew out from the far side of the building. It sped past, screeched around the corner and was gone.

Guy's whole body was trembling as he sat frozen in a sickening moment of confusion. He raised his head and peeked out the window. The street was dark and empty. He sat there, at a loss for what to do, when Gary came limping out of the building. He leaned against the wall, then collapsed to the sidewalk. Guy got out and ran over to him.

Gary's eyes were rolling around, and he was squeezing his right thigh, where blood had soaked his pants. He vomited when Guy tried to lift him up. Guy got behind him, grabbed under his arms and dragged him across the street. One of the Steves opened the rear door, then they hauled him into the back of the wagon. Guy took off his shirt and ripped it to fashion tourniquets that he tied on and above the wound.

"They shot me," Gary said, grabbing Guy's arm. "They fucking shot me in the leg. They took the stuff and one of them comes over and shoots me in the leg."

He started pounding the back of the seat, grimacing, wailing, and going into shock. With a prolonged moan of "Oh no," Guy stepped on the gas and drove blindly, hoping to find a hospital or a sign to one. He pulled up to the first person he saw, an old man carrying a bag of groceries on a residential street.

"Where's the hospital?" Guy demanded. The man stopped and just stared at them. Guy screamed again. "The nearest hospital—how do I get there? My friend's been shot!"

The man put his groceries down and came over to the car. "My house is on the next block. You sit tight and I'll go call an ambulance."

"No—there's no time for that. Just tell me how to get there."

He leaned in and saw Gary, who was semiconscious.

"You go straight up here till it becomes one-way. Then turn right, then left at the next stop sign. Turn right, that's the only way you can turn there. You'll get on Ogden in ten blocks or so. Keep going towards the city. You'll see the signs two or three miles on. You'll see it."

Guy took off, only half-understanding the directions. He blasted through stop signs, went the wrong way down a busy arterial, and narrowly avoided two head-on collisions before finding Ogden. He sped along, missed the exit, and backtracked to the hospital. He found the emergency room and parked the car up on the sidewalk. He ordered the Steves to stay put, then got out and dragged Gary inside.

"This man's been shot!" he shouted to the first uniformed person he saw.

"Calm down, calm down," the orderly said, then signaled for someone to come help. They got Gary on a gurney.

"How long ago did this happen?"

"I don't know. Ten minutes. Fifteen. Twenty."

They examined the leg. "Missed the artery. Small caliber. No exit wound. He's going to need surgery."

He was rolled away, and Guy was left standing there. A woman with a clipboard approached him and asked for Gary's name, then his. He lied both times.

"What's your relationship to him?" she asked.

"I'm a friend of his," Guy answered, his beady eyes shifting in this brightly lit space.

"What happened?"

"We were out walking and got jumped."

She wrote this down, cast him an appraising look, and said, "Sit down over here. We have procedures to follow for gunshot wounds."

He moved slowly over to the waiting area she indicated, then bolted down the hallway.

"Stop him!" she shouted.

Guy ran into the parking lot, chased by a security guard. He darted among the cars, crouched in the posture of a scurrying rat, and doubled back to the station wagon. The Steves had fled, leaving the rear doors open. He threw it in gear and tore off down the sidewalk, the rear doors flapping wildly as he squealed away. In a daze he somehow got to the freeway and headed back to Door Prairie, the only place he could think to go, his dark way lighted by the flares of the steel mills.

13

Friday was a day Carl always looked forward to, but he was more keen on this one than usual. Russell, Victor, and Manny were all getting together for a night out. He hadn't been out at all lately and couldn't remember the last time the four of them had been together. It must have been sometime before Russell had left town, before Manny got married and Victor shipped out.

It was going to be good to loosen up. He'd been devoting himself solely to getting along with Ellie, to trying to make things as good as they could be between them. For the most part his efforts were meeting with success. At least they had worked out a peace of sorts; both of them resigned to the fact that they were going to face parenthood together.

At first he'd resisted taking Manny up on the offer to go out tonight, but Ellie encouraged him to go. She was feeling the need for some time alone, and told him to have fun and not to worry about her. So he left work as soon as he could and made his way to Dick's Bar in Door Prairie, where they were all to meet.

As he approached the bar, he noticed Victor's car, with Victor and Russell sitting in it. He parked and walked over to them. They were involved in a conversation, which they terminated when they saw him coming.

"Hey," he greeted them, leaning into the car. "What are you doing out here?"

"Oh, hi," Russell said. "We didn't see Manny's car, so we were just waiting."

Carl smirked. "What? You need him to go in?"

"Well, no, but—" Victor started, then shrugged. "We were just talking."

"Come on," Carl said, gesturing toward the door. "Let's go talk inside and get a drink. I know I can use one."

When they entered, they saw Manny sitting at the bar having a drink with someone. He acknowledged them with a slight nod and continued talking to his friend. They found an empty booth and sat down.

"You were waiting for him, but he apparently wasn't waiting for you," Carl said, craning his neck to survey the scene. "Maybe he'll even join us."

He ordered a pitcher of beer for them all, and a shot of bourbon for himself.

"How you guys been? It's good to see you—Vic, you especially, 'cause Russ here's been around awhile. You having a good furlough or whatever you call it?"

"Yeah, yeah. Real good. It's all good, " he said. The pitcher arrived and Victor filled their glasses.

"Well, all right then." Carl raised his glass of whiskey to them.

Manny finished his drink at the bar and patted his friend on the back. He took a dollar out of his wallet and waved it to catch the eye of the bartender, signaling that he wanted a pickled egg from a jar on the counter. The bartender told him to help himself, which he did, slurping it down on his way to his friends.

"Hey, you finally decided to show up."

He sat next to Carl, across from Russell and Victor. Carl regarded the remains of the egg.

"Ugh. You eat those things?"

"What? They're good."

He swallowed the last of it and slapped Carl on the shoulder. "What's up, man? Glad you could make it. It's been awhile, huh, since the four of us hung out together like this?"

When the waitress walked by, Carl ordered another round. He checked her out as she walked away, sighed, then turned his attention to Russell.

"Hey, I saw you and Helen were getting pretty friendly at that party. What's up there, you and her?"

"Oh," he started, somewhat at a loss. "Yeah, we've been hanging out a lot together since I came back. A whole lot lately. I've always liked her, but I never thought we'd be sleeping together. I do really like her, but it's strange. When I'm with her for a long time she sort of drives me nuts—sometimes she talks nonstop and just loses me, and all I can hear is this long string of words that stops making sense. After a while I just want to get away from her. Then, after I'm away awhile, I start wanting to see her again. Like today, I knew she was going to be working, and all I wanted to do was go hang out with her."

Carl raised an eyebrow, gave half a smile and shook his head. "Well, isn't that sweet!"

"I don't know what it is. It's something, though. Whatever it is, it's weird. She's weird. The whole thing is weird."

Carl laughed. "Well, that's the name of the game when it comes to women, ain't it? Hell, live it up—I would if I were you. Helen's pretty damn hot. I saw her at that party. Ouch!"

Russell shot him a look and snorted. "Hey, Ellie's pretty damn hot, too, you know."

"Oh, I know, I know," Carl chuckled. "That's all well and good. We've just been together so long."

"You make that sound like a bad thing," Russell said.

"Oh, it's not bad, but—" he gestured to Manny. "You know how it is."

Manny shrugged. "Maybe, but Carmela's all I can handle. Maybe more than I can handle." He refilled his half-empty glass and continued. "I just wish she'd get off this 'save the widow's farm' kick. I'm hoping it'll be like some of her other obsessions—that she'll just burn out on it. Because this project's a big deal, and if she scuttles it and they find out at work that it was her, I'm screwed big time."

Carl nodded sympathetically and asked, "How'd that all play out with Nestor and Luis?"

"Nestor's vanished," Manny replied, snapping his fingers. "Him and that Cheryl both—poof—off the face of the earth. No one's seen or heard from them since that night. And Luis, poor guy, he's going down in a gin-fueled tailspin. It's all pretty gross."

"Family," Carl began. "Ain't it swell? You marry her, you get all of them. Me and her folks, we started out on the wrong foot and it's been all fumbles since. They were waiting for her to get rid of me for years, and now that we're married, well, let's just say they're less than thrilled. They're always looking at me like they're taking notes on what a failure I am so they can point it out to her later. You know?" He downed another shot and coughed. "Of course, then she's stuck with my family. But they love her, and she really digs them, too. She'd feel different if she was raised by them, I can tell you that."

They could all go on about their messed-up families, and frequently had when they were younger. But they hadn't talked in so long that they all paused and steered their own courses around the topic. They drank silently during the lull. Manny turned to Victor and ventured a question.

"Just what is up with you, Vic? You've been in and out, here and there—I've been seeing a lot of you but we haven't really talked. What's going on? No one hears from you for years, now you show up and you won't say why. What gives?"

"Yeah," Carl chimed in. "What gives?"

Victor looked at Russell, who gave him a weakly encouraging smile.

"Well, I left the Navy."

Manny looked at him askance. "What do you mean, you left the Navy? You don't just leave the Navy."

"You mean you got an early discharge?" Carl suggested.

"No, I just left."

Manny leaned in and whispered, "You mean, AWOL?"

"That's what they call it, yeah. Or maybe it's technically desertion."

Carl smiled. "Isn't that, like, a federal offense or something?"

"Oh yeah. Big time."

Manny took a gulp of beer, wiped his mouth with the back of his hand, and said, "OK, start over here. Take it from the top now."

Victor proceeded to tell the story he'd earlier related to Russell.

"Well, my first assignment was in the office that issues IDs. Pretty soon I figured out there were these guys making fakes for their friends so they could get into bars. So, I started making them on the side, too."

"Wait a minute," Manny interrupted. "You were making fake military IDs?"

"Uh-huh."

"Oh Jesus."

"I know. Well, they got busted. I got busted. Somehow I managed to convince them not to throw me in the brig. Had to cop to alcohol and drug addiction as part of a plea. So they demoted me as low as I could get and had me going to these AA and NA meetings every week with all these losers. Miserable. They had me on paint detail. You know what it's like to paint a Destroyer? You're swinging on a little wooden seat on the side of this massive ship for twelve, fourteen hours a day. Gray paint. Fourteen hours a day of gray paint on this little swing. Day in, day out, no end in sight. Christ almighty."

He picked up his glass and drained it, then filled it from the last of the pitcher. Manny lit a cigarette and waited for him to continue.

"So, one day they bring me inside. There's a sealed compartment deep in the interior that needs to get painted with this special spray paint. I had to get into this suit, right, like a space suit, with this long air hose, because I had to go down this real narrow compartment and coat everything with this heavy-duty, toxic paint. This stuff's got skulls and crossbones all over it, and they hand it to me and tell me to get in there and start spraying. So I go to the far end and start spraying, working my way back, and I don't know what happened—a kink in the hose, or it got wrapped around something or what—but all of a sudden I lost my air. I couldn't breathe and I panicked. And here I have this high-power spray gun loaded with this deadly paint, and I'm just thrashing around and trying to find my way back, and the paint's going everywhere and I can't see and I can't breathe and I swear to God I thought I was dead. I don't know how, but I stumbled out of there and ripped the helmet off that suit and blacked out. When I came to, I saw all these horrible faces, all these ugly guys standing around looking down at me and laughing and telling me how lame I was."

He took a drink and shook his head.

"I decided right then and there: I'm outta here. There's nothing here worth another minute of my life. The next time there was an NA meeting—those are held off base at a church—I was let off for that and I just never went back."

Manny rested his cigarette in an ashtray. "Whoa. This is something. Whoa. Oh, man. Let me wrap my brain around this. Now, they've probably already called your mom, right? Does she know?"

"Yeah, but she told them she hasn't seen or heard from me, that we're not close anymore."

"Oh, that's great," Manny scoffed. "You've got your mom lying to the federal government for you."

"Well, it's not like she's going to rat me out. I don't want to get her involved, so I'm not telling her where I'm going or what I'm going to do, and I'm staying away from her place. She wants me to turn myself in, though. She says they'll probably only give me a dishonorable discharge, just to get rid of me. But what a hassle—seems to me I'm already dishonorably dis-

charged, so why make it official? And they could lock me up. That I definitely do not want to happen. So, I'm moving on. Going to California."

Carl laughed. "Right, because the Navy's never heard of California.
Christ, dude, if you get pulled over for anything at all, you're a goner."

"Victor Van Donkersloop would be a goner. Fortunately, I am Dwight
Richardson." He produced a license from Virginia. "Pleased to meet yas."

It was too much for Manny. He got up and went to throw some darts
and think this over. They followed him.

"I'm not telling Carmela," he told Victor. "And if you're caught with
me, I'm totally ignorant of any of this, OK? As far as I know you're here
on legitimate leave and that's that." He ran his hand through his hair.
"When are you taking off?"

Victor shrugged. "I was just talking that over with Russ this
afternoon."

Manny turned to Russell, his look of concern turning to bafflement.
"You're going with him?"

"I'm thinking about it."

Manny threw his darts. "Oh, God. Well, you can still stay with us
until you figure it out, but be cool around Carmela, all right? I don't want
to mix her up in any of this."

As they stood huddled around the dartboard, they were greeted
with an effusive, "Hey, fellas!"

They turned to see Tim Zataine and his entourage. He was a school-
mate of theirs, whom they had met through Carmela. She had a crush
on him for a long time, until he finally came out to her. They had met a
lot of people through him over the years, notably Lydia Perigrue and her
crowd. But he hadn't been around much lately, occupied as he was now
owning and operating the town's only strip club, The Shake Shack.

"It's been about forever since I've seen you all. How are things with
you guys?"

They chatted a bit while Tim's troupe drank their glasses of wine and
puffed their slim cigarettes.

"Hey," he told them with a conspiratorial look, "we've been having
all-nighters out at the Shack, after hours. We close the place down, and
then things get really wild. So come down there tonight for sure. Just show
up before closing and we'll get you hooked up. Lots of fun—guaranteed
good time."

With that, he and his followers walked out the door. Manny looked around.

"This place is really filling up. You want to go drive around a little, get some fresh air?"

It was agreeable to them all, so they finished their drinks and walked with Manny to the Imp, parked in the alley behind the bar. They piled in, and Manny ripped off down the main drag. He looked at Victor, started to say something, stopped, shook his head and laughed.

"Well, Vic, or Dwight, or whatever the hell you call yourself —you know, I never would have gotten in the jam you're in, so I don't know what to tell you. I guess you're doing what you think is best, but it sure seems crazy to me."

Victor just smiled.

"Let's get some food," Carl said. "I'm starving."

Manny took them to the drive-in, where they all ordered hot dogs. He laughed again as they ate.

"Just look at us, would you? Carl married to Ellie, baby on the way. Me and Carmela and, well, kittens for now. Vic on the lam and Russ— heck, I don't know what Russ is doing, because Russ doesn't know what he's doing. Life. How about it?"

When they had finished eating, Carl asked if any of them wanted to take Tim up on his offer to close down the Shake Shack.

"Oh no, no," Manny shook his head. "No, you guys can if you want, but that's not my scene at all."

Victor and Russell were likewise disinclined, neither of them having much money to blow. Russell, besides, was hoping to talk with Helen tonight about taking off for California.

"I suppose I should be getting home anyway," Carl reluctantly con- cluded, and with that Manny drove back to where their cars were parked.

"All right," Carl said, somewhat miffed at these guys for wanting to cash it in so early. "I guess it's been a night. Take care. Vic, Russ—don't leave without coming out to say goodbye, OK?"

Carl drove off. He didn't know exactly what he'd hoped would hap- pen tonight, but this wasn't it. He was pleasantly inebriated, and he hated the thought of wasting his good buzz by going home. Besides, Ellie had said she wouldn't wait up for him, so he had the whole night ahead of him still. They all used to hang out until dawn, and he was expecting at least a late night. Things had certainly changed, but he wasn't sure exactly how, or what he needed to do in order to meet the mysterious requirements of his new life. He accepted that the circumstances he found himself in were the result of his own choices, yet at the same time everything seemed beyond his control. With a jerk of the wheel he turned around and headed back to town.

Victor and Russell followed Manny's car until they stopped at a red light that he ran. They both quietly contemplated the idea of traveling across the country together. Manny was waiting for them when they arrived.

"OK, not a word about any of this, right? She doesn't need to know."

Carmela was eating popcorn and watching a movie on television.

"Hey, you're back earlier than I thought," she said by way of greeting, then shushed them so she could catch an interesting part of the film. Manny settled in beside her. Victor swatted a gnat that was hovering around him.

"You guys have bugs."

"They came in on you," Carmela told him.

Russell went to the kitchen to call Helen. He got her answering machine, which informed him that there was no room for new messages. He really wanted to see her, or at least talk to her. It was still early for a Friday night in summer, and he was all wound up about Victor and California, so he decided he'd go for a ride and knock on her door if the lights were on. He informed the others that he was leaving.

"You coming back?" Manny asked.

"I don't know. Maybe."

"Well, you've got your key, right?"

He did, and having said his goodnights he got on his bike and rode off.

Not only were her lights on, but the door was open. He was about to knock when he looked through the screen and saw a man with tattooed arms and a long greasy ponytail sitting at her table, gnawing a cigar butt and brooding over a cup of coffee. He saw Russell standing there and called out, "Yeah?"

"Uh," Russell stammered, "is Helen here?"

"Helen!" the man bellowed. "You got company!"

She came around the corner in her bathrobe, rubbing her wet head with a towel.

"Oh, hey there. What is this, party at my place? Someone should've told me. I come back from my jog and Jim here's on the porch. I take a shower and you show up. Guess I'm Miss Popularity."

She draped the towel over a chair and ran her hand through her now short hair. Russell liked the new look, and told her so. She smiled.

"Russ, you've never met my brother Jim. I've talked about him, but here he is in the flesh. Jim, this is my friend Russ."

They greeted one another from across the room, Russell with a little wave and Jim with a nod.

"Hey, Jim, I've told Russ about you some, but now that I have you both together you've got to tell him about the phone booth."

Jim stopped chewing on the cigar and squinted at her.

"What? Why?"

"It's a good story, and Russ loves a good story. And he'd get it, he'd totally get it."

"It's stupid is what it is. I don't want to talk about that."

She touched his shoulder. "Oh, come on."

Jim gave Russell a tired look. "You like hearing stupid stories?"

Russell sat down and said, "Well, now I think I have to."

Jim cleared his throat, looked at his sister, then at Russell.

"It was the stupidest damn thing ever, and it changed my whole life. I was a kid, barely fifteen, and I was totally in love with this girl, Melanie Minnich. Totally crazy about her. Last I knew she was married to a cop in Gary. Go figure."

He scowled and shook his head, then drained his coffee and dropped his cigar in the empty cup. "But I became real obsessed there. And she, you know, she was friendly enough, but I'm sure I creeped her out, and her parents didn't want me hanging around either. So I get the idea that I'll make her feel sorry for me. I'm going to fake a suicide, and then she'll be sorry; and then I can come back from the dead and she'll be so happy she'll marry me or something."

He stopped and shook his head again, a smile struggling across his rough face. "I told you it was stupid, right? So one night I sneak out and go to a phone booth with this pipe bomb I made. I used to make pipe bombs all the time and set them off in fields. Anyway, I call over there to her house and she gets on the phone and I tell her I'm going to kill myself over her. I left the phone dangling so she could hear, then lit the bomb and ran off. Goddamn that sucker blew, too—glass and metal everywhere—bigger than I thought it would be. Could've killed myself for real, or someone else. Needless to say, she never did fall in love with me for that. I got carted away and sent to juvie, and now I'm an ex-con working at the Poor House, right back where I started. No getting away from it."

Helen looked at Russell. Russell looked at Jim. Jim grunted.

"Now, aren't you glad you know?"

While Russell mulled this over, Helen and Jim started talking about someone named Jill and when and where they were getting together with her tomorrow. That plan settled, Helen asked him to make a repair on some work that Larry had botched.

"You have to get Mom and Dad to can that guy, or at least get someone to do the real jobs and let him do the lame ones. I'm sick of covering for him."

"I can't get Mom and Dad to do anything, let alone fire Larry. They've known him since high school; he's like family; blah, blah, blah. Just won't happen."

They griped a little more, then Jim got up to leave.

"So, I'll see you over there around nine," he said to his sister. He turned to Russell and gave a slight nod goodbye.

After he left, she got up, dumped the cigar in the garbage and put the cup in the sink.

"So, what are you up to?" she asked.

He wanted to tell her about the possibility of leaving town with Victor, but this didn't seem like a good time to bring up the subject, so he said, "Nothing, really. Just thought I'd see what you were up to."

"This is pretty much it. I'm about ready to call it a night. We're helping my cousin move tomorrow, it's going to be a big day. It's good to see you, but call me and I'll make sure we can have some more time together."

"I did call. I got your machine, and it was full."

She glanced at the telephone. "Yeah, I should get around to clearing that. But let's get together soon."

She gave him a quick kiss and walked him to the door.

"Hey, do you want to help with the parking gig for the fair? You could make some easy money and maybe catch another good story or two."

"Sure," he accepted.

"Good. We'll talk about it later. Call me."

The door closed and he stood on her dark porch a moment, listening to the crickets in the still night air. He picked up one of the glass paperweights on her windowsill and placed beneath it a piece of paper on which he'd written a few lines for her.

> Your head is like a muskmelon,
> framed by curly tendrils.
> My head is like a can of creamed corn,
> with two protruding knobs.
> And together our shadows roam,
> looking to cut what needs to be pruned.

14

A shot rang out at Bloodstone, cracking through the air and sending Guy scrambling behind the moldy old couch. The spent shell landed in the pit with a dull clink.

"Fish in a barrel," Gary's voice boomed, echoing down the hole. He approached on crutches, flanked by two men in sunglasses carrying large handguns.

"A fish in a barrel," he repeated while Guy peeked out over the edge of the couch.

"Jesus!" he shouted. "Come on. What the hell!"

"That's what I want to know," Gary shouted back. "What the hell! I get shot doing your lame ass a favor, and you just up and bail on me? Tell me what the hell! Tell me why I shouldn't take you out right now."

"I drove you to the hospital, dude. I got you help. What do you want?"

"You took me there and just left. That's how you treat me, leaving me alone in a hospital in fucking Cicero?"

Guy spluttered and then blurted, "What did you want me to do? Stick around and hold your hand so we could all end up in jail?"

Gary took his crutches to the rim of the pit and leaned over. "What do you mean, end up in jail?"

"I've got warrants out; you know that."

"I know you're full of shit, you coward. I woke up in that hospital, hooked up to machines, no one knows who I am or where I'm from. I got cops questioning me, and I got to make up a story, and I don't know where you are or what you told them. Then I had to call my dad, man, and that scene is now whacked. I've got big bills, and you're going to pay them."

Guy slumped and sighed, then reached for a duffel bag. Gary's men aimed their guns at him.

"Cool it," Guy said with his hands up, then kicked the open bag over, knocking out a coffee can filled with money. He tossed it out of the hole.

"Eight grand. It's all I got."

Gary sent one of his bodyguards down into the hole to search, but he didn't find anything else of value.

"I told you, man, that's it."

"Well, hand over the rest of the hash."

"It's gone," Guy lied. "The Steves stole it, and everything else, too."

He had cleared almost everything out of Bloodstone, taking it out to the cabin, which he felt was more secure. There he had already stashed his drugs, crates of cigarettes, a few cartons of booze, a couple of rifles and a shotgun. He was going to hole up there until he could figure out a course of action. It was just the kind of luck he'd had lately to get caught unarmed here now as he was picking up the last of his gear.

Gary squinted and leaned forward on his crutches. "You trying to tell me you let those losers rip you off?"

Guy shrugged. Gary sent the other man to search the car while his partner stayed down in the pit, gun at the ready. He came back empty-handed.

"I'm telling you, they cleaned me out. That coffee can, that's all that's left. Now will you call your goon off? Or else tell him to shoot me and get it over with already."

"I'm not going to put you out of your misery," Gary sneered. "I'm going straight over to the Collector and tell him exactly where to find you—those mob guys can track you down and take care of you. Better start hopping, rabbit—the hounds are coming."

———◆———

Guy was lying in wait in full combat mode, wearing a flack jacket and gripping a high-powered rifle. He had strings tied through the brush all around Bloodstone, each leading to his hiding place. If one moved, he'd know someone was coming and from what direction. No one was going to get the satisfaction of hunting him down—if they were coming for him, he'd give them a surprise and take at least a couple of them out with

him. He'd been popping speed all afternoon, and was itching for something, anything, to happen.

A string moved. Someone was approaching from the east. He ori-
ented himself and crawled on his belly to get into the best position for a
clear shot.

"Guy? Hey, Guy?" a bewildered little voice croaked. "Guy, you out
here?"

It was his brother. He sprang up from his cover, giving Bob a fright.

"Bob? Holy crap, I just about blew your head off."

Bob was more puzzled than usual.

"What? Why? What are you doing?"

Guy ran his hand over his sweaty face. "Oh, Jesus, I can't even tell
you. Why are you here?"

It was then he noticed that Bob had a black eye and swollen cheek.

"What happened to you?" he asked, bending toward him for a better
look.

Bob turned away. "You never came back to fix that window in the
basement, and Dad found it. Then he started yelling about how I shouldn't
let you in the house, and he was drunk."

Guy stood frozen, his mouth half open, eyes glazed. He threw his
arms around him and held tight. Bob began to cry.

"He killed my guinea pigs," he managed to say between sobs. "He
squeezed them and wouldn't let go." He doubled over and held his head
in his hands, then dropped to his knees. Guy grabbed him and pulled
him to his feet.

"Oh, Bob, oh, I'm sorry. I meant to, but I forgot. I'm so sorry."

He embraced his brother, then grabbed his shoulders and shook
him while looking him in the eyes.

"This is it, man. I've got to leave town, and you've got to get out of
there. Come with me. I know some guys who went down to Houston a
while ago. We can go down there and hook up with them maybe. We just
have to go somewhere far away. I set up a bank account in your name, for
when you finally decided to move out. You've got close to twenty thousand in there now. We'll go to the cabin the rest of the weekend, and come
Monday we'll close your account and head out of here."

He hugged him again. "Come on, man. I'll take care of you."

Victor and Russell were sitting on a trestle above some train tracks on the outskirts of town.

"Ever think about plants?" Victor asked. Russell gave a snort of bemused laughter.

"Yeah, all the time."

"There's so many of them," Victor observed, waving his hand at the greenery surrounding them. "The whole earth is covered with them, practically. I mean, just think about grass—how much grass is there in the world? How many individual blades of grass? How many leaves? I tell you, if these plants ever get any ambition, look out."

"Look out how? Like they'd take over the world? Seems to me they have it just the way they want it anyway."

Victor was good for wasting time in meandering conversations like this. They had climbed up the trestle to sit here and wait for a train, as they had done when they were young boys. The trains came less frequently now than they had then. The brick building that used to be a foundry had been long abandoned; doves now nested in the empty windows. They kicked their dangling legs lazily in the humid afternoon.

"You know anyone in California?" Russell asked.

"Nope. You?"

Russell didn't.

"I just always wanted to go there," Victor said. "I figure, if not now, when?"

Russell nodded in affirmation. Something had changed about Victor, beyond just growing a few years older and becoming a fugitive. He had always been a dreamer type, someone prone to impulse and whimsy, but there was a look in his eyes now, as though he were staring at something in the distance that no one else could perceive.

"So, what do you still have cookin' around here?" he asked Russell.

"Well," he began, "I still haven't talked with Helen about it. I've sort of got myself involved there, and I can't just up and split on her without talking about it first—see how she feels and all. She wants me to help out parking cars at the fair in a few days, so I'll bring it up then. That'll make a little money, too."

"Yeah, money's good," Victor opined. "How much do you have, anyway?"

"A thousand, maybe. Something close to it. But, you know Guy Bogel?"

"Kind of."

"Well, he still owes me some more for weighing out this hash for him, but I've been avoiding him for weeks."

Russell then told Victor the story of his involvement with Guy, up to the night Lester told them the jig was up, which was the last night he had spent with them.

"You think he's still around?" Victor asked.

"I have no idea. But we have to go out to his camp at some point, because I've got some stuff there. That is, if they haven't stolen or sold it."

"No time like the present," Victor said. "Come on. Let's go check it out."

They climbed down and drove off. No trains ever did come by.

The sun was beginning to set when they trudged through the weeds around Bloodstone.

"I'm sure he's gone," Russell said as they got near the pit. "We'd know by now if he was out here—we'd get some sort of welcome. He's got it set up that way."

They came to the edge of the hole in the gathering twilight.

"Yeah, he's gone."

Russell led the way down the stairs. He was surprised to find all of his things there, and proceeded to pack them up.

Victor smiled. "What's that they say about honor among thieves?"

"I wouldn't credit these guys too much," Russell replied.

"So, you think they're gone for good?"

Russell reflected a moment. "Probably. I don't know, though. There's a place he took me once that he said was where he'd stay in the winter. Maybe he's gone out there, but I don't know."

Victor pressed him to go, and so they did. Russell had only been out there once, in daylight, and had a hard time locating the trail. They found it, and walked through the silent woods.

With a wild yell, Guy rushed out from the dark trees, shotgun leveled at them. They screamed and reflexively put up their hands, their wide eyes focused on their assailant. Guy halted, scrutinizing Russell with a malevolent squint.

"Christ almighty, you goddamn deserter."

At this, Victor shot Russell a look that he returned with an amplified expression. Guy lowered his firearm and approached Russell.

"You looking to get yourself killed?" He sized Victor up and declared, "Who the hell are you?"

Victor started to recount some encounter they'd had years ago, but Guy cut him off, saying, "I can't remember every punk I ever sold liquor to."

He led them to the cabin. "You're fucking lucky, both of you. I'm not exactly in the mood for unexpected visitors." As they got near, he called out to Bob to relight the lantern. He did, then sat staring blankly into it. Guy opened a bottle of whiskey, took a slug and passed it around. They drank while he told Russell about all that had gone down.

"So, Bob and I are out of here—at least for a while, maybe for good."

Bob intercepted the bottle as Russell was passing it to Guy.

"Since when do you drink?" Guy asked his brother.

"Since now."

He sniffed the bottle, recoiled a little, then took a sip. His eyes bulged and he puckered his cheeks, but managed to swallow. Guy patted him on the back.

"It gets easier the more you do it," he assured him.

They sat quietly by the glow of the small lantern. Cicadas buzzed above the chirping crickets and croaking frogs. Victor glanced at Russell, prompting him to state his business.

"So, wow," he started. "Well, I'm glad I caught up with you before you left. See, you said you'd pay me for weighing that stuff out for you."

Guy looked at him, a weary smile slowly curling his dry lips. He took a drink, put the bottle down and cackled a raspy laugh.

"You want to get paid, huh?" He coughed. "Well, I'm a little short on funds right now, old chap."

His cough became a laugh as he walked into the cabin.

"Here's the stuff you weighed," he said, sorting through the contents of a canvas bag. "I'm keeping all that. I hate bagging." He took out an unweighed block the size of a brick and handed it over. "Take it. The shit's got a hex on it anyway. Spread the bad vibe around, maybe it'll catch up with you before it gets me."

That was worth a lot more money than Russell expected to receive, so he took it with no question. The bottle went round again; then Victor and Russell got up to leave. Guy reached in the bag and tossed Russell a glass vial containing a small pinkish crystal.

"Might as well take this, too. I don't know what it is—it's what Skutch was smoking. I don't need any souvenirs from that dude."

With that, they started to walk away.

"See you in hell, Pinske," were Guy's final words to him.

15

Russell was up at first light, a time of rising he usually avoided if he could. Today he couldn't, because he was going to help Helen with the parking lot she managed for fairgoers. Exactly what he'd be doing wasn't clear, but she wanted him there, and he wanted to see her. He hadn't yet told her that he was considering leaving with Victor, and was hoping to find a good time today to tell her. One detail he'd omit was Victor's trouble with the Navy. It just seemed like something that it would be best to keep quiet about.

It was Saturday. Carmela and Manny were still asleep in their room, and Victor was snoring on the couch. He showered and got ready to go. He wanted coffee but didn't want to make the noise to brew some here. Besides, Helen always had a pot on, even if it usually wasn't the best. She was into greeting the dawn and going jogging and all like that, so she was probably already waiting for him, pumped up and ready to go. He pumped himself up as best he could, got on his bike, and took off around the lake. The calm water was tinged with the lingering colors of sunrise, the cool air fragrant with the bloom of summer. He enjoyed riding through this bright morning, appreciating the pretty town he was soon to leave.

On his way he rode by the free house that no one had laid claim to. The fine, old place had been reduced to a pile of fine, old rubble. He thought about all the people who had lived there over the last hundred years or so: all the children who had played in the yard and climbed the trees; all the visitors who had come to call and had sat on the porch on summer nights, listening to the crickets and greeting the neighbors. Soon no one would even remember the house had ever been there.

He knocked on Helen's door and stood waiting. A woodpecker's percussion accompanied her faintly tinkling chimes. He knocked again. There was a doorbell, but he didn't think it worked. He began to fear she'd already gone, but surely she would have left a note. Before he knocked again, he sensed movement behind the curtains. She opened the door and stood slumped in a bathrobe, droopy-eyed and disheveled.

"Oh, God," she muttered upon seeing him. "Is it that time already?"

She waved him in. He followed, feeling bad for having awakened her, but also confused because the last time they talked she had told him to come over as early as he could make it.

"Guess I'd better wake up," she drawled, and walked toward the bed-room. "I'll go get ready. Why don't you make some coffee?" She shuffled down the hall, tightening the belt of her robe and loudly yawning.

OK, he'd make coffee. That is, he would if he could figure out how to work the contraption she called a coffeemaker. It was sleek and black and modern and completely devoid of any clues as to its proper operation. There was a multitude of buttons tagged with allegedly universal symbols that he, for one, could not decipher. Why a coffeemaker needed more than a place to put the water, the coffee, and a power switch was beyond him; this thing was loaded with dozens of functions, not one of which was clearly labeled for the plain and simple brewing of a pot of coffee. His first impulse was to give up, but he kept jabbing at the buttons long enough to hit the one that got it to do what it was ostensibly designed to do.

He took a deep breath and settled down. This morning was off to a rougher start than he had been prepared for. He reminded himself that he wanted to be here to do this parking lot gig and to find the right time to tell her of his plans.

She walked into the kitchen in a T-shirt and shorts, running her hand through her wet hair. She yawned and moved toward the sink, where she took a pot from the dish drainer and started filling it with water.

"Want some oatmeal?" she asked.

"Sure," he answered, glancing at her, then at the coffeemaker. She fol-lowed his gaze, and her eyes landed on a carton of milk on the counter.

"Did you get that out?" she asked him.

He shook his head no. She put the pot of water down heavily on the stove and sighed.

"Cripes. I left it out last night." She grabbed the milk, gave it a whiff, then sighed again. "Well, we'll have oatmeal and coffee without milk. Great." She put the carton in the sink and shook her head slowly while she stared out the window.

He'd never seen her quite like this before. Sure, she'd been cranky plenty of times, but she was always able to laugh at herself through her crankiness. This morning her mood was severe. Maybe it was just because lately she'd been so flirty and funny with him. She was showing another side, one he wasn't sure how to relate to.

The coffee was done. He walked over, got a cup, and stood next to her, putting his hand lightly on her shoulder.

"You OK?" he asked. She turned to him.

"Yeah. Why?"

"You just seem out of sorts is all."

She scowled and gave a little shrug. "It's nothing. Or, at least, it doesn't have anything to do with you."

"Well, if something's bugging you, you can tell me about it, if you want."

He sipped his coffee. It wasn't bad. She reached for the carafe and poured a cup for herself.

"It's just everything lately," she said, and took a sip. "Whoo—you like it strong, huh?"

She poured a little out and diluted it with water from the tap. "It's just everything," she started, stirring the cereal with a wooden spoon. "Lately it's just everything. There's something seriously wrong somewhere, but I don't know what it is. One thing I know is that I'm sick and tired of working for my parents. It's just been too much for too long, all the stupid little hassles have been piling up. I've been thinking a lot about when I was down at the school in Indianapolis, doing some good work, I thought, helping people become self-sufficient and getting them what they needed to live the lives they wanted to live. Now what am I doing? I'm dealing with one stupid little mess and another stupid little mess, lowlifes skipping out in the middle of the night, a drunken so-called handyman who can't even hang a towel bar." She shook her head and stirred the pot some more, pausing before continuing.

"And for what? For my parents, who don't even care, and who get on me day and night for everything. Myrtle, for instance. She's two months behind on rent. I don't even want to know why. But they want me to give her notice to move out. Christ, you know I'm not her biggest admirer, but frankly I don't give a damn if she pays rent or not. She can just live up there till she dies, for all I care. But they sure care about getting her money. You'd think they were never in charge of the Poor House, the way they act now."

She took the oatmeal off the stove and spooned it into a couple of bowls.

"I'm sorry," she said. "It's just a frustrating time for me. I really want to put my degree to work, get back into something I feel is more in line with what I want to do, start making some money, get a place of my own and not have to rely on them."

She handed him one of the bowls, then fixed her eyes on the soured milk.

"And it's all coming out in things like leaving the milk out. That's not like me at all. But here it is."

She took the offending container and dumped its contents down the drain.

"The thing is," she continued, walking over to the table with her bowl of cereal and mug of coffee, "I don't know how to get out of whatever arrangement I have with them, because it's never been formalized. Not only that, but I don't have anything in sight to do if I did get out. So, I'm just feeling really stuck right now. Guess that's one of the reasons I like you so much—you know what it's like."

She leaned her head on his shoulder. He loved her and wanted to tell her that. Then he remembered he was about to leave town, and her, too. He felt his heart pound. Should he tell her now that he was going away? How could he? Was he even certain he was going to leave? After all, he could do whatever he wanted. But if he stayed here, what good would it do her—or him for that matter? He was all muddled up, which wasn't unusual for him, except that he thought today's agenda was going to be pretty clear—that he'd work with her, tell her about his plans, and they'd come to some resolution. Now things had gone and gotten even more complicated. He stabbed at his gummy porridge and downed a spoonful.

"Not terribly palatable, eh?" she said, looking at him with one eyebrow raised.

He shrugged and swallowed. "It's OK."

"Not the oatmeal," she said. "My problems. It's being heavy, and I don't want to be heavy on you."

"You can be heavy with me, if that's how you feel."

"Well, I don't want to." She took their unfinished portions to the sink and rinsed them clean.

"Let's go," she said, and bent in to kiss him just before he finished his coffee.

———————

"Look at this crap," she proclaimed. They were stopped before a half-completed new duplex. "There was a beautiful old home here, rundown a bit, but it was solid, good craftsmanship. They tore it down for this."

She walked onto the lot and into the structure, waving for him to follow. He looked around, not sure they should be trespassing, but no one seemed to be on the site. They walked up the framed-in stairs and stood on the landing between floors.

"Look at this lousy stuff they call plywood these days," she said, thumping it with disdain. Then she grabbed the supporting struts and jumped up and down and rocked around. The whole building shook and swayed.

"Cheap and shoddy crap!" she yelled. "Just the way we like it now!"

She gave it a final kick, looped her arm in his, and they walked on.

"That reminds me," she said, tapping his hand. "I've got some pamphlets for Carmela from the People Involved in Preservation group. There's a good one on their first project, the old Russian bathhouse in Hammond that they saved. Some developer was going to tear this beautiful, old, historic building down—this thing's just a jewel, with tile mosaics and everything. They were going to raze it and turn it into a parking garage. Goot got on it and found someone to invest in refurbishing it, and they turned it into a high-class health spa. Now people make reservations months in advance to get in there. That's how the whole PIP thing got started. She'll like that."

As they continued on their way, a grizzled man rode up beside them on his elaborately outfitted bicycle, hauling behind him a wheelbarrow filled with scrap metal. Bicycle Bill, as he was known, a man who rode around town collecting all sorts of junk for resale or recycling. He was something of a fixture in the town, but few really knew anything about him. Apparently, though, he knew Helen because he stopped to talk with her.

"Well, what do you say, there; what do you say?" he stuttered in greeting, his face twitching with multiple small spasms.

"Hey, Bill. How's tricks?"

"This guy comes up to me and says, 'Bill, haven't seen you around, thought you was dead.' That's what he says to me, 'thought you was dead.' Now, what kind of thing is that to say to someone, 'I thought you was dead?' Come on now, how do you answer that, 'I thought you was dead?'"

She shrugged. "I guess you just say you're still above ground and kicking."

"That's what I did." He growled a gruff laugh. "That's just what I did. I said to him, 'Sorry to disappoint you. But you're invited to the funeral when the time comes.' That's what I said." He laughed again and cleared his throat. "What a thing to say to a man, 'I thought you was dead.'"

"Well, the best thing you can do is keep living and show 'em all," she encouraged him.

"That's just what I intend to do," he said. "Just what I intend, all right. Tide's coming in." With that he rode off, whistling tunelessly.

Russell pointed at the receding figure of the mysterious man who had been the subject of much speculation among him and his friends throughout their childhood.

"You actually know him?" he asked her.

"Oh, sure," she replied. "He'll talk to anyone who'll listen, tell you his whole story, although it changes a lot. He'll stop and gab whenever he sees me. He's got his own thing going on, you know, been going on a long time, too—he must be pushing seventy. He's got this shack he's homesteaded forever, just north of town. Manages just fine, as far as I can tell. My folks tried to get him into the Poorhouse for years, but he wouldn't hear of it, and they finally gave up. Good for him, I say." She pumped her fist in the air. "Keep on pedaling, Bicycle Bill!"

Some people were milling around on the lot when they got there. A passel of children ran about, chasing each other and squealing. She introduced him to her friends and relatives, and after chatting awhile they started getting things set up, bringing out folding chairs and coolers, and putting out signs. Russell helped one of her cousins put out orange pylons to mark lanes. They opened for business, and cars began to arrive. At a loss for anything to do, Russell wandered over to where Helen was discussing something with someone who was counting money. She greeted him with a little wave and continued talking. He stood around, wondering what there was for him to do. She wrapped up her conversation, then came over to him.

"Hey, looks like we're all good to go here. I have to run into town for a little bit. Tell you what, why don't you hang here and walk around the lot and do basic security stuff. Remind people to lock up, and just keep your eyes open. You should be good for that. I'll be back in a few."

So he was left alone to wander this parking lot. She was right. If he was good at anything, it was walking around and checking things out. He got to it.

The day was warming up quickly, with only a hint of a breeze. He watched a bumblebee crawling on clover and thought about how much of his life he'd spent alone, wandering and daydreaming. His entire childhood seemed like one long summer day, lived with no regard for the future, not beholden to any past. In that timeless space all things actual and potential mingled in a fluid swirl, his dreams as real as the blue of the sky above.

Countless small scenes have played countless times upon this noble land, this dry sea of grass and wind, of sighs and yearning. Countless lives have been lost in the toils and snares of living, their daily problems and chronic worries threshed out of their stories in the end, leaving kernels of joy and grace to be warmly toasted for the ages. But the shifting wind filled with trouble and care stirs the dry grass as long as it's there, world without end.

Time was when parties were held as the chestnut trees came into bloom in the warmth of the spring. These were pretty events, gay and festive, and all manner of niceties were observed. Picnic lunches were enjoyed, and fancy cakes, and great amusement was gained from many merry games. And in the evening the rowboats would go out by lantern light; whispers could be heard across the lake, and laughter, too, across the spreading ripples.

She found him in his reverie in the shade of a broad oak tree.

"Having fun yet?" she asked, and gave him a little punch in the arm.

"So far, so good."

"Sorry I took so long—got tied up in a bunch of stuff and nonsense."

Until she said that, he hadn't been aware that hours had gone by. It was now past noon.

"Feel like going in, see what's going on, get some fair fare?"

It seemed like a fair proposition to him, so they informed the other attendants and walked across the street to the admission gate. He started to get out his wallet, but she motioned him to put it away.

"Hi, Walter," she greeted an elderly man in a seersucker suit and straw hat standing beside a turnstile.

"Well, hello, young lady. Haven't seen you in a long while. Where you been hiding?"

"Oh, here and there, you know, keeping busy."

"Oh sure, sure. And how's your father? Haven't seen him in some time either."

"He's as ornery as ever. You know."

"Well that sounds about right. And your mother?"

"Very well, thank you. They're both getting on very well."

Russell stood by during this exchange of pleasantries, which culminated with their being ushered through without charge.

"Do you, like, know everybody?" he asked her as they entered the midway.

"Oh, not everybody. Just enough to get by."

They walked around among the rides and games and sideshows, and got some sausages that they ate while they wandered the midway. They finished their sandwiches and entered the grange, where they walked past rows of vegetables and preserves, attempts at art and homespun crafts. Russell suggested that they find Carmela and check out the stuff she had for sale. They found the booth. Her friends from the cleaners were there, but Carmela wasn't.

"This sure is nice work," Helen said, looking through a stack of embroidered tablecloths. "I might just have to get something later. We'll see how we do this year."

Back on the outer loop of the midway they passed a dunking tank where a fat clown named Bobo was heckling the crowd and calling out his refrain in a raspy voice: "High and dry! High and dry!"

She stopped and waved at a tall, lanky man walking with a woman and a baby.

"Hey there, Joe Tanner."

She walked briskly over to him, and Russell followed a pace or two behind. The man stopped and looked at her a little apprehensively. The woman took a step back as Helen greeted him effusively.

"Hey, Joe, where you goin' with that stroller in your hands?"

He let out a weak sort of laugh and said, "Hi, Helen. How's it going?" The woman gave them an appraising look and he thought to introduce her. "Helen, you know my wife, Beth?"

And so they were introduced, but Helen didn't think to introduce Russell, who turned his attention to Bobo, now aggressively taunting a group of girls.

"Judy, Judy," Bobo ranted. "Judy with the big booty. You want a piece of me?" He growled, then paused and leaned in close to his microphone. "You want a piece of Bobo the Clown?" He leaned back and droned, "High and dry. High and dry."

The girls talked among themselves in a tight cluster while Bobo continued to needle them.

"Gabby girls, gabby girls; gabby, gabby, gabby girls. Come and get me, gabby girls. I'm high and dry. Step on up, Judy with the booty. Come and get a piece of Bobo. High and dry."

The girls rose to the bait. One put her money down and took aim. Her throw failed to make it even halfway there.

"Ha, you throw like a girl! Gotta have balls to throw one!"

One of her friends took a turn and fast-pitched it, but it went way off the mark.

"Nice try, Butch. Whoo-hoo!"

The next throw winged the target, but not hard enough to dunk him.

"High and dry!" he shouted triumphantly. The girls walked on, and Bobo turned his sights on Joe.

"Hey, family man. Hey, hey, family man. What do you know about steppin' out, family man?"

They all ignored him but Russell, who was removed enough to see Bobo in his cage, Joe and his family and Helen, and behind them all the amusement rides spinning and twirling. The hot air smelled of dirt and animals and fried food.

"Family man don't know nothin' 'bout steppin' out. High and dry."

He heard Helen ask how his home projects were coming along. Again Joe wheezed a halting little laugh and mumbled, "Oh, yeah, yeah—slow but sure, you know."

His wife looked impatient, and the infant started to squirm.

"Well," he said, starting to move on, "good to see you again, Helen."

"You bet. Give my regards to Elzoon."

The couple left and she turned to Russell.

"Nice people," she told him. "I met Joe a few summers ago, when I took that exterminator job I told you about. We gassed a lot of varmints, Joe and I."

They walked on while Bobo's droning jeers faded behind them.

"Who's Elzoon?" Russell thought to ask.

She chuckled. "It's sort of an in-joke with him."

"Oh," he replied.

"You see, he bought this house out in the country," she began, screwing her face in a perplexed expression. "Well, do you have something to write on?"

He did, and handed over pen and paper.

"So, he bought this old fixer-upper way out in the country, and I asked him for his address. He wrote it down for me—it's one of those funky rural routes that reads like map coordinates, you know? Four eight six east twelve hundred north." She wrote it out for him: 486 E 1200 N.

"Well, he just scribbled it real quick on this scrap of paper. Later on I wanted to send him a card when I heard he'd had a kid and all. I found that scrap and couldn't make it out. To me, it looked like '486 ELZOON.' So that's how I addressed it. And I'll be darned if it didn't get to him. So from then on, that's where he lives—Elzoon."

He looked at her with a curious squint. "OK," he said, and took back his writing utensils. "I see."

"We'd better get back to the lot and see what's going on."

So as she directed they did, while the sun slowly set.

———◆———

The lot was more or less full, with people coming and going all over the place. Children scampered and screamed. The lights from the midway grew louder as the twilight deepened. She went off to check in with the others, then came back and hooked her arm to his.

"Well, these guys are going to camp out here and take the night shift till this thing shuts down, so they'll be here first thing when it starts back up. Why don't you and me make ourselves scarce and head on back to my place?"

He liked the sound of that, and they started walking that way in the cool of the evening. Crickets chirped and fireflies flickered. This seemed to him like a good time to discuss his coming departure.

"So, you remember my friend Victor?"

"The guy with the big head? Yeah."

"Right. Well, he's heading out to California and I was thinking about heading out there with him."

She looked at him with a smile slowly spreading across her face, then she gave his arm a tight squeeze. "Good for you," she told him. "I've been wondering how and when you were going to get out of here."

He wasn't sure what sort of reaction he was expecting, but he was pretty sure this wasn't exactly it.

"So, that's OK with you, then?"

"Well, of course. It's what you want, isn't it? Ever since you got to town you've been talking about getting out, so, good for you—you've found your way out."

They reached her porch and stopped there.

"So, we're good, then?" he asked.

"Well, sure we're good. We're more than good." She slipped her key in the lock, then turned and kissed him before opening the door. She walked to the kitchen and pulled out one of her perennial bottles of half-finished champagne. They clinked their glasses in a silent toast to they knew not what.

"Really, I don't want to belittle what we have going on here," she began, "but, it's a summertime thing, right? I mean, I don't think things would have gone the way they've gone between us if it hadn't been for the situation, you know, with you just here for a while before moving on again. Right?"

He supposed that was right, but he wasn't quite as sanguine about their temporariness as she seemed to be.

"We can talk more about it later, if there's anything to talk about," she said, then refreshed her drink. "Let's just enjoy tonight."

They touched their glasses together again.

16

"When did they move out here?" Victor asked Russell as he drove them to Carl and Ellie's in Stillwater.

"Few years ago, I guess. Before they got married. It's a place her parents own, I think. Part of it's a daycare. I've only been there once. Way out in the middle of nowhere. It's OK, if you like that sort of thing."

Victor nodded, a suggestion of a smile on his face.

"Were you at their wedding?"

"No, no one was. Eloped. Happened pretty fast, I guess. I just came out to visit that one day and they told me. Hadn't told anyone else, from what I understand, except their folks."

Victor nodded again. "Yeah, everyone's got their own thing going on now. Not like it used to be, when all we had to do was hang out together."

He had just stated an obvious fact that had eluded Russell's powers of articulation. Things were indeed much different now, and getting ever more strange.

The thick, yellow sky shimmered in the afternoon heat. As the marshy scenery streaked by, Russell contemplated the flimsy vehicle he was riding in. Any collision with anything at all and this thing would crumple like tinfoil, which material, he surmised, it was likely built of. This contraption was to carry him halfway across a rough continent? Was he crazy? He looked at his driver, who himself was certainly half mad.

"So, they're going to have a baby, eh?" Victor asked.

"That's what they say, yeah."

Victor scratched his chin. "First of our little group to spawn. At least, that I know of."

Russell put up his hands. "I haven't spawned anything. Don't intend to, either. You know, Manny and Carmela want to, but it just hasn't happened yet." He turned to Victor, who was squinting in the sunlight. "You want kids?"

He looked thoughtful, biting his lip lightly before he responded.

"I'd like to. Little kid to play with, mess around with. You know, teach it cool things and stuff."

"Yeah, the playin' and the messin' is the fun part. The other ninety-nine percent ain't so much fun, I bet."

"Well, now, you've become a right crusty old sinner, haven't ya?"

Russell shook his head. "I'm just sayin', man, there must be a reason our dads acted the way they did, you know? It cracked their nuts; it'll crack ours, too."

"If we let it."

"I'm not giving it the chance."

Victor smirked. "Well, I'm just keeping myself open to all possibilities."

"You go ahead and do that," Russell said, turning to look out the window. "Let me know how it works out."

———————

"This is the place?" Victor asked, pulling into the driveway.

"Yeah, looks like it."

"Boy, this really is out in the middle of nowhere, isn't it?" He looked up and down the country road, where there were no other houses in sight. "People bring their kids to daycare here? Where from?"

Russell could only shrug. They walked around back, where they saw smoke drifting from the patio.

"Hey guys," Carl greeted them while tending to his grill.

"Hey guys," Ellie repeated in a flirty tone. She was reclining on a lawn chair, wearing sunglasses and sipping lemonade. "Glad you could make it."

"Yeah," Carl grinned, poking at his glowing briquettes. "Good to see yas."

"Quite the homely scene you've got," Victor commented, pulling up a chair.

"Suits us homely folks just fine," Ellie drawled through a crooked smile.

Russell sat next to her. "How's things?" he asked.

"Things are things," she told him.

He accepted this with a nod and looked around. Stray toys were scattered on the lawn. Weeds sprouted from cracks in the concrete. The woods buzzed with insects. A few swallows swept the grass for their supper.

"Hey, hon," Carl called to her, covering the grill and wiping his hands on a towel, "I'm going to take these guys into town to get the steaks, OK? Keep an eye on this, will you? Throw a few coals on it if it seems to be dying out, but I think it'll be fine. We won't be too long."

"Righto," she placidly intoned.

"We'll take my car," Carl said, leading them to the garage. "I don't think that thing of yours can support the three of us."

"Hey, now," Victor objected. "It's a good car. It's friendly. It's weird, like I've bonded with it somehow or something."

"Baraka," Carl stated, nodding his head and repeating, "Baraka."

"You all right?" Russell asked.

"It's when you sense an inanimate object has a personality. Like, something you use all the time, a special tool or a car or something like that. At least, I heard that somewhere along the line. Don't remember where, or what language it comes from."

He started the car and drove out of the garage.

"There's a word for everything," he continued. "In some language or other. No matter what you can think of, there's a word for it."

"You think so?" Russell asked.

"Name something there's not a word for."

Leaving his passengers to puzzle on that, he started down the road and changed the topic entirely.

"Had to kill a cat the other day. Don't tell Ellie. She'll be all upset that I didn't try to save it. There was no saving it. I backed out of the driveway and felt this thump, and there it was, all squashed and mangled. The thing would've just bled out, there was nothing to do for it, so I lined its head up with the tire and backed over it again. Dumped it in the ditch for the crows."

"That's brutal," Victor offered.

Carl nodded. "It's the way of the world, my friends. Should I have just left it to die on its own?" He shrugged. "Maybe. But it seemed like the thing to do at the time. Not that I'm proud of it or anything. I'm just sayin'.

"What's with all this glass back here?" Russell asked.

"Don't even get me started," Carl said, but he had already started and proceeded to tell the tale of the night he spent with Mira and how his car had been broken into.

"The thing is, I haven't seen her since, but she's got my phone number, see? I don't know why I gave it to her, but I did, and so now every time the phone rings I jump a little. But I can't change it, right? That'd be pretty suspicious. What am I going to tell Ellie why I'm changing it? So I'm just hoping Mira never calls, although a couple times I've picked it up and I know someone's there, but it'll just be a long pause, then 'click,' and that's all." He shook his head and muttered, "Shit's fucked up."

He glanced back toward his house, which was now out of sight.

"Hey, about that night we went out? We were all out together till six the next morning, OK? You know how you all cashed it in so early? Well, I took Tim up on his offer to party at the Shake Shack. Oh my God, I've never seen so much blow before. It was a cocaine blizzard, dudes, just the wildest scene I've been at in some time. Perigrue was there, too, and asked about you," he turned to Russell. "Or, at least she asked if 'Rupert' was with me. I assume she meant you. But anyway, she ends up on the stage, writhing around and begging for people to touch her. Lots of people did, too, I tell you. It was just wicked in biblical proportions. And Ellie doesn't need to know anything about it. We were all just out together cruising till dawn."

Russell didn't need to know this, either, and didn't like being enlisted in his friend's deceit. Victor laughed.

"Carl, man, you got a wife and a kid on the way."

"Tell me something I'm not painfully aware of."

"Well, you know, don't you think you should cool it with all this sneaking around?"

Carl looked at him squarely for a moment. "Yeah, yeah. I know, I know. And I'm trying, I'm trying, but I just feel like I'm over my head in all this responsibility all of a sudden. Work, work, work all the time, no end in sight. All the worrying about her, worrying about the baby, worrying about money and everything else. I just feel like I have to blow off some steam sometimes, go crazy deliberately instead of keeping it stuffed down until I go crazy for real. You know, I actually got into a fistfight with my dad about this a couple of weeks ago. Came to actual blows."

The speeding car rattled and bumped when Carl drove squarely over a pothole.

"Damn it!" Carl shouted. "I swear I'm going to bust an axle out here one of these days. Then I'm going to sue. That was a new one, too. I know most of the big ones along here, and that's a new one. The pothole fairy comes out here in the night just to mess with me."

At his friends' urging, he continued telling them about the tussle with his father.

"Should've known better than to go talk to him about anything that matters. I'm over there having a beer with him, you know, and he's pretty well hammered already, and I'm unloading on him about all the responsibilities I suddenly have and how to deal with it all, and he just comes out and says that my life isn't my own anymore, and that I'd better get used to it. And I'm, like, 'When was it ever mine? Guess I missed that part.' And he tells me, 'Don't blame me if you fucked it up.' And I don't know what it was, but it just got to me and I hauled off and smacked him in the jaw. And, oh man, he came down on me like a ton of bricks, the son of a bitch. One hit square in the eye and I went down. He told me to get out, and I did. Should've seen the shiner I had. That was a hoot, going in to work looking like I've been worked over. Haven't talked to him since then, month ago or so, and don't intend to anytime soon, either. The shitty thing is, the fucker's right, though—I just didn't need to hear him say it the way he did."

He directed their attention to the road ahead. "This is the scariest intersection ever. Three roads cross this road up here. All three of them have stop signs, but this one doesn't. And there's this curve coming up, see, so you have to slow down as you approach the intersection, and the other cars see you slowing down, and they think you have a stop sign too, but you don't, and they pull right on out, 'cause they think you're coming to a stop. I've had some close calls out here. Every year someone gets creamed. I've taken to speeding up on the curve and blowing my horn, even if there aren't any other cars in sight. I got the right of way, damn it, and I'm a takin' it!"

He shot through the intersection, horn blaring, with Victor bracing himself and Russell screaming that he was too young to die. They sped along without incident and drove to town on a road along the Kankakee River. Russell relaxed and sat back. Huge willows hunched along the banks, among cattails and sweet flag. Carl was in one of his manic moods today for sure. Sometimes he could be very quiet and withdrawn. Other times he was right in the center of things, regaling anyone and everyone with his stories and observations.

"A few weeks ago I picked up this guy around here, only going the other way." He told them, pointing vaguely at the side of the road. "He's an old dude, wearing suspenders. He's got a beat-up suitcase and he's thumbing a ride. I had to stop, right? So he gets in, and I ask him where he's going, and he asks me where I'm going; so I say Chicago, to go to work; and he doesn't say anything to that, and so I ask him again where he's going, and he says he guesses he'll go to Chicago, too, so OK. We're going along, and then he opens up his suitcase and takes out a tambourine and starts singing Jesus songs. I let him go on for a while, but I can only take so much tambourine, so I told him, you know, 'Jesus is all right with me and all, but cool it, pops.' And he does for a time, then I ask him what he's going to do in Chicago, and he starts back in with the tambourine and the promised land and all, and I told him to can it or get out. Then he starts in real loud, shaking that damn thing like it was on fire, so I pulled over and left him there with his suitcase shouting his hallelujahs and hosannas to the trees. Probably still out there."

Stillwater was a town of small, neat houses on shady streets around a grain elevator next to the train tracks. They drove down the main street, past the post office and library, the hardware and dime store, and pulled into the parking lot of the IGA supermarket. A hint of rain hung in the humid air, the sky pale in the late summer heat. A string of firecrackers popped off in the distance, ringing through the steady hum of cicadas.

"Remember Hobby Rohrman? He's working here now, stocking shelves. I remember watching him get busted at the bar, when I was working there. He was drinking alone and the cops walk in; he gets up, slams his drink, and walks out with them. I looked up the case in the police blotter, 'cause I've always wanted to now what his real name was. I mean, I didn't think it was 'Hobby,' maybe something like Hubert or Hugo or something, but, no, it's really 'Hobby.' Anyway, he was into some small-time hoodlum stuff and got sent away for a couple of years."

"Who names their kid 'Hobby?'" Victor wanted to know.

"Maybe that's what he was to his parents," Russell offered.

"Kid as a hobby, huh?" Carl considered. "That's a thought. My dad could've used a hobby. Other than drinking and whaling on me, that is."

Victor and Carl crossed the parking lot to the store entrance, while Russell lagged behind, allowing a car to pass. A young couple with a baby walked by, and Russell tried to imagine Carl with a child, but he just couldn't. When he rejoined them, they were standing next to a soda machine.

"Hey, check it out. It's a talking Coke machine. I like to mess with it. Here, watch." Carl put a nickel into the coin slot. The machine hummed, then a flat electronic voice came out of a tinny speaker. "Thank you for—" it paused, then continued: "five cents." It paused again, then informed them: "You need to put in more money." Carl laughed. The machine repeated: "You need to put in more money."

"Yeah, yeah," Carl laughed as he walked away and the machine kept repeating its demand for more money. "Ain't technology great? Talking Coke machines. What next?"

They made their way to the door. Russell noticed a littered puddle near a crack in a cinderblock wall where a dragonfly hovered, a flashing iridescence in the leaf-filtered sun. It was something glanced in passing, a perfect little mess, and while he watched, he heard a woman say, "You know, twenty years from now—" but he never heard the rest, as she walked through the door into the store. He went in and was greeted by a blast of conditioned air that rustled the papers on a bulletin board, one of which caught his eye: an advertisement for a lost parrot.

"Oh, guys, I haven't seen you in so long," Carl said, stopping to take a plastic basket that stuck to the others below it so that he had to shake it free. "Talking about the bartending days got me to thinking about his guy, Keith Spellman. Russ, I almost sat down and wrote to you about this dude. He's a real trip. Used to come in pretty regular, usually already loaded by the time he showed up. He'd nurse a few and tell me all this shit about how he's a great studio musician, played on all these albums with all these guys; blah, blah, blah, you know, always telling me how famous he is, and I'm, like, yeah, you're so great and famous you're trashed every night here in freakin' Door Prairie, Indiana, right? That's what you're famous for, pal."

He laughed and proceeded to the produce department.

"So, one night Keith's way too drunk, and it's closing time, and I took his keys from him and told him I'd drive him home in my car, and he'd have to find a way back in the morning. He starts bitching me out, and

I told him he could drive off a cliff as far as I was concerned, but I didn't want him killing anyone else. Eventually he gets in my car and he's giving me directions, taking me way the fuck out west on the lake, way out past Beverly Shores and that area, and he has me pull up to this fucking mansion, right on the water, with these huge windows looking out across the water, the lights of Chicago and all, real cool place and I'm, like, 'What are we doing here?'"

He interrupted himself to direct their attention to a thickset man with long hair, stocking canned goods on a shelf nearby.

"That's Hobby, there. That asshole used to make my life miserable in grade school, junior high. Never actually hit me or anything, there was just this constant threat from him, which is even worse, really." He cracked a smile and said, sotto voce, "Stock them real nice and neat now, boy, real nice and neat."

Picking up the thread of his other story, he continued: "So Keith asks for his keys, and I give them to him, then he gets out and goes up to the door. I yell at him to get back in the car before we get in trouble, but I'll be damned if he didn't unlock it and go right in. I'm sitting there, wondering what the hell, so I got out and went in, too. The place was all decorated with this real sleek furniture, modern art everywhere, and he's walking down a hall to where he has this whole home studio set up, and there are all these gold records on the walls, all these album covers, and I'm just freakin' at this point. Then he picked up a guitar and proceeded to wail on it, playing all these heavy blues riffs, just letting it rip, completely tearing it up. He puts it down after a while and says, 'You didn't fucking believe me, did you?' And I just shook my head, I was totally blown away. Here I thought he was a wannabe, and it turns out he's a has-been."

They got some ears of corn, then went on to the meat aisle, where they lingered over packaged steaks. Carl motioned them to observe a young woman walking by. They shook their heads and rolled their eyes in response.

"What's the matter with you two? If I were single, I'd be all over that."

"You'd be all over it anyway," Russell told him, "if we weren't here to hold you back."

Carl conceded the point with a little grunt of a laugh, and craned his neck to catch a last glimpse of her before she turned the corner.

Having made their selection, they headed to the checkout. They stood in line and read the tabloid headlines to each other while they waited. Carl added a pack of batteries to his order, commenting to the cashier, "Almost forgot I needed these."

"That's the whole idea of putting them there. Sometimes we make you remember to buy things you don't even need."

She smiled and rang up the remainder of his purchases.

"Haven't seen you around here before," he said.

"Well, I guess it's your lucky day," she replied, handing him his change.

"Could be," he began, then was pushed along by his friends.

"Did you see her?" he asked them as they left the store. "Damn. One of you should've followed my lead there." He elbowed Russell. "But I guess you've got your hands full with Helen, eh?"

Russell looked at him curiously and said, "What?"

"Oh, come on. Don't tell me you're not, 'cause I know better."

"Yeah, well, it's complicated," Russell said.

"It always is. It always is."

They passed the vending machine that was still broadcasting its need for coins.

"Get a job!" Carl yelled at it. "One of these days it's going to follow me home," he said as he unloaded his groceries into the rear of his car. They got in and he drove behind the building, slowly prowling past the loading docks. He stopped, got out, and pushed a shopping cart over to the car, putting it right up against his front bumper. He got back in.

"This is one of my favorite sports lately," he said, and slowly pressed on the accelerator, pushing the cart ahead of them. He got up to a good speed, then hit the brakes. The cart took off on its own, then began to shake violently, its wobbly wheels unable to sustain its velocity. In a shower of sparks it tumbled end over end and slid a fair distance before bouncing off a Dumpster with a tremendous crash. Carl sped off, laughing so hard he was crying.

On the road home, he asked, "Hey, remember my cousin Janet, the one who burned off her eyebrows at the dunes that one summer?"

They both knew to whom he was referring.

"Well, she's always had this big lump on her back, like the size of a walnut or so. They said it was a cyst, but she had it looked at a little more and it turns out that it's what's left of what would've been her twin. Freakiest damn thing. Imagine carrying that around. No one had any idea at all. She's wondering if she should get it removed or not, and what to do with it if she does. So now every time I see her I ask about her sister. Get it? 'Cyst-er?' Man, I tell you, you hear all sorts of shit. I've been reading a lot about babies and birthing and all, and there's just so much that can go wrong. So much."

Victor looked at Russell, then at Carl. Carl met his eyes and glanced back at Russell.

"Hoping for a boy or a girl?" Victor asked.

"Yes," Carl deadpanned, then snorted. "Perfect set-up, straight man. Seriously, as long as it's got the right number of limbs and digits and they're all in the right place that's all I care about."

Russell leaned forward. "What about names?"

"Names," Carl said thoughtfully, raising a finger for emphasis. "Names are important. Really. Names have a kind of power, you know, if I'm not being too weird." He acknowledged his passengers. "Seeing as how I'm talking to you two, I'd say not. There's a lot in a name, though, so we can't go about this naming business lightly. Hitler grew up named Schickelgruber until he was adopted. You could say that he'd never have risen to power as Schickelgruber. Can you imagine it? 'Heil Schickelgruber?' There's no way."

Victor raised an eyebrow and scratched his head. "So, you're going to name it 'Hitler?'"

"Yeah," Carl drawled, slowly shifting his gaze over to him. "Yeah, that's what I'm going to do. Actually, it'd probably be popular with a lot of the yokels around here. Had ourselves a good ol' cross burnin' out here not too long ago. I swear, some of the shit that goes on in this goddamn place. I sure wouldn't mind moving to the city, but Ellie won't even hear of it, a dead-end issue." He chuckled, then got back on topic, saying, "But you know all about the power of a name, don't you Vic? Or, I mean, Dwight?"

Victor nodded contemplatively and stared straight ahead. Carl cleared his throat and caught Russell's eyes in the rearview mirror.

"Hey, you still in with Bogel and his guys? The stereo that got swiped from me was one I got from them. Think you can hook me up before you split?"

Russell told him about all that had gone down with Guy and the gang.

"Damn. I'm not about to pay retail, but driving to work without even a radio is just maddening." He thought a moment longer, then asked,

"Hey, so do you have any of that hash you had at the party? That stuff was too good. I could use a little of that, you know."

"Sure," Russell said. "I've got more than I know what to do with. Want some?"

"Well, sure."

"It's in Vic's car. I'll get you some when we get back."

"Well, wait now. What's it going for?"

"Heck, man, I'll give you some. No money between us, come on."

Victor interrupted. "Uh, you know, that stash is going to help bank-roll this little expedition of ours. Anything we can turn into cash is a good thing. In case you haven't noticed, we're not exactly rolling in it here."

Carl spoke up. "Yeah, and, you know, I've got a little weed money to spend."

Russell wouldn't hear of it. "I'm not taking your money."

Victor and Carl looked at one another. Russell looked at both of them and asked, "What?"

"Nothing," Victor said. "It's just—well, it is your stuff."

When they arrived back at Carl's place, Russell removed a cushion from one of the rear seats and broke off a healthy hunk of the dope for his friend.

"Hey, wow," Carl said gratefully. "Thanks. You sure you don't want something for it?"

"You're cooking dinner, right? Come on and feed me."

"Right," Carl said, putting the hash in the glove compartment of his car and picking up the bag of groceries. "And, um, mum's the word to the missus on the contraband combustibles, natch."

—◆—

"Hello, boys," Ellie greeted them upon their return. She was leafing through a magazine and sipping lemonade under a beach umbrella. Carl gave her a kiss and put the bag down.

"I hope the fire's OK," she said. "It seemed to be fine, so I didn't do anything to it."

He took the grill lid off and poked around a bit. "Looks great, hon." He slid the glass door open and walked into the kitchen, calling out to ask if Victor or Russell would like a beer.

"It's OK with you?" Victor asked Ellie.

"What? Oh, God, yes, of course. I don't mind at all. It's not booze I miss, it's caffeine. God, I'd kill for a good cup of coffee."

Russell sat next to her. "You get headaches without coffee?"

"Not anymore. But it's just that I'm dragging a lot lately, especially in the heat, and I really wish I could get a good jolt, you know? Of course, when my mom was having us kids she was drinking and smoking and everything else. They didn't know back then, and still we came out OK for the most part. Now we do know, and we're all still coming out OK for the most part, so who really knows? But I just can't take chances."

The warm day was settling into a lazy evening. The tall grass of the meadow rippled softly in a faint breeze. Wisps of silky cirrus streamed across the soft sky. Smoke from the barbecue wrapped around the patio and drifted off around the house. Carl returned and gave his friends opened bottles of beer, the stuff that Manny's friend brewed. It was welcome refreshment, and Victor and Russell settled in while Carl got busy with the steaks. He slapped them on the grill amid hissing flashes of searing flame.

Ellie swatted a bug with her magazine, then stood up.

"Should I get things put out?" she asked Carl.

"Sure. Just a few more minutes here."

Russell got up to help and followed her to the kitchen. She handed him a bowl of potato salad and a stack of napkins. He took these out to the table and she followed with a bowl of coleslaw and a plate of deviled eggs. Carl served up the grilled steaks and corn, and they began their dinner as the first hues of sunset touched the sky.

"Saw your mom a week ago or so," Ellie told Victor. "She's really worried about you, you know."

Victor stopped eating and looked at her. "Worried?"

"Well, sure she is. I am, too."

"Does she—" Victor began to ask Carl, who laughed and shrugged.

"Yeah, I told her. You know I don't keep anything from her."

At this Russell caught his eye for just a moment before he turned away. Victor sat looking like he was considering what to say, then took a drink.

"Look," he said. "I don't really want anyone to worry about me, 'cause I'm not worried about it. Things'll work out."

Ellie looked at Russell, who smiled at her. She returned the smile weakly, making it clear she was not at all convinced things would work out well. Carl got up to bring back another round of beers, and when he did he found Russell rhapsodizing over his wife's coleslaw.

"Seriously, this is the best coleslaw I've ever had. I don't even like coleslaw so much, but this, this is something beyond coleslaw."

"Hey, hey, steady there, buddy," Carl said, patting him on the back. "It's only cabbage, son."

Russell ate another mouthful and shook his head. "This is no mere cabbage." He went on. "You have to tell me how to make this. This is just too good."

"You can take some with you, if you'd like," she offered, puzzled by his enthusiasm.

"Yeah, that's good, but I still want the recipe."

The phone rang, and Carl fairly leapt out of his chair. Ellie shot him a questioning look.

"Startled me," he apologized. "I'll get it."

Victor asked Ellie about her daycare, and what the plan would be after the birth of their child. Before she could answer, Carl returned with the phone.

"Your sister," he said, handing it to her.

She excused herself and took the phone back inside. Carl sat down, blew some air through puffed cheeks and looked at his friends.

"I just have to find a reason to change our number." He shook his head and took a drink. She returned with the phone to her ear and stood near her plate. She used her free hand to mimic incessant talking, then took a bite of food while she continued to listen to her sister. She propped the phone to her ear with her shoulder, picked up her plate and carried it to the kitchen, finishing her meal as she walked and saying "uh-huh" between bites.

She rejoined them in time, saying to Carl, "Jack's in one of his moods again. Everything's going to hell, blah, blah, blah."

"Yeah, like last time. And then when you try to get involved they close ranks and it's like, 'Who are you coming between us?' That whole scene is truly screwed up."

She sighed, and leaned back in her chair, allowing the cool of the evening to flow over her.

"Hey," Russell addressed her. "You know what? At the grocery store there was a sign for a lost parrot. How do you get a parrot back?"

"Maybe its wings were clipped," Victor suggested.

"Well, then, how did it get away?" Russell wanted to know.

"Maybe they're really fast runners."

Ellie laughed and said, "I heard there's a whole flock of feral parakeets down in Florida. Escaped pets that all hooked up together. That must be a sight."

The sky deepened in the twilight, and the first fireflies appeared, with the cricket chorus beginning in earnest.

"Well, I'm going to go in and take care of a few things," she said, and got up. She walked over to Victor and Russell and gave them both a kiss on the cheek.

"Be safe. And write or call or something."

She went inside.

"Leave the dishes," Carl called after her. "I'll take care of it all later."

———————— • ————————

They sat in the warm night with their cold beers. Carl went to the garage and returned with a pipe full of hash. The smoke filled the patio with its musky fragrance.

"It'll be a while before we all hang out again," Russell observed.

"It's been a long time already," Carl added. "Just a finite number of times we'll get to be together, isn't there? Not like when we were kids and time really seemed infinite, you know?"

"That's kind of morose," Russell said.

"Morose," Carl repeated. "Now, there's a word."

"Yep," Victor concurred. "That'd be your word, right there."

Carl commented on the fireflies. "They're really out in force tonight."

They stared across the field at the sparkling display. Russell leaned in to share some of the arcane knowledge he'd acquired. "They're remarkable creatures, you know. The energy they use to make light is almost all given off as light, with very little heat. Unlike, say, a light bulb, which gives off a lot more heat than light."

"Like a politician," Victor quipped.

"Yeah," Russell paused and looked fondly at his friend. "That's right. But they do it by a chemical reaction, something called 'luciferan' that they extrude in these little tubes inside them."

Carl interrupted him and pulled up closer.

"Say what? What's the name of that stuff?"

"Luciferan," Russell repeated. "They extrude it in these little tubes—"

Carl put up his hand and interrupted him.

"Brilliant," he declared, then withdrew his tape recorder from his pocket. "Oh, that's just brilliant," he said again, then rushed inside.

Victor looked over at Russell, but before he could say anything Carl came bounding back with a tape deck and inserted his cassette of found sounds.

"What's going on?" Victor wanted to know.

"Hang loose, good buddy, all will be revealed. Listen."

After the angry growling of a dog they heard Carmela exclaim, "Oh, I just love topiary!" This was followed by Victor proclaiming, "That'd be your word, right there," and finishing with Russell: "Luciferan. They extrude it in these little tubes."

Carl laughed riotously, his face turned to the sky in the glory of his creation.

"That's your copy, guys, the latest and most up-to-date."

"Oh, gosh, thanks," Victor droned.

"Maybe you should name your kid Luciferan," Russell suggested.

"Yeah, maybe," Carl considered. "Hitler could be his middle name. Got a nice ring to it, but I don't know."

Moths beat around the light, and June bugs crawled on the door screen. A train whistle cut through the stillness.

"Whoa, it's later than I thought," Carl said. "That's the midnight train."

Russell took out his pocket watch, but it had stopped at half past eight.

"Nice old watch," Carl observed.

"Yeah, it's real useful when I can remember to keep it wound," he replied. "Got it from my grandfather. One of the few things I have of his. Besides his genes, I guess."

Victor looked at him skeptically. "You're wearing his jeans?"

Russell shook his head and closed his eyes.

The beers were dry; the bowl was cashed. Carl got up and stretched.

"Well, you guys are welcome to stay if you want, or hit the road, or whatever. I'm going to check in on the little woman."

Victor and Russell stood and embraced him, and with that they said farewell.

17

The season of hedge apples was upon her. They didn't usually start appearing until later, in the fall. Yet here it was, in the heat of August, and they were all over the place. The sight of them was always a little unsettling to Helen—for what reason she couldn't tell. Maybe it was because she never noticed them growing on the bushes, just saw them when they suddenly showed up: wrinkled green fruits the size of softballs, littering the lawns and sidewalks, looking for all the world like alien invaders. The cranefly population was booming, too. She'd been shooing them out of her house every day for over a week now. There was no accounting for some things.

All this foretold for her the end of summer, the end of long afternoons, and the end of the year as she reckoned it. She preferred an academic or agricultural calendar, marking the beginning of the year with the autumn equinox, making a fresh start psychically charged with the summer. To mark a new year in January, in the middle of the cold and dark, seemed an unnecessarily gloomy approach to her.

Russell was on his way over to say goodbye. He'd soon be off to wherever he was going. It was good for him, and she was truly happy he'd found his way, but she'd be sad to see him go. He was a confidante, someone she could trust implicitly. She knew a lot of people, had many dear friends, but he was something else. He was someone who saw things the way she did. They had a sort of shorthand communication that she treasured. Although she regretted his departure, she knew, too, that if he stayed, if he got stuck here, if he didn't follow through on his plan, she would have lost some respect for him and would have had to call an end to their current state of affairs. So what was happening was all for the good. They could part as lovers as well as friends and keep things open should they cross paths again.

He rode up on his bike. He gave her a broad smile with a little wave and swung his right leg over the rear wheel, coasting on one pedal and coming to a stop at the foot of her porch steps.

"Impressive dismount," she said, gently rocking the porch swing.

"Sorry," he replied, leaning the bike against her house.

"Sorry?"

"I didn't mean to impress you."

He joined her on the swing, where they hung silently for a moment. Her carpet of wildflowers was all but gone now, just a few splashes of color left hiding among the brown grass. She put her hand on his knee.

"Hey, I really have to take a leak," he informed her.

"You know where it is," she said, and kept swaying a little while he went inside.

He washed, and while doing so noticed that the arrangement of her mirrors was such that, by angling the door on the medicine cabinet just so, he could bounce the reflection off a mirror opposite it, creating a serial regression of the image. He amused himself with this curiosity, creating a curving recession of his own image and contemplating his infinite self.

"Back here," she called out when she heard him leave the bathroom. He turned and went to her cluttered back room, where she was rifling through some cardboard boxes. He noticed the scraps of her unfinished quilt sitting on a dusty shelf. She waved him over.

"Take these brochures for Carmela that I told you about." She handed some to him, reading aloud about various preservation and restoration efforts. "And here's some of their newsletters. *The PIP Squeak*. Their motto is: 'the squeaky wheel gets the grease.' Goot's got a good sense of these things. I keep telling him he should run for mayor."

He took the papers from her, then she rummaged through another box and gave him a stack of old magazines.

"Here's a little on-the-road reading for you. I salvaged them from the Poor House. They're from when it used be the loony bin, back in the thirties."

He read the title: "*The Journal of Mental Hygiene*." He leaned toward her, cracking a smile. "Mental Hygiene? Does that require mental floss?"

She shook her head wearily. "I knew you'd say that. I mean, really, I just knew you would."

"Guess I'm pretty obvious, huh?"

"Sometimes. But I appreciate that about you, Russ. I never have to guess too much about where you're coming from."

Their eyes met.

"You know, I'm probably not going to make it back over here before I split. We're leaving the day after tomorrow."

"I know," she said, then put some things in boxes and closed the lids. "And I'm sorry, but I totally forgot when I asked you over that I have to go out tonight. Aunt Winnie and Uncle Ted's fiftieth anniversary at the Legion Hall. Big doings, you know."

"Sure," he replied, disappointed that they wouldn't be spending the evening together. But he was just here to be here and wasn't really expecting much of anything.

"Should I go?" he asked.

She looked up from what she was doing and reached out to him. "Oh, no, no. It's not till later. I'm not rushing you out, believe me. You can even come along tonight, if you want to. Although, I don't think you'll probably want to."

She was right about that.

"I'm just sorry we won't have more time together," she told him, and put her arm lightly on his.

A wordless moment passed, then her eyes surveyed the room and she said, "Let's get out of here. This room reminds me of all the crap I need to deal with."

She led him down the hall, and as they passed the bathroom he commented on the mirror trick he'd discovered.

"Oh, yeah," she said. "I found that out the day I moved in here. Had fun with it for a while—a zillion Helens bouncing around. Bit too much, don't you think?"

He thought it probably was. What was it he wanted to tell her? It seemed there were many things, but he couldn't articulate a single one. He felt he was in some sort of dance, but wasn't sure who was leading or what any of the expected moves were. She was always telling him he was good at going along with things, and he believed it was true. So along he went, and ended up in her living room. A train was lumbering down the tracks. He stood staring out the window, then turned to her as she settled on the couch.

"Ever get tired of the trains going by here all the time?" he asked.

"Oh, they don't go by all the time. And no, I don't mind it at all. The place wouldn't be the same without them."

He watched the trailing end of the train sway around the bend and vanish behind some trees. She yawned, stretched, and relaxed on the cushions. Somehow he knew this moment was being permanently etched into his consciousness. She looked so pretty in the late summer light, and this place was so warm and comfortable. He was about to go off into something totally unfamiliar, and likely neither warm nor comfortable. He was acutely aware of what he was leaving. Did she realize that this was the last time they'd be together like this, maybe forever? Of course she did, he knew, and he also knew that it had to be. He felt himself beginning to get hung up.

She was thinking about tonight, who would be there, what to wear. She also wondered about him, and whether she'd ever see him again. Something told her she would, but her intuition wasn't always trustworthy. She didn't really want him to go, but hated saying a prolonged goodbye. It was good she had somewhere to go, to make a clean break of it and call it a night already. Right now she kind of wanted him to leave, but when the thought of him actually going came to mind, she wanted him to stay.

"Say, you're a notary, right?" he asked, remembering he had a bit of business to tend to.

"Yes sir," she said, flashing a smile. "Whatcha got?"

"Well, I was with Manny when he got into this accident," he began, and took a piece of paper from his pocket. He looked at it, then handed it to her. "He had me write a statement, since I won't be here when he takes this woman to court to get her to pay damages. An affidavit, I guess. He wanted me to get it notarized. I don't know if it's really necessary, but I said I would."

She took the paper over to her desk, and got out her register book.

"I just need to see your driver's license," she told him.

"You know who I am."

"Sure, but I need to record that I verified that with official ID."

He sighed and frowned. "Well, I don't have one."

She stopped writing and looked up at him. "You don't?"

"Well, I let my driver's license expire."

She scrutinized him with eyes almost imperceptibly squinting.

"You're on a road trip with no license?"

He nodded.

She thought for a moment, rolling her tongue against her cheek. "God bless America. OK, then, just tell me your social security number, and I'll write that down. Its fudging it, but no one should ever be the wiser."

She wrote it down, then read his statement. "Enid Kartch!" she exclaimed. "That old witch was my fourth-grade teacher, and she was just plain mean. I'm sure she hated kids. You don't forget a bad teacher like that." She stamped the paper and handed it back to him. "I'll waive the fee. And I hope she has to pay for everything. Which reminds me, I have something for you."

She reached in her desk and handed him an envelope of money.

"It's from the parking lot."

He gave it back. "But I didn't even do anything."

"You showed up," she said, insisting that he take it. "You were willing to do what you were asked, you just weren't asked for much. Take it. You'll need it."

He thanked her and put it away.

"I have something else, too." She walked over to a shelf and picked up a box that contained a medallion of Saint Christopher on a silver necklace.

"Even if he's not a saint anymore, it can't hurt," she said as she put it on him.

He held it and thanked her again.

"Where exactly are you going, again?"

"California for sure, but I don't know where."

"Well, be sure to wear some flowers in your hair," she said, and turned away. "I should be getting ready to go." She sighed, putting her hand on his shoulder. "But don't you go, not yet. Stay awhile, and we can have a toast for the road, OK? I won't be long."

"Take your time," he said, and meant it. He had hoped they'd have all night together, but that obviously wasn't going to happen. She went to her bedroom and he sat on the couch for a minute, staring at the uneven plaster of one of her walls. He got up and started looking around, taking inventory of her stuff. She surrounded herself with an odd assortment of baubles: hand-blown glass paperweights, seashells, souvenir shot glasses, ornamental bowls, wax fruit. The place was quiet, save for the soft ticking of a clock.

These front rooms were so tidy and neatly arranged, and those back rooms were such utter chaos. There was so much about her that he'd never get, and probably there was a lot he wouldn't want to know. Yet during these past couple months, he'd felt closer to her than he'd ever felt to anyone. His feelings were difficult to reconcile, a slowly roiling mix that didn't seem like it would resolve into anything coherent anytime soon.

She returned, adorned with dangling earrings and a sparkling necklace. She wore a pink blouse, lavender skirt, and white pumps.

"Wow," he greeted her as she entered the room. "You look lovely."

"Why, sir, you are a gentleman."

She shot him a coy look and went to the kitchen to fill a couple of tumblers with some of that half-flat champagne she always kept around.

"Hey, good news I almost forgot to tell you. I hooked up with an old friend of mine, Roger, who, it turns out, is now training guide dogs for a state program. I used to do that back in college. So, I'm going to start with him in the fall. It's going to be great. I'm really looking forward to doing some rewarding work for a change."

He was happy for her, but sorry he wouldn't be around to see her doing something she really liked, something she was obviously enthusiastic about.

"Next time I see you, I'll know how much I've missed you," she said, tipping her glass to his. They drank.

"I don't spend a lot of time sitting around missing people," she said. "You know. But when I see someone again after it's been a while, it's, like, hey—I've really missed that person."

She finished her wine and put the glass in the sink.

"So, show up again sometime, and I'll tell you about how much I've missed you."

"OK," was all he could think to say.

"But we won't be all that far apart anyway," she went on to tell him. "We'll meet in the 'Elzoon Zone,' address unknown, but our messages will get through nonetheless."

"Nonetheless," he repeated.

After that there was not much more to be said. He finished his drink, then she had to go. He rode off into the fading dusk, muttering "Elzoon" to himself over and over.

18

Russell had been awake all night in anticipation of the trip ahead. He was in the shower at dawn, going over everything in his head to make sure he'd packed it all. Victor walked in and used the toilet.

He called out to Russell, "You going to be done in there pretty soon?" Then he flushed.

"Ouch!" Russell screeched. "Like, now!" He shut off the water and stepped out.

Victor began undressing. "Good. I'm next."

Russell rechecked his pack then hauled it out to the kitchen, where he set about making coffee and toast. Carmela shuffled into the kitchen, yawning and stretching in her old bathrobe. Russell thought her beautifully bedraggled in the soft morning light.

"Coffee," she pleaded wearily. He poured some for her and she plopped into a chair at the table. He took his plate and sat beside her.

"Toast?" he offered.

"No thanks," she declined. "Just the coffee for now."

She gave a wide yawn, and he ate his breakfast.

"I've never seen you this awake at this time of day," she commented.

"Yeah, well, I'm all jazzed up about getting this started."

"Sure, sure," she said, and sipped her coffee.

Victor came in, wearing only his shorts, still toweling himself off.

"Oh, hey," he greeted her, rubbing the towel over his hair. "Didn't know you were up, too."

"Barely," she replied. "But the coffee's helping."

He went over and got a cup.

"What's that you're eating?" he asked Russell.

"Toast and peanut butter."

"Got any more?"

"Already made? No. You know where the bread is."

Carmela shook her head. "You two are going to make great roommates."

They sat together in the light, quiet kitchen, eating and drinking, three old friends comfortable and at ease. Russell reflected on the past few months and how he'd ended up bound for California, where he knew no one and had no prospects for a livelihood. For a while he'd been considering this summer as a prelude to something else, and that something else seemed to be coming right up.

Carmela finished her coffee. "Well, I'd better see about getting Manny up. He can be such a bear sometimes."

She took her cup over to the sink, where she noticed a vase of flowers that had wilted. She took them out and threw them in the garbage, then dumped the water from the vase down the drain. The smell of the murky water shocked her and she turned her head away.

"Oh God, that's nasty." She set the vase down and held her stomach, breathing deeply. With a little shiver she composed herself and walked out of the kitchen, leaving the two of them eating in silence and contemplating their imminent departure.

Victor and Russell sorted and stowed their gear. They didn't have much, really, but it nearly filled the rear of the small car. Manny walked out of the house and across the lawn, carrying a cup of coffee.

"Getting ready, huh?"

"Yep," Victor replied. "Just about there."

"Well, don't go anywhere yet," Manny told them. "Let me wake up a little first before we send you off."

Victor followed him back inside. Russell took one last look through his pack, then locked the car and went in to join the others. Victor was sitting at the table with another cup of coffee. Manny had retired to the bathroom. Carmela came bounding in, looking a little too perky to Russell.

"What's up?" he asked her.

"What? Nothing," she said. "What should be up?"

"Well, you're all, I don't know—all bubbly."

"All bubbly? I think not," she protested. "But it is exciting, isn't it? Aren't you excited?"

Russell admitted that he was. Victor shrugged his shoulders. Carmela drew back one of the lace curtains and looked out at the sun on the lake. Russell noted a hint of autumn in the slant of the light and commented on the coming season.

"I love this time of year around here. I forgot how nice it is."

"Hmm," Victor hummed by way of reply, returning to his coffee.

Manny emerged from the bathroom and made his way back to the kitchen, where he grabbed his mug and headed out to the porch for a cigarette. The others drifted out, too. Manny blew some smoke in the general direction of Victor's car and said, "Well, you two are braver than me, that's for sure, heading out in that deathtrap."

"Hey now," Victor defended his vehicle. "It's a sporty little car. I'm thinking of painting some flames on it."

"Ha!" Manny coughed. "Boy, you'll be lucky if it doesn't burst into flames for real."

Victor scowled and downed the last of his coffee. Carmela leaned over the railing and cooed at her cat below, with her entourage of kittens following.

"It's sure been good having you here and all." Manny extinguished his cigarette. "Place is going to seem kind of empty without you."

He looked over at his wife, who was still trying to entice her pets up on the porch.

"What route you planning to take?" he asked Victor, who shrugged.

"After we get past Chicago, I don't know. We'll play it by ear for the most part, I think. I'd like to stay off the freeways, take the state roads and see what's going on out there."

Manny cracked a smile and looked at him a long moment, then went inside. Carmela had succeeded in coaxing a couple of the kittens up the stairs and was dangling a bit of string for their amusement when Manny came back with an envelope.

"This is yours," he said, handing it to Russell. In it were the wages he'd earned from his time with Arturo. "You never did tell him you were quitting, did you? He couldn't figure you out, but he gave me that cash and told me to make sure you got it. He's a good guy."

Russell thanked him and put it in his pocket, then said, "Well, should we get this show on the road?"

Victor slapped his thighs and stood.

"Wait," Carmela stopped them, then went to get a shirt she'd made for Russell, and a few embroidered handkerchiefs for Victor. She beamed at them when they accepted her gifts, and hugged them both. They all walked to the car, Carmela stopping along the way to scoop up one of the kittens. Goodbyes were repeated all around, then Victor went to open his door, finding to his dismay that it was locked. He looked over at Russell, who was waiting by the passenger door.

"You locked it?" Victor asked.

"Well, yeah—it's got all our stuff in it."

"Including the keys," Victor informed him. He looked around at the quiet neighborhood. "Who did you think was going to come steal our stuff while we were on the porch?"

"Well, I don't know," Russell responded. "How was I to know you'd left the keys in it so anyone who wanted to could drive off with everything we own?"

Carmela laughed. "Oh, you two are going to make great roommates."

"I'll go get a hanger," Manny offered, but Victor stopped him.

"There's a rusted spot down here," he said, wriggling under the car. He put his arm through a hole in the floor, reached up onto the seat and retrieved the keys.

"Holy shit!" Manny exclaimed. "What is that? Your Fred Flintstone brake system? Jesus! Now you two aren't going anywhere—just hold your horses, damn it."

He marched off to the garage while Victor and Russell sat on the lawn with Carmela, who had several kittens scampering around her. Manny returned, dragging a couple of ramps that he placed under the front wheels.

"OK, drive it up on these, buddy," he instructed Victor, then added, "but, actually, you could probably just hold it up for me, couldn't you?"

"Real funny," Victor mumbled. He drove the car onto the ramps while Manny went back to the garage. He returned with a toolbox and a piece of sheet metal.

"Goddamn," he growled, then put on a mask and lit a welding torch. He fit the piece of metal over the hole, spot-welded it in place, then drove in a few bolts to reinforce it. He completed his work, then Victor backed the car down.

"That'll at least keep your feet from falling through," Manny said, packing up his equipment. "But it doesn't do much to shore up the structural integrity of the heap. It's rusted pretty bad in a lot of places."

All of Russell's second thoughts came rushing to the surface, but he stuffed them down again.

"Take a kitten." Carmela handed Russell one. "Take two kittens," she insisted, picking up another.

"What?" said a perplexed Russell, suddenly holding a fuzzy little gray thing.

"Take two kittens," Carmela repeated matter-of-factly.

Manny shook his head. "Hon, there's barely enough room in there for the two of them. They don't need a couple of kittens."

"Sure they do," she insisted. "We've got to give them up soon anyway, so go ahead and take a couple and make a good home for them."

Russell glanced at Victor, who gave him a look like he couldn't care less if they had kittens along for the ride or not. "They're yours if you take them," he told Russell.

Russell looked back at Carmela, who was holding a little white furball with a pink nose.

"OK," he finally said, not sure it really was OK. But he put the kittens in the car, where they went wild, climbing up the seats and running over the gear.

"I'll get you some things," she said brightly, then ran off to the house.

"That's just the way it is, isn't it?" Manny commented. "All you want is to get out there and do your thing and—poof—you got kittens to take care of." He let out a weary little chuckle.

Carmela returned with a foil-lined box top filled with litter, and a bag of supplies for the trip.

"Really," Manny said, "you don't have to take them."

"No, no," Russell shook his head and fit the stuff into the car. "No, I'll take care of them. They'll be good company."

While he was in the car he remembered the preservationist papers Helen had given him for Carmela. He rummaged around in his pack to find them.

"Terrific!" she said, leafing through the pamphlets. "Sign me up."

Manny rolled his eyes. "Great, just what she needs to put me out of work."

She swatted him with a copy of the *PIP Squeak*.

"All right, then," Manny smiled and held his hand out to Russell, who clasped it and received a zap.

"Hey!" he yelped.

Manny laughed and held up his joy buzzer. "You gave it to me," he reminded Russell.

Victor cranked the ignition and they rolled out of the driveway with their friends waving them on. Russell turned around to see Carmela and Manny walking slowly back to the house. He knew how they'd be spending the rest of their day and thought about that, thought about everyone he knew here and what they would be doing tonight when he was hundreds of miles away. As they headed out of town, they stopped to wait for a train just down the street from Helen's. Russell caught glimpses of her place in the spaces between cars as the train chugged along. It passed, the gates swung up, and Russell asked as they pulled away, "When did trains stop having cabooses?"

Victor had no answer.

The cats initially created quite a bit of chaos in the car. On the entrance ramp to the highway one of them got under the brake pedal and almost caused them to rear-end a semi, but by the time they approached Chicago things had settled down. The white one slept in Russell's lap, while the gray one napped in the litter box on the floor in the rear.

"Going to name those cats?" Victor asked.

"Sure, at some point. You have any good ideas?"

"No, not really. Too bad Carl isn't here. He seemed to have a thing for naming stuff."

They entered the city and headed north along the lake.

"Hey, you want to look up Zane Peters?" Victor asked Russell, who did. Zane was one of their circle of friends whom neither had seen in some time.

"I ran into one of his sisters the other day. She gave me his address in the city. I say we stop by and see if we can unload some dope on him, make a little quick cash."

It seemed like a plan to Russell, so they went in search of his Uptown apartment. They found a teetering old tenement, with its door high above an alley, accessible only by a flight of steep, rickety stairs. They locked the car tight, climbed up, and knocked. Their first attempt went unanswered, so they tried again. When that too went unheeded they turned to leave. The door opened and a fat, disheveled man in his underwear bellowed at them.

"Yeah?"

Victor turned to address him. "Uh, sorry. We thought this was Zane Peters's place."

"Still is for the time being," the big guy said. "He's at work. Or at least he better be—he's behind in rent again."

Victor asked where Zane worked. The roommate gave them the name of a restaurant across town and added, "If he owes you guys or something, you can stand in line behind me."

He slammed the door and they returned to the car. Russell cleaned the litter box, then they headed off to find the restaurant. They located the place, only to learn that Zane had called in sick. So they gave up the search and sat down to order some lunch.

When the waiter brought their food, Victor asked if he knew Zane.

"Maybe if I saw him, but I'm new here. I don't know everyone's name. You could ask Mattie, up front."

He gestured to the blonde woman who had seated them, and who had told them Zane was out. They finished their meal, and took the check to her.

"So, do you know Zane?" Victor asked as he paid. "We were hoping to see him today."

She looked up from the register, then handed Victor his change. "All I know is he's supposed to be here, and he's not."

"Well, we're friends of his, and we're just in town for the day."

She turned to Russell, who smiled and gave a little wave.

"Friends of his, eh?" She clucked her tongue.

"Yeah, from his hometown. We're on our way to California, just passing through, and thought we'd look him up. We went to his place, his roommate said to come here. You have any ideas where else he might be?"

With her lips pursed, she took a scrap of paper and wrote a number on it.

"That's his cell," she told them.

They thanked her and walked to a pay phone near the door. Victor dialed, and Zane answered. He shouted when Victor identified himself.

"No way! I thought you were overseas or something."

"Well I'm back. Sort of. And I'm here with Russ Pinske."

"No fucking way," Zane's voice crackled through the receiver that Victor withdrew from his ear and held at some distance. "Where is he? Where are you guys calling from?"

Victor recounted their search thus far, which had brought them to this restaurant. Zane said something, but the transmission was garbled.

"What?" Victor said. "I didn't get any of that."

There was silence for a moment, and Victor thought the connection had been lost, but Zane came through again amidst a buzz of static.

"Don't make on like you found me, all right? I'm up here in Rogers Park. Meet me at this café called the Bean Bag. Just go north on Clark till you get to Rosemont. It's around there; you'll see it. This thing's running out of juice, I gotta go. The Bean Bag, North Clark, half an hour."

They turned to go and found Mattie staring at them.

"Did you get a hold of him?" she asked.

"Uh, no," Victor ineptly lied.

She gave them a cockeyed smile and said, "Well, good luck to you guys."

Russell spotted the café, but they had to circle several blocks before they found a place to park. They left the windows open just a crack, and locked the kittens in the car. It worried Russell that he wouldn't be able to keep an eye on them, but he figured they'd be OK for the amount of time it took to visit with Zane.

The Bean Bag was a light-filled space with a high ceiling, a long bakery counter and an elaborate espresso machine of gleaming copper and brass. Zane wasn't there, and they felt they had to order something while they waited, so they got some coffee and sat near an open window. The street was busy in the bright, warm day.

"So, what are you thinking?" Russell asked. "You want to check out Zane awhile and then get going again, or what?"

"Or what," Victor shrugged and sipped his drink. He grimaced a little and set the cup down. "Let's just see what he's up to and take it from there."

"Yeah, but, you know," Russell began, "if we hang out here with him for too long, we're not going to get too far today."

Victor shrugged again. "So?"

"Well, I kind of thought we'd get farther than Chicago on the first day out."

"I didn't know you were in a big hurry."

With a single gulp Russell downed his coffee. "I'm not. But the thing is, if we're this close I could maybe spend another night with Helen."

Victor smiled. "I'd advise against that."

Russell wanted to know why.

"I think you've already said goodbye, and that should be it. That's what she's expecting. Don't you think it would be awkward, coming back the same day you've supposedly left? You have to move on. It's best to keep facing west at this point."

Russell thought about this a moment. The coffee was making him queasy and a bit edgy, and he went to go check on the cats. They were asleep and apparently comfortable, so he left them alone and returned to the café. Zane was sitting across from Victor. He looked like a larger, sturdier version of the kid Russell had known. As he approached, Zane caught sight of him and stood. He'd always been taller than Russell, but he seemed even more so now when he bent over slightly to give him a hug. He had thick, dark hair, a long aquiline nose and a rich voice in service of a dry wit.

"What the hell. How are you?" He snorted, and patted Russell on the back. He pulled a chair from another table and they all sat together.

"Headed to California, are ya? I'm glad you guys looked me up. Let's make a night of it. Listen. Sit tight for a minute. I've got to see this guy here, then there's a few things I need to take care of, and then we can do it up right." He stood and slapped the table. "Yeah, this'll be good. Just wait here—I'll be right back."

They watched him walk over to the barista. He spoke with her, and she waved him behind the counter. He walked down a hallway and was gone for a couple of minutes. When he returned he began talking about other stops he needed to make to attend to what business he had.

"One thing," Russell interrupted as they made to leave. "I have two cats in the car. I don't want to keep them cooped up in there for too long, you know. If I can leave them at your place or something, I'd feel better."

"Cats?" Zane asked with a laugh. "You guys are traveling with cats? You crazy mothers. Well, Vic said you went to my place, but it's not really my place anymore—I just haven't told Big Roland yet. I left some of my junk there so the fat bastard thinks I'm coming back, but I'm not. I'm pretty much moved in with my girlfriend now. We can take them over there."

Russell was doubtful. "Really? She won't mind?"

"She loves cats," Zane told him. "She had one for years that died last winter. Besides, if you're friends of mine, you're welcome to my place. And your cats, too."

Zane walked them over to a Vespa that made Russell shake his head in disbelief. It was almost identical to Helen's, only this one was white and in better shape. As Zane took his helmet off the seat, Russell asked about it.

"Is it a '73?"

"Seventy-four. Why? You into them?"

"Helen has a yellow '73, a lot like this one."

"Who's Helen?" Zane wanted to know.

"Russ's new, long-lost love," Victor answered. "Bound to be an epic, with a violin score and everything."

Zane gave them a puzzled look, then said, "She sounds swell. Hey, let's take your car. We can come back here later to pick this up, but I better take the helmet with me—I've had two stolen already this year."

They carved out a space in the backseat for Zane, who crawled in the rear and sat surrounded by their stuff and the scurrying kittens. He steered Victor to the apartment while asking about Carmela and Manny, whom he hadn't seen in years, and other mutual acquaintances. Russell told about his summer in Door Prairie. Zane laughed to hear about Guy, with whom he'd had his own dealings. Victor pulled the car up in front of a brick building blackened with age. Zane led them up to the apartment, a handsome old place, spacious and with an expansive view over jumbled rooftops. Russell first brought up the cat's stuff, then went down again for the animals.

"Are you sure this is OK? She's not here, and I don't want her to get all freaked out when she comes back and finds cats in her place."

Zane assured him he'd leave her a note, and that everything would be fine. They shut the cats in the kitchen, left the note on the door, and went out for a night on the town.

The first stop was a falafel joint. Zane had them pull into a parking lot, then went in alone. He returned after a few minutes, and they went to a bar a few blocks away. After two more such stops, Russell asked him what he was up to.

"Just running some numbers, you know. Making some payments, picking some up, taking my percentage. A couple more stops, then we're going to this swank joint to party proper."

After the last stop, Victor produced the hash pipe and handed it to Zane.

"We've got some of this to sell. You interested?"

Zane took a deep hit, tried to hold it, spluttered and coughed.

"Oh yeah," he groaned.

The pipe went round as they drove across town to the place Zane was intent on going. It was in a sleek, modern building on the lake. Russell was worried that they were underdressed, but Zane just laughed and led them inside. He talked with someone while they waited by the door, then he introduced them to Tim, who seated them in a prime spot and started them off with a plate of antipasto and a carafe of Chianti. Twilight touched the water and shimmered through the window in glittering waves.

"Uh, this place is pretty upscale," Victor commented while looking around. "Where's the menu? We should check the prices here."

Zane shook his head and poured them all glasses of wine.

"Don't worry about it. We don't need a menu. Tim's bringing us the best from the kitchen. He knows what's good."

"Yeah," Russell began, "but we're kind of on a limited budget."

Zane laughed and swatted him on the back. "No worries. Just relax and enjoy."

After the antipasto came minestrone, bread, and a carafe of Montepulciano. Soup was followed by salad; then plates of braised boar and roasted vegetables, served with a bottle of luscious Tignanello. Russell's culinary sensibilities were delighted by these courses, and he luxuriated in them. For the first time since he'd left work, he felt like returning to the kitchen to practice his craft. By the time they picked through the cheese cart, they were full and tanked, but they topped it off with a baked Alaska and cordials. They talked about times they'd had together and caught up on the years in between. Twinkling lights ringed the black lake.

Tim came by when the brandies were dry and handed the bill to Victor. He looked at it, his eyes grew wide, and he passed it to Russell. The total came to over four hundred dollars. Russell gave it to Zane, who looked it over and gave an approving nod before handing it back to Tim. He leaned in toward them, tore it in half, and tucked it in the pocket of his apron. With a wink he bid them goodnight and walked away.

"That about covers what he owed me," Zane explained. "But I'm sure he wouldn't mind it you left him a tip anyway."

They walked along the lake a little in the warm night, and wound their way back to the car.

"You're really taking this thing to California?" Zane wanted to know.

"We're really doing that," Victor answered, feeling a little dizzy with the wine and the prospect of what lay ahead.

"Crazy mothers," Zane muttered as he crawled into the back. He guided them to the café where he'd left his scooter. He strapped on his helmet, telling Victor to follow him to the apartment.

Along the way, Zane sped through a yellow light and Victor had to stop at the red. They drove on after the change, searching for Zane, who pulled out in front of them but stalled a couple of blocks later. He had to push-start the scooter to get it running again, and they made their way to his place. The lights were on and the kitchen door was open. Zane walked down the hall to the living room, with Victor and Russell following a few paces behind.

"Hey, Matilda," Zane greeted the woman reading on the couch. Victor and Russell recognized Mattie from the restaurant.

"These are my friends, Russ and Vic. I guess you met their cats."

"Uh-huh. And I met these guys, too." She turned from him to them. "So, I see you did find him."

"We got your number from her at the restaurant," Victor told a confused-looking Zane.

Russell picked up the white kitten. "Sorry if they've been a nuisance—I just didn't want to leave them in the car."

She petted the gray one, curled beside her.

"It was surprise," she said with a sigh, then got up and stretched. Zane followed her into another room.

Russell and Victor stood for a moment, then sat on the couch. The kittens started scampering around. Russell tried to in vain to contain their rambunctiousness. He was attempting to corner one behind the TV when Matilda came back, with Zane lagging behind. She sat in a chair and Zane slumped on the couch beside Victor.

"So, I guess you're staying here tonight," she said.

Victor nodded. "That'd sure be nice."

Zane nudged Victor. "How about firing up some of that hash?"

Victor looked at Russell, who excused himself to go down to the car. He returned with their sleeping bags and other gear. From a pocket of his backpack he produced a slab of hash the size of a deck of cards and handed it to Zane.

"Whoa, there. I don't think I can afford that."

Russell shook his head. "No, man, it's yours. Forget about it."

Victor stopped himself from objecting. Zane filled a pipe and gave it to his girlfriend. She smiled her approval. It was passed around, and after a few hits each they all took to watching the antics of the kittens.

"So, you're taking these little guys with you?" Matilda asked.

"I asked them that, too," Zane said. "Truly nutty."

"Well, if you wanted," she began, picking up the white one, "I've been going back and forth lately about getting a cat or two. I don't know, but it seems like a hassle to take them on a road trip. So, I'm just saying, if you want you could leave them."

She had addressed herself to Victor, who put up his hands and said, "They're totally Russ's responsibility."

The kitten had squirmed out of her hands and was wrestling with the other at Russell's feet. It did seem sort of crazy to have them along. They were certainly making things more complicated. But he liked them, and was feeling a sense of duty toward them.

"I don't know," he said. "They were kind of thrust upon me, but I have to think about it."

She smiled. "Sure. But it's really OK—I'll take good care of them."

When the old friends resumed discussing youthful antics with people in places Matilda didn't know or care about, she rose and said goodnight and goodbye. She kissed Zane on the forehead and shuffled off to bed. A few minutes after her departure, he rousted himself and went rummaging through a closet. He took out a box and set it on the floor.

"You guys have a camp stove?"

Russell did. Zane unpacked his device and said, "I bet it's not as cool as this. Check it out."

It was a single burner on a tripod, attached to a steel cylinder that was about the size of a pocket flashlight. Zane opened a valve and lit it. For such a small thing it put out a large, bright flame.

"You can't buy these in the states. My brother got this one in Portugal. It runs on just about any liquid fuel. There's unleaded gas in there now, but you can run it on alcohol, paint thinner, kerosene. Anything like that. Probably even whale oil."

They sat and watched it awhile. Russell thought about what a way it was to start their trip, running around the city, that outrageous meal, and now sitting around a camp stove in Zane's living room.

"You can take it, if you want," Zane offered. "I never go camping. Extra burner could come in handy."

He turned the thing off and let it cool down, then handed it to Russell, who thanked him. It was then that he noticed the wooden floor beneath the thing had gotten deeply burned.

"Oops," Zane said, his eyes wide. He got a throw rug from another part of the room and covered it up with a smile and a wink. Then he went to the kitchen and brought back some cognac for a nightcap.

"To California." They raised their glasses to the golden state.

"I've been thinking about going somewhere else," Zane said. "Montreal, maybe. Quebec is calling me."

"What's there?" Russell wanted to know.

"I don't know. What's in California?"

"No idea," was Russell's reply, delivered with a shrug.

Victor yawned and said, "I've always wanted to go there. And I was on my way when I ran into Russ, who was looking to go somewhere. So there's your serendipity right there."

Zane raised his glass again. "Serendipity, synchronicity, good old coincidence."

They all drank to that.

With their glasses drained and the hash turned to ash, they began to drift off. Zane went to his bedroom, Victor sprawled on the couch and Russell slipped into his sleeping bag on the floor. The cats remained awake and active all night.

Victor and Russell both sort of woke up when Matilda was walking around getting ready for her day, but went back to sleep again when she left. Then Zane got up and nudged them awake.

"I have to get going, you guys. Been slacking off too much at work lately, so I better put in my time. It was awesome seeing you again, though. I'm really glad you looked me up." He pointed to the cats and asked, "Are you leaving them here?"

Russell shook his head. "No, they're coming with me. They're road kitties, I think."

"Good. I was going to try to talk you out of it if you were. I don't want cats. No offense to them, but just in general. So, you guys can take showers, make breakfast, coffee, whatever. Or, there's a diner around the corner."

After admonishing them to make sure the door was locked behind them, he left, saying, "Send me a postcard."

They were both hung over and moving slowly. Victor went to shower while Russell tried to sleep a little longer. But the strangeness of the place and his pets mewing for food forced him to get up. He fed them, then showered. They gathered their belongings and loaded the car, then Russell went back for the cats. He wrote a note of thanks, rounded them up, and locked them in the car while they went to the diner.

"I know you're all into meandering and everything," Russell said while they ate. "But I'd really like to make it across the Mississippi."

"You have a destination in mind? What kind of hobo are you?"

"Who says I'm a hobo? What does that even mean, anyway?"

"Just seems like the adventure is in getting there."

"Yeah, but there's got to be a there to get to at some point, right?"

They ate and thought about it, then Victor went to the car and came back with an atlas that they spread on the table. Russell studied it, keeping in mind the idea of avoiding the interstates in favor of alternate routes. He pointed to Clinton, Iowa.

"Let's head here," Russell stated. "There's just something psychological about crossing that river. I want to do it today."

"Well, by all means, let's be psychological," Victor concurred.

On the street they saw a half a dozen kids carrying stacks of boxes, calling to pedestrians and pestering cars at intersections.

"Chocolate bars. Box of good chocolate bars, five dollars."

One of them approached Russell. "Five dollars, good chocolate." He opened the box to show him the bars. Russell looked at Victor.

"Lot of chocolate for five dollars. Is it good?"

"Sure it's good, man. Truck spill, you know, this morning."

"Truckspill chocolate?" Russell asked.

The kid tried to explain, slowing the rhythm of his speech. "A truck spilled, right? Get it? Stuff all over the street, boxes everywhere. Come on, five dollars."

Russell handed the kid a fiver, and he hurried off.

After refueling they returned to the freeway and left the city. The kittens got all riled up again and began scampering around the car. One of them crawled under Russell's seat and nudged out a small tin box.

"What's this?" he asked.

Victor glanced over and saw what he was holding. "Oh, that. Yeah, it's weird. First night out I camped in this field in Maryland, I think it was. Anyway, when I woke up that box was right next to my head. I guess I hadn't noticed it in the dark. There's something rattling around in there, but I can't get it open."

Russell used a toothpick he'd taken from the restaurant to spring the lock.

"Didn't try too hard, did you?"

Victor was surprised. "No. I mean, yes. I tried, but couldn't."

Russell opened the lid.

"What's inside?" Victor wanted to know.

There was some dust, a frayed red ribbon, the nib of a fountain pen, and a penny from 1928.

"Then nothing, really," Victor said.

But Russell wasn't so sure. He locked the box with those things inside and slid it carefully beneath the seat. The radio broadcast top country hits above the drone of the engine and the rush of wind through the open windows.

"Yee-haw!" Victor called out with a wide smile. "Here comes the river, and the rest of the U.S. of fuckin' A."

They were a few miles from the bridge when Victor pulled over at a rest stop. They got out and stretched. Victor went to use the facilities first while Russell kept watch. When Russell came back, he saw Victor crawling in the weeds, looking for the cats.

"Damn it!" he was shouting. "Get back here!"

Russell joined in the search and after a while nabbed the little gray kitten, but the white one bounded farther away, until it was lost.

"Oh, man," Russell groaned.

"Well, we got one of them," Victor tried to console him.

"Yeah, but we can't just leave that other guy out there on his own."

So they locked the one kitten in the car and went searching for the other until it seemed futile. Russell was crestfallen to abandon him but didn't know what more to do. He resigned himself to losing him and returned to the car. They looked around a last time, then decided they had to drive on. As they pulled away, Russell spotted the kitten running across the grass. Victor slammed on the brakes and Russell rushed to get it, alternately scolding and caressing it on the way back to the car.

Victor was looking through the box of chocolate that had fallen to the floor and spilled open.

"Man, we got ripped off."

Beneath the top layer of chocolate bars, the rest of the box was filled with Velamints. Russell looked through them.

"Dozens of packs of Velamints. Ten chocolate bars. Damn."

"Hardly a deal," Victor appraised.

"Unless you like Velamints," Russell said in an attempt to mitigate their disappointment, but neither of them knew anyone who did. Russell repacked the candy and tucked it away while Victor got them back on the road.

"Hey, that rest stop was pretty freaky," Victor observed.

Russell was busy petting his prodigal kitten and musing on his feelings of responsibility toward it.

"What do you mean?" he absently replied.

"Well, you know, it's kind of out in the middle of nowhere. I was just thinking I bet it's really creepy at night, you know? No one's around, and you pull in to use the head—who knows what's lurking in there? Could be real creepy, like vampires and stuff."

He looked over at Russell, who was still stroking his pet.

"One of us should write something like that."

"What? 'Vampires of the Rest Stop?'"

"Yeah, sure. Great pulp fiction. It'd sell, I bet."

Russell nodded and said, "Sure. Maybe." He thought about what it might take to write such a book. He was pretty sure he didn't have whatever it was.

"So," Victor spoke again after some time. "What happened to that crystal Guy gave you?"

"That stuff they said Skutch was smoking? I've still got it. Why? You want it?"

"Oh no, no," he said slowly. "I was just wondering if you still had it. What do you think it is?"

"I have no idea," Russell replied. "Why don't you try it and see what happens. Maybe you could channel Skutch through it."

Victor considered this. "Well, I was just wondering is all. Keep it around in case we find someone who wants to try it out."

The sun was in the west when they crossed the river at Clinton, the hills and bluffs awash in a warm glow.

"Hey, um," Victor began. "You notice anything weird between Carmela and Manny?"

"Anything weird? Weird like how?"

"You know, like, tense, especially when I was around?"

Russell shook his head. "Especially when you were around? No. Why? Should I have?"

Victor scratched his chin. "Well, it was just a little weird for me," he said. "I was wondering if it felt weird to you is all."

"I don't get what's supposed to be weird," Russell said.

"It's just that, well, Carmela and I had a thing going there for a little while."

Russell blinked rapidly while processing this information. "What? When? What kind of thing?"

"Back a couple of weeks before I shipped out to boot camp. The three of us went out one night and got pretty wasted. We ended up back at Manny's apartment, where he passed out. So I walked Carmela back to her place and, well, one thing led to another."

"So, they weren't married yet?" Russell said, trying to understand this news.

"No, but they were engaged. I shipped out in the fall, they were married the next spring. And it wasn't just the one drunken night, either. We hooked up a few more times before I left."

Victor let this sink in, then continued. "So, it was weird for me, because I didn't know if she'd ever told him. I seriously doubt it. It doesn't seem like it. But I was wondering if you were picking up any weird vibes."

"No," was all Russell could say.

"Yeah, well, she and I were both totally acting like it never happened. Neither of us even really looked at each other for too long, you know? So, I guess that's just what it is."

After a while Russell said, "Man, I didn't need to know this."

"Maybe you didn't," Victor responded. "But I felt like I needed to tell you."

Russell slumped and closed his eyes in the glare of the sun on the horizon.